Hitler's British Nazis

Fasces
In ancient Rome, the word *fasces* referred to a weapon consisting of a bundle of wooden rods, sometimes surrounding an axe. Used by Roman authorities to punish wrongdoers, the fasces came to represent state authority.

Fascism (definition)
a political philosophy, movement, or regime that exalts nation and often race above the individual and that stands for a centralized autocratic government headed by a dictatorial leader, severe economic and social regimentation, and forcible suppression of opposition.

Characteristics of European inter-war fascist movements
(*A History of Fascism*, Stanley G. Payne)
- Fascist negotiations: anti-liberalism, anti-communism, and anti-conservatism.
- Ideology and goals: a new type of authoritarian state, corporatism, expansionism, and the creation of a new modern culture.
- Style and Organisation: an emphasis on aesthetics, mass mobilisation, militarisation, violence, an organic male dominated view of society, exaltation of youth, and leadership principle.

Hitler's British Nazis

The Hidden Story of the Fascist Movement in the UK

Norman Ridley

AN IMPRINT OF PEN & SWORD BOOKS LTD
YORKSHIRE – PHILADELPHIA

First published in Great Britain in 2024 by
FRONTLINE BOOKS
an imprint of Pen & Sword Books Ltd
Yorkshire – Philadelphia

Copyright © Norman Ridley, 2024

ISBN 978-1-39903-334-3

The right of Norman Ridley to be identified as the author of this work has been asserted by him in accordance with the Copyright, Designs and Patents Act 1988.

A CIP catalogue record for this book is available from the British Library.

All rights reserved. No part of this book may be reproduced or transmitted in any form or by any means, electronic or mechanical including photocopying, recording or by any information storage and retrieval system, without permission from the Publisher in writing.

Typeset by Concept, Huddersfield, West Yorkshire, HD4 5JL.
Printed and bound in England by CPI Group (UK) Ltd, Croydon CR0 4YY.

Pen & Sword Books Ltd incorporates the imprints of Aviation, Atlas, Family History, Fiction, Maritime, Military, Discovery, Politics, History, Archaeology, Select, Wharncliffe Local History, Wharncliffe True Crime, Military Classics, Wharncliffe Transport, Leo Cooper, The Praetorian Press, Remember When, White Owl, Seaforth Publishing and Frontline Books.

For a complete list of Pen & Sword titles please contact
PEN & SWORD BOOKS LTD
47 Church Street, Barnsley, South Yorkshire, S70 2AS, England
E-mail: enquiries@pen-and-sword.co.uk
Website: www.pen-and-sword.co.uk
or
PEN & SWORD BOOKS
1950 Lawrence Rd, Havertown, PA 19083, USA
E-mail: uspen-and-sword@casematepublishers.com
Website: www.penandswordbooks.com

Contents

List of Plates vii
Introduction ix
1. The Radical Right in Britain Before 1914 1
2. The Emergence of Fascism in Italy and Germany 9
3. British Fascist Movements in the 1920s 15
4. The Suffragette Movement and Fascism 27
5. British Press Coverage of Nazi Germany in the 1930s 33
6. Lord Rothermere 41
7. Nazi Camp Followers 47
8. The Mitford Sisters 69
9. The Cliveden Set 81
10. Oswald Mosley and the British Union of Fascists 87
11. Olympia 101
12. Mosley after Olympia 107
13. The British Legion 127
14. Edward VIII and Mrs Simpson 131
15. Lord Londonderry 143
16. Sir Barry Domvile 147
17. Archibald Maule Ramsay and the Right Club 155
18. The Windsors after the Abdication 163
Appendix: Edward's Abdication Statement 173
Notes 175
Bibliography 183
Index 187

List of Plates

Emeline Pankhurst being arrested outside Buckingham Palace in 1914.

Rotha Lintorn-Orman, founder of the British Fascisti.

Flag of the Imperial Fascist League.

Arnold Spencer Leese, sentenced to six months' hard labour for seditious libel.

German ex-servicemen parading through Whitehall on 21 January 1936.

Lord Rothermere and Adolf Hitler at Berchtesgarten in 1937.

Diana Mitford and Bryan Guinness on their honeymoon in Taormina, Italy, 1929.

Daily Mail headline on 15 January 1934.

Crowds giving Mosley a rapturous reception at Olympia in June 1934.

Mosley receiving the adoration of his followers.

The British Legion chairman, Major Francis Fetherston-Godley, meeting Hitler in July 1935.

Philip Henry Kerr, 11th Marquess of Lothian, with one of his favourite books.

Mosley being pelted by an angry crowd in Liverpool on 10 October 1937.

Edward VIII and Wallis Simpson.

Boca do Inferno, where the Windsors stayed in Portugal.

A wounded William Joyce after his arrest on 29 May 1945.

Introduction

Fascism is a system of political authority and social order intended to reinforce the unity, energy, and purity of communities in which liberal democracy stands accused of producing division and decline. Perceived inadequacies of the liberal state were seen as condemning the nation to disorder, decline, or humiliation where the political right was no longer able to wield power alone, but refused to share power with a growing and increasingly significant leftist movement. The resulting polarisation of civil society threatened deadlock within the political system. It is difficult, however, to define fascism. Its characteristics have been engraved on the public consciousness in the form of crude, primary images. There is the chauvinist demagogue haranguing an ecstatic crowd as disciplined ranks of marching youths go past. Uniformed militants are seen beating up members of some demonised minority. There is an obsessive preoccupation with civic decline and humiliation compensated for by cults of unity, energy, and purity, pursued with redemptive violence.

To find the roots of fascism one must go back to 1860 and the American South, just after the Civil War, when the Ku Klux Klan was formed by some former Confederate officers, fearing the vote being given to African Americans. They set up an alternate civic authority, parallel to the legal state militia, with the aim of restoring an overturned social order that, in their eyes, no longer defended their community's legitimate interests. However, when one looks at the types of fascism that arise in different societies, there are not as many common factors as one might expect. Germany's fascism under the Nazis, with its militarised regimentation, was quite different to the more relaxed fascism of Mussolini's Italy. During the 1930s many regimes that were not functionally fascist borrowed elements of fascist decor in order to lend themselves an aura of force, vitality, and mass mobilisation.

George Orwell wrote, in 1936, that for an authentic fascism to succeed in Britain it would have to be much more soberly clad than under the Nazis. Perhaps Sir Oswald Mosley's Blackshirts might have had more success if they had worn bowler hats and carried well-furled umbrellas. Each national variant of fascism draws its legitimacy not from some universal dogma but from what it considers the most authentic elements of its own community identity. It does not rely on formal philosophical positions with claims to universal legitimacy and certainly does not base its claims to validity on any such. For the fascist, faith triumphs over reason. What matters is blood, prowess of the race and Darwinian triumph of the strongest community with no pretensions to an intellectual position in pursuit of an historic destiny.

Robert Paxton has identified seven 'mobilising passions' in fascism:

1. The primacy of the group, toward which one has duties superior to every right, whether universal or individual.
2. The belief that one's group is a victim, a sentiment that justifies any action against the group's enemies, internal as well as external.
3. Dread of the group's decadence under the corrosive effect of individualistic and cosmopolitan liberalism.
4. Closer integration of the community within a brotherhood whose unity and purity are forged by common conviction, if possible, or by exclusionary violence if necessary.
5. An enhanced sense of identity and belonging, in which the grandeur of the group reinforces individual self-esteem.
6. Authority of natural leaders throughout society, culminating in a national chieftain who alone is capable of incarnating the group's destiny.
7. The beauty of violence and of will, when they are devoted to the group's success in a Darwinian struggle.[1]

Chapter One

The Radical Right in Britain Before 1914

During the years before the First World War, the ideas that prepared the ground for fascism were abundantly evident in British politics and society. Like other European countries, Britain's idea of fascism evolved from traditional concepts such as a sense of community, nationhood, kingship and hereditary leadership all solidly rooted in native traditions and influences and which embraced, at heart, a hostility towards economic and political liberalism. British fascism developed as a force opposing the party political system, which it saw as bogged down in factionalism and endless argument rather than necessary action. It was this, above all else, the argument went, that was the root cause of the decline in British imperial power. Socially, fascist ideology urged the regeneration of society through racial purification and the Nietzschean concept of the 'will to power' whereby necessary action was taken by strong leaders who would stir up popular revolt in the national interest. It is clear, however, that this British fascistic trend was in no way comparable to the French Action Française that posed such a threat to the Third Republic during the years before the First World War. That movement had aimed to achieve a restoration of the French monarchy by means of a coup d'état involving a transitional authoritarian government. Neither did it have much in common with the 'blood and soil' German 'volkish' nationalism that had anti-Semitism and romantic nationalism at its heart and which would go on to play such an important part in the subculture underpinning Nazism in later years.

British fascism, much like its European equivalents, grew out of the social tensions acting on society at the time. The engine of change was modernisation that was accelerating at an unprecedented pace, threatening the role and status of agrarian elites and a middle class that were incapable of reacting and responding to the changes in a timely fashion and creating within these groups a sense of insecurity. For them, the first real signs of change were seen after the unification of the German state that followed the defeat of France in the Franco-Prussian War. The emergence of Germany as an economic power after 1871 coincided with a period of British economic decline after decades of industrial supremacy and then the large-scale imports of cheap grain from North America triggered a long-term decline in agriculture, which left a generation of country gentlemen and aristocratic landowners feeling the pinch and unhappy with the conventional conservative politics that was failing to protect them. All of this and the early signs of worker unrest was encouraging some within these privileged classes to look for alternative political solutions to their problems and made them fertile ground for the sowing of extremist ideas.

The growing disquiet felt by these groups was expressed through the Die-Hards, a right-wing faction within the Conservative and Unionist Party who claimed that they would rather 'die in the last ditch' than witness the political emasculation of the aristocracy. It is generally accepted that the ideas of British fascism and diehard Conservatism have a common origin, in domestic rather than European politics, and in particular, the Edwardian radical right and diehard peers. Their philosophy manifested itself in a paternalistic conservatism that lauded a 'glorious' imperial past and opposed political liberalism but their ideas were vague and unrefined, leaving no single coherent idea around which they could rally. There was strong backing for such ideas from the military, who were always on the lookout for civil unrest, and general support from those who feared that the Home Rule element in Ireland were poised to further undermine the Empire. There was also a much more widespread opposition to 'alien' immigration, but these negative tendencies existed alongside a radical right-wing sense of urgency to modernise British society to keep pace with the industrial might of Germany that was now a real threat to British imperial power. Germany's industrial achievements, especially in the fields of chemicals, steel and optics, were laying the foundation of a vibrant modern state with considerable military offensive capability.

Alarmed by the pace of social change that was taking place in Britain, the rise in power and influence of the labour movement, and frustrated by its own impotence to compete, sections of the Edwardian radical right began to display a dangerous disillusionment with conventional politics. Baffled by the complexities of urban, industrial Britain, they sought to recreate a deferential rural past by looking for simple, immediate solutions to what they perceived to be the nation's decline and yearned for a patriotic, virile leader. There grew a sense that a whole new set of ideas was required rather than a rehash of the old dogmas that were seen as suffocating necessary innovation in the political and social spheres. The search for these new ideas looked for answers both in an idealised version of the past and a revolutionary new vision of the future encompassing new modern values and power structures. Much of the blame for society's ills was laid at the door of the late Victorian and Edwardian ruling elites, who were seen as having failed to recognise the need for change in the face of the growing power of mass movements rippling the surface of social stability.

The years between 1900 and 1914 saw a whole series of campaigns and agitations that reflected alarm about imperial decline and increasing anxiety about the apparent sharp deterioration of Britain's international position. The dominance of maritime trade was being reduced as rapid improvements in land transport allowed continental powers to mobilise their resources much more efficiently. Politicians such as Joseph Chamberlain and Leo Amery warned of the domestic implications for a country that was becoming unable to defend its interests against those of emerging continental powers. Despite evidence that any threat to national security could arouse a strong public reaction over a short period, neither man was under any illusion that a singular act was sufficient to reverse the national trend and that there could be no expectation of popular support for the sort of complicated changes required over an extended period. The public would simply not understand and grow bored.

British party politics appeared to be unable to respond to imperial concerns. Both the journalist and editor of the conservative British publication *National Review*, Leopold Maxse, and the Cabinet Minister Lord Milner were contemptuous of what they called parliamentary posturing, which robbed politics of principle. Democracy, they said, was an inefficient form of government run by mediocre individuals where secondary issues would often be given precedence over matters of national importance. Cabinet government was seen as unresponsive and indecisive during periods of national crisis.

Someone who would influence the growth of the fascist movement at the turn of the century in the way he opposed free trade as a means of protecting British manufacturing was a man who showed himself to be arrogant and contemptuous of weaker minds and aristocratic privilege, who chose to apply his formidable political skills towards achieving personal goals rather than in support of his party or the greater good of the country. Joseph Chamberlain was not above fomenting popular revolt and allowing it to degenerate into street protest and violence. As British

Secretary of State for the Colonies, he would go on to advocate policies based on racial superiority of the Anglo-Saxon nations. Chamberlain was an extremely disruptive politician who split the Liberal Party over Home Rule for Ireland and later did something similar to the Unionists over protectionism. In later years, Adolf Hitler is known to have drawn on Chamberlain's anti-Semitic writing for his own race theory.

As noted earlier, central to the ideas of the radical right during the Edwardian era was the sense that British power and influence in the world was in sharp decline, unable to stand up to the growing industrial challenges of Germany and the United States, and was becoming 'a working museum of industrial archaeology'.[1] The somewhat lamentable performance of British forces during the Boer Wars further emphasised the erosion of British ability to influence world affairs. Government policies were characterised by the radical right as being woolly and liberalistic, undermining the moral fibre of the nation. Many policies later advocated by Oswald Mosley, who would become what one observer called 'the intellectual heir of the most extreme wing of Chamberlainism', had their roots in pre-war Chamberlain ideas of social-imperialism, including the protection of domestic industries against cheap foreign imports, and the boosting of the home market to offset the negative effect of Britain's diminishing foreign export outlets.[2]

Along with the loss of confidence in British power there grew a sense that Germany was becoming the nation most to fear and this engendered a sort of spy-mania aimed at wealthy German Jews. For some years around the turn of the century, German immigrants in Britain had been the target of hostile propaganda and were portrayed by some as populating the lowest levels of criminal and immoral society. A great deal of popular fiction depicted Germany as casting off its more admirable traits of high culture in favour of overt militarism, and a number of best-selling novels, such as Erskine Childers' *The Riddle of the Sands*, had a German invasion of the British Isles as a main theme. The national press, such as the *Daily Mail*, led campaigns castigating German residents as potential spies and agitators and blamed German Jewish financiers for inveigling Britain into the disastrous Boer Wars to erode its imperial power. The government took advantage of this fear to launch an attack on political freedom in the 1911 Official Secrets Act, which passed with scant discussion on a quiet Friday afternoon in an empty House of Commons. This legislation allowed the authorities to arrest and prosecute anyone on the mere suspicion of harbouring an intention prejudicial to the safety or interests of the state.

The radical right took the view that state power should hold sway over liberal economics and expounded the Social Darwinian concept of survival of the fittest through military and economic power. This meant greater military expenditure. This, however, was a view that did not take account of political realities. There was little consensus between the Liberal and Conservative parties. Indeed, there was division within the parties that forbade any possibility of radical right policies gaining any traction in Parliament and there was no appetite at that stage for any challenge to the parliamentary system.

Significant numbers of Jews had arrived in Britain after 1871, fleeing persecution in Europe, but they aroused little public comment and, indeed, apart from some prominent Jewish families such as the Rothschilds and Montefiores who discouraged further Jewish immigration presumably on the grounds that it would imperil their own status, were generally welcomed with open arms. There were, however, active groups such as the ultra-nationalist British Brothers' League, who conducted propaganda campaigns to discourage immigration at source and also encouraged the repatriation of Jews. Although the strength of anti-Semitic sentiment in Britain was much less than in Russia, France or Germany at this time, Jewish immigrants were, in the words of some, characterised as 'paupers and useless parasites' who constituted 'a grave danger to the [resident] Jewish community'. The Jewish Board of Guardians equivocated, on the one hand adhering to the British tradition of granting asylum to the oppressed and on the other describing immigrants as 'undesirables, criminals and other dissolute classes'.[3]

Anti-Semitism has always played some part in British life and it has even, at times, been a factor in British politics. As early as 1253, Henry III had brought in the Statute of Jewry, which placed a range of restrictions on Jews, including segregation and the wearing of a yellow badge. It would nevertheless be unrealistic to suggest that it ever reached the scale of continental anti-Semitism. Public feeling, except in certain restricted circles, was never virulent enough, nor did the British political situation provide the uncertainty that, in the case of continental regimes such as the French Third Republic, enabled anti-Semitism to be exploited as a major political weapon.

At this time also, beliefs were formed that would go on to become fundamental to the ideology of many fascist groups during the middle part of the twentieth century. Concepts of race, culture and evolution would be imported into Britain from mainland Europe, discussed and developed and recycled back to the Continent, where they would play important roles in the emergence of Nazi doctrine in particular. In Britain, there was a view that the British possessed innate qualities of leadership and wisdom that justified their right to impose dominion over indigenous groups throughout the Empire. One viceroy of India called it 'British gentlemen engaged in the magnificent work of governing an inferior race'. This was most clearly expressed in the concept of Social Darwinism, an idea that had the support of a significant portion of the scientific community at the time. According to theory, certain groups or races were superior to others by virtue of genetic traits that should be protected from 'dilution', and the total lack of evidence for such a mechanism did little to diminish enthusiasm for the idea within the fascistic mind. Many intellectuals of the time believed that a liberal society encouraged the procreation of the least fit members, which was a certain recipe for industrial, military, and imperial decline. They saw eugenics as an appealing remedy.

Houston Stewart Chamberlain, in his book *The Foundations of the Nineteenth Century*, believed that Britain was threatened by racial impurity or mixing, the worst agents of which were the Jews. He believed that the state had a clear duty to encourage selection with a view to maximising the proportion of pure Teutonic blood in the population; the logical conclusion was the elimination of the 'degenerate' elements in the national stock.

The radical right placed a strong emphasis on discipline, service and duty; all seen as essential ingredients in the evolutionary life struggle. The state, whose technical and military efficiency was crucial for national survival, was almost deified as the supreme authority in all things and individualism was antisocial, hindering the task of state efficiency. This instrumentalist model of the state sanctified its role as the interpreter of the peoples' will, and the guarantor of their welfare.

Lamarckian fascism was not so much an ideology of racial supremacy through genetics as a cultural evolution, which held that racial characteristics grew out of a culture and so if people were exposed to a certain culture then they would absorb its values and psychological attributes and so develop to a point where they could become part of the racial elite. 'Lower races', however, who were seen as culturally deficient, could not benefit from this process since they were deemed to have reached the limits of their evolutionary development and were no longer capable of responding to the challenges of modern life. These groups essentially included all peoples of non-European origin. The role of the state as an instrument of racial improvement was to enhance the nation's racial character in order to improve its prospects of survival in a hostile world. Emigration and the curtailing of progressive welfare reforms were put forward as remedies to deter procreation among supposedly inferior categories and so redress the perceived imbalance in fertility levels between the higher and the lower social orders, thus checking the process of 'race deterioration'.

Chapter Two

The Emergence of Fascism in Italy and Germany

One of the consequences of the First World War was the way in which, for those who had fought, extreme hardship and violence had become normalised and accepted as part of the new world order. Many returned from the trenches with an urgent desire to restore stability and return to a civilised way of life, but others had become politicised by the violence and were eager to change society by exercising their new power as a mass movement. In Italy, the end of the war was seen by some as 'a bloody dawn of a new era of Italian history, consecrated by the blood shed by the heroes and by the martyrs to give life to the new Italy'.[1] The wholesale redistribution of national boundaries after the Treaty of Versailles saw nationalistic movements that challenged the new order, and paramilitary organisations throughout Europe created a febrile, unstable environment where conventional political elites struggled to maintain control of events.

The First World War was the most decisive immediate precondition for fascism in Italy and the National Socialist movement in Germany.[2] Had there been no war, fascism would probably have remained a marginalised, sectarian movement. This does not mean, however, that war was the only cause of the success of these movements. The frailty of democratic and representative institutions, and later the catastrophic consequences of the economic crisis, were other factors that must be taken into consideration.

Germany, in particular, reacted to Versailles with an emotionally and moralistically charged groundswell revolutionary movement that a fragile Weimar Republic struggled to contain. The most direct link between the war and the post-war fascist movements is to be found in the special units set up during the conflict who would migrate into the fascist militias. Men who had served in elite German *Sturmtruppen* and Austrian *Frontkämpfer* units, which had been distinguished by special uniforms and better food rations, were ideologically driven to join the fascist militias, while in Italy it had been the *arditi* special units, conceived by General Luigi Capello, which would take on a similar role and become 'a new type of man ... who has achieved the highest intensification of all human qualities and blended them so harmoniously and yet so violently'.[3] In Germany, the extreme right condemned parliamentary democracy for disunity and weakness in the country.

By the end of the war the *Sturmtruppen* in particular had become deeply frustrated and humiliated by what they saw as a meek acceptance of defeat, which was blamed on the traitors or 'November criminals' that had exposed Germany to the brink of a communist revolution. Soldiers returning from the trenches took to the streets and formed marauding bands of paramilitary groups. They wore uniforms, took part in parades, wore medals, relived the camaraderie of wartime, and generally tried to bury the shame of having lost a generation-defining conflict. Nationalist and class sentiments saw the rise of irregular volunteer *Freikorps* and *Einwohnerwehren* units, which had existed in some form since the eighteenth century but which were now reinvented as the idealisation of militarised masculinity, physical power and the absence of emotion, and energised by a desire to oppose revolutionary movements such as Rosa Luxemburg's Marxist Spartacus League (Spartacists).

Street violence was widespread but there were also mass killings of civilians as well as prominent German politicians and members of the Communist Party. In the spring of 1919, *Freikorps* troops violently terminated the short-lived Council Republic in Bavaria and brutally suppressed communist supporters in Berlin, where some 1,000 people died as a result of the fighting, which included aerial bombardment and artillery fire. The Baltic region saw extreme violence and a deliberate targeting of civilians suspected of being Bolshevik sympathisers. In Mitau (Jelgava) alone, *Freikorps* soldiers executed some 500 Latvian civilians and a further 325 were killed in the towns of Tuckum (Tukums) and Dünamünde (Daugavgrīva).

When the *Friekorps* survivors returned to Germany in 1919, many of them joined illegal right-wing terrorist groups such as the infamous *Organisation Consul*, whose members murdered famous politicians, Matthias Erzberger among them, who had signed the armistice at Compiegne in November 1918, and the Jewish Foreign Minister of the Weimar Republic, Walther Rathenau. Their displays of violence, terror, and male aggression and solidarity would later create a bedrock of the fascist Nazi philosophy.

The Emergence of Fascism in Italy and Germany

After Hitler's abortive Bürgerbräukeller [Beer Hall] Putsch in November 1923, which had been inspired by Mussolini's March on Rome, Hitler was jailed, supporters of extremist parties in Germany were diminished, and violence temporarily eased off, largely because of the relative political and economic stabilisation in Germany. However, by 1929, the country was already plunging once again into crisis and violent disorder. The Great Depression, which began with the stock market crash on Wall Street in October 1929, did more than any other event to end the Weimar Republic's brief era of relative stability. Germany was more adversely affected by the Depression because its economic recovery was largely the result of short-term American loans that were now recalled, pushing banks and businesses across the country into bankruptcy. Many voters increasingly began to see the Nazis as the only viable alternative to the Communist Party.

In Italy, most of the *arditi* units were disbanded at the end of the war, but many of the membership harboured a frustration that their sacrifices were unrecognised and found it difficult to reintegrate in post-war life. The political extreme right wing regarded the *arditi* as the potential vanguard of a movement with a sincere desire for radical political, social and moral renewal, and found common ground with the *Fasci di combattimento* founded by Benito Mussolini in March 1919 at a meeting in San Sepolcro Square in Milan. However, the *arditi* did not take to Mussolini and favoured Gabriele D'Annunzio as their honorary president, which saw the movement separate from Mussolini's fascists. Unlike the *Freikorps*, which after 1920 lost much of its political power due to its support for the abortive Kapp Putsch, the *arditi* promoted a vague programme of social and political renewal without violence but, despite the popularity of its leader, it failed to attract significant support and many followers drifted away to join Mussolini's more pro-active fascist movement.

One notable characteristic of the early fascist movement in Italy was the intense and systemic use of political violence through the use of well-organised paramilitary militias that had been brutalised by war. There was a clear propensity towards violence both in the language and daily actions of the militants. The fascist *squadrismo* action squads, composed mostly of young, middle-class opponents of revolutionary socialism, would become a political phenomenon that was not afraid to employ violence and the use of force in its abandonment of rules of decency and good taste as it took the path of civil disobedience in support of the fascist movement. The Italian *squadristi* stood at the centre of a new political movement centred on Bologna and Florence and would show themselves to be more aggressive in their fight against 'all those who threatened the rebirth of an energetically-combative nation' than their German counterparts, primarily because of their greater access to arms. In both cases, however, the political leaders who used the movements for their own ends often found them difficult to control. A number of *squadristi* leaders were hostile to Mussolini's leadership, which they saw as pandering too much to the left, and even went as far as to call Mussolini a traitor to fascism. At this stage, Mussolini was not strong enough to withstand *squadrismo* pressure and was forced to abandon his plans for the formation of a fascist Labour Party. However, in making this concession he won recognition as the undisputed leader of the newly renamed national Fascist Party.

Right from the start of his fascist movement, Mussolini had admirers in Britain. They looked on the Italian fascists with wonder and admiration. The country was moving from chaos to order and general living standards were rising. The dukes of Westminster and Buccleuch, Sir Oswald Mosley and Harold Nicholson all made pilgrimages to Rome to pay homage to the new Italian leader. Even Winston Churchill was enthralled and praised fascism by saying, 'Fascism has rendered a service to the entire world ... If I were Italian, I am sure that I would have been with [Mussolini] entirely from the beginning [for] providing the necessary antidote to the Russian poison.'[4] The Italian nation, however, was looked on as a lesser power and while fascism seemed to be working for them, it was of little relevance to a world power such as Britain. Churchill's apparent admiration was tempered by his observation that 'we have our own way of doing things'. Austen Chamberlain called Mussolini 'a wonderful man [who was]working for the greatness of his country' but he said that it would be a mistake to 'apply British standards to un-British conditions'. 'Mussolini,' he averred, 'would not be a fascist if he were an Englishman in England.'[5]

It is not true to say, however, that post-war fascist movements were necessarily populated predominantly by bitter ex-combatants. There were, in fact, a higher percentage of the *squadristi* who had been too young to fight in the war. It is more significant, especially in the case of Germany, that membership was seen to include a high percentage of young people who had not fought but who had been old enough to experience the massive patriotic propaganda put out at the end of the war in which an apparently united national community had fought heroically and, in the end, been betrayed by the politicians. It was a focal point of Nazi propaganda that these young people would be motivated to redress the sacrifice of their fathers.

The paramilitary militia that sprang up in Italy and Germany immediately after the war were emulated by other extreme right-wing groups: from the Romanian Iron Guard to the British Union of Fascists (BUF), from the Spanish Phalanx to the Rexists of Léon Degrelle. They also evoked the war in their symbols and rites. Although many of the members of these militias were too young to have actively participated in the war, they were influenced by the symbols and cultural legacy of the conflict.

Chapter Three

British Fascist Movements in the 1920s

Fascist movements usually start off with a small, hardcore group who are bound together by a shared ideology and devotion to a leader, and the vast majority get no further. British politics in the 1920s has its fair share of such organisations that never got beyond this embryonic stage. In as much as the development of fascism in its early years can be thought of as a movement at all, it is clear that it was by no means a coordinated or homogenous undertaking and in no way can it be asserted that it was anything but a fringe issue in British society that went largely unnoticed by the vast majority of the population. Politically, however, the Die-Hard element within the Conservative Party was giving the Conservative Party leader Austen Chamberlain sleepless nights. 'I am fighting for my political life,' he wrote in November 1921, 'the Die-Hards are organising fiercely and strenuously,' but revolt from the right was primarily focused on imperial decline and the Die-Hards failed to make inroads, not least because they failed to attract any presigious political figure to lend coherence and stature to their movement.[1]

Although the core values of fascism were similar across continental Europe and Britain, different national traditions are key to understanding why fascism succeeded in the former and failed in the latter. The German people, in particular, had suffered a huge traumatic crisis as a result of the way its leaders had capitulated in 1918. Large sections of the population had felt betrayed by democratic values that had served them so badly. In Italy, the catastrophic defeat of its army at Caporetto had also shaken national morale and confidence in its political system. In contrast, the British people had their faith in their institutions reinforced by victory. There was no demand for an overhaul of the system as there was in Germany and Italy.

The First World War influenced fascist ideology in a number of very different ways and the responses were mixed. The democratisation of

British society and breakdown of the traditional social class system as a result of the conflict was seen by some as a retrograde step threatening ultimate collapse of the social fabric and the traditional elitist traditions that underpinned imperial power. The Bolshevik Revolution in Russia had scared some, who saw its shadow falling over Britain in the form of the socialist Labour Party becoming the major opposition party in Parliament. Others saw it as an opportunity to mobilise the masses in a national movement to create a new sort of society that relied not so much on parliamentary democracy as strong leadership unencumbered by internal dissent. Overall, British fascism inherited from the war a keen sense of nationalistic pride in Remembrance Day rituals, but most of all was energised by the increase in economic and social problems, which were seen as having been accelerated by the war. The continuing failure of Britain to make any significant military breakthrough in the long years of trench warfare encouraged some influential observers such as Arnold White to imply that forces had been at play within the British ruling class, especially those of German or Jewish extraction, to secure a German victory.

The immediate post-war period was a time of deep anxiety as Britain confronted the problems of readjustment and reconstruction. The enormous loss of aristocratic officers during the First World War had a destabilising effect, leaving the older generation without direct heirs and adrift in grief and nostalgia and unable to come to terms with a changed world. There was an atmosphere of insecurity and uncertainty provoked by the Bolshevik Revolution, the Spartacist rising in Berlin, and the establishment of 'Soviet Republics' in Bavaria and Hungary during 1919 and then further heightened by the formation of the Communist Party of Great Britain in 1920. This atmosphere was to prove conducive to the emergence of a number of radical right and proto-fascist groups such as the National Party (NP) and the British Commonwealth Union (BCU). While none had significant numbers of members, the totality of such movements indicated a strong undercurrent of reactionary anti-socialist and nationalist sympathies. Britain, however, was spared the worst due to having been granted 'such generous terms on which to negotiate [its own decline] and such favourable circumstances in which to adjust to the new global distribution of power'.[2] It had avoided military defeat and destruction of its social framework. No patriotic revolt had got anywhere close to challenging and exposing the incompetence of its political elites, who still bestrode the world stage helping to redraw the map of Europe at Versailles and who still, with diminishing confidence, ruled the Empire.

The radical right in Britain exhibited a number of elements that were not observed elsewhere. Much as on the Continent, there had long existed racist, and anti-democratic groups but it was some five years after the armistice, much later than elsewhere, that the first explicitly fascist movement in Britain, the British Fascisti (BF), was formed on 6 May 1923, based on Benito Mussolini's National Fascist Party in Italy. It was really no more than a Conservative movement, obsessed by the dangers of civil emergency and dedicated to the 'struggle against all treacherous and revolutionary movements now working for the destruction of the Throne and Empire'.[3] Unusually for the time, it was founded and presided over by a woman, Rotha Lintorn-Orman, described by her critics as 'a mannish woman' and even derided by fellow fascists as 'abnormal'.[4] She had served with the Women's Reserve Ambulance and Scottish Women's Hospital Corps during the First World War and had twice been awarded the Croix de Charité for gallantry in Salonica. However, it was still thought prudent to give the movement a more traditional character by having a male president, Lord Garvagh.

Lintorn-Orman largely funded the movement from her own resources (more to the point, her mother's resources). As with other fascist movements, the character of this organisation reflected that of its leader. While the movement did not advocate ethnic cleansing or any 'revolutionary rebirth' ideology, and did not have charismatic leadership, it was important from the point of view of introducing figures who would become important in the following decade. These included Arnold Leese, Nesta Webster, Neil Francis Hawkins, E.G. Mandeville Roe, H.J. Donavan, and William Joyce, who began their involvement in fascist politics there and would become major players in the 1930s. Leese, however, would later call it 'Conservatism with knobs on'. He had never actually believed in female suffrage, which he though was against the laws of nature, and Lintorn-Orman did not fit into his developing vision of fascist virility and male-supremacist racialism.

The party's main appeal was its 'heroic mission' to save the British middle classes, and ultimately the Empire, from the socialist 'menace'.[5] It presented the movement as made up of super-patriots, gentry and military men, who harboured an intense aversion to Bolshevism, radical socialism and militant, direct action trade unionism. It endeared itself to those who were anxious to protect their property and status in the face of a perceived socialist threat and whose views were expressed through pressure groups such as the British Empire Union, the Middle Classes Union and the National Citizens Union. Despite its name and adoption of the Italian fascist salute, it went to some lengths to emphasise its quintessential Britishness, which owed little to continental ideologies and, indeed, had only a limited understanding of Italian fascist doctrine.

The BF was really only able to come into existence because of a new outlook and approach to the role of women in society that had been brought about by their war work and, on the home front, involvement in patriotic societies, such as the Red Cross Society, the Prince of Wales Fund, and the Soldier's Parcel Fund. Many women had emerged from their wartime experiences with a renewed sense of patriotic endeavour.[6] It was less a fascist movement and better described as one promoting constitutional right-wing activism.[7] Membership peaked in the mid-1920s at around several thousand but showed a high turnover, not least because of Lintorn-Orman's eccentric and fractious leadership, and failed to make any significant impact on British political and social life.

It did, however, set a precedent for organisation through military discipline and a tendency to encourage political violence in pursuit of its objectives. Many of its senior personnel had hailed from military, naval and aristocratic backgrounds. The group was divided into various sections including intelligence, transport, and propaganda and publicity, as well as an infantry section who would become the Fascisti shock troops primed to confront the communist revolutionaries on the streets in times of civil emergency. They adopted a distinctively British fascist regalia of blue shirt, dark trousers or skirts and a blue beret or fedora. One example of this penchant for violence was when a group of hard-line anti-Semitic members of the BF broke away to form the National Fascists, which was a more virile brand of fascism more closely approximated to the Italian model. This small group of activists adopted the black shirt associated with Mussolini's *squadristi* that Lintorn-Orman had eschewed for fear of being too closely associated with the Italian fascists. They had no qualms about confronting communist opponents with street violence and even saw its own leadership arrested for common assault in an internal power struggle that involved a drawn sword and loaded pistol.

Lintorn-Orman became ever more dependent on alcohol and drugs and began to exhibit extreme tendencies. She financed strike-breakers in 1926 and endlessly pestered the police with claims of Soviet-led communist plots to overthrow the government in violent revolution. However, the failure of the General Strike to usher in a wave of communist insurrection exposed the weakness of the BF's alarmist rhetoric and went a long way towards depriving it of a core element in its ideology, resulting in a loss of political direction. It did not remain idle, however, but in a bid to remain relevant, took on a more distinctly fascist character to recover its purpose and dynamism. Alongside its anti-Bolshevik rhetoric there now emerged a more reactionary position of anti-trade union policies that sought to outlaw strikes, and several political reforms, including the disenfranchisement of persons in receipt of poor law relief for a period of six consecutive months. A more extreme reaction was evident early in the 1930s when BF policy hardened and developed into a full-blown anti-Semitism that advocated the removal of Jews from official offices in the state and depriving them of their voting rights.

When the BUF emerged in 1932 it proceeded to occupy the ideological high ground on the fascist right. The BF discussed a possible merger with the BUF, but Lintorn-Orman and others rejected the idea. Many of its senior figures and activists had already migrated to the new organisation, however, and the refusal of the BF to be swallowed up led to violence when its headquarters at 22 Stanhope Gardens were attacked by more than fifty BUF Blackshirts. They smashed the ground-floor window, entered and upset office furniture. During the raid they injured four members of the BUF, including one woman, Mrs Florence Waters, who was struck on the head with a chair and had to be treated in hospital. The BF then suffered a mortal blow when its financial base was undermined by Lintorn-Orman's mother withdrawing her allowance, forcing it into bankruptcy with debts of £1,706, and eventual dissolution in 1934. She told police that her daughter had held drunken orgies where undesirable practices took place. Other BUF members, she said, were guilty of 'plying her with drink and drugs, with a view of extracting money from her'.[8]

It is generally accepted that the BF attracted very little public interest and made little impact on the political landscape, being characterised by some as 'innocuous and often farcical'.[9] The BF's wayward policies meant that it was quite unable to compete when faced with a rival fascist organisation of greater ideological and programmatic substance, superior resource potential and possessing a more capable and charismatic leader. Historian Julie Gottlieb says that while the BF had cultivated a set of ideals that placed them firmly on the radical right, it lacked a coherent understanding of fascism. However, its mobilisation of ultra-patriotic men and women and its encouragement of female activism secures its place in the history of fascism in Britain.

It is important to appreciate what the public attitude towards Jews was in the years before the Holocaust. It was based on the traditional hostility of Christianity to Judaism, and hence Jews had been persecuted in Europe since at least the Middle Ages. In much of society, anti-Semitism was not only perfectly acceptable, but often the only form of discourse in relation to this topic.[10] Jews were portrayed as vulgar 'money-grabbing' capitalists and revolutionaries and were easy targets for conspiracy theorists to concoct stories about Jewish control and manipulation of the political agenda for their own enrichment. Jewish jokes in the worst possible taste were common currency, and many establishments such as golf clubs barred Jews from membership.

Though persecution of Jews has a history of at least two millennia, the late-nineteenth and early twentieth century witnessed a high-water mark in hatred against them, especially in western Christian societies. There are a number of well-argued theories as to why this occurred. One theory has it that European states had become less dependent on wealthy Jewish financiers and Jews experienced a new status characterised by a loss of real power while remaining holders of major wealth. But this fails to explain why levels of popular anti-Semitism tended to be higher in Romania and Germany than in Great Britain and Italy. A popular explanation for the rise of anti-Semitism is the scapegoat theory, which posits that in times of national crisis, people instinctively seek groups upon whom to assign blame for their misfortunes, but again there are exceptions such as the fact that in Italy, during a period of dramatic political and economic turmoil, Italian Jews remained untouched by events and anti-Semitism was relatively non-existent.

What made anti-Semitism different from other forms of xenophobia was that Jew hatred was more multifaceted than other kinds of prejudice. Popular anti-Semitism incorporated religious, economic, racial, and political prejudice, meaning that Jews were disliked and feared for their religious beliefs and attitudes, their so-called racial characteristics, perceived economic behaviour and power, and their assumed leadership or support of subversive political and social movements. This may help explain why Jews rather than other minorities were frequently sought out as scapegoats or useful targets during periods of both worldwide and national difficulties.[11] Although not necessarily the views of the Christian Church as a whole, the Moderator of the Church of Scotland, the Right Reverend

James Black, in March 1938, attacked the Jews for remaining 'unassimilated' and felt the need to assert that, in his view, the 'Jewish problem' could only be solved by converting them to Christianity.

In Britain, generally, there was much admiration for the way that the Nazis had revitalised the German state and while treatment of the Jews and other minorities was frowned upon, most people gave it little thought and most of those who did saw it as an internal problem of social reform for Germany to deal with in its own way. In the early years of Nazism, at least, the full extent of repression taking place in Germany did not impinge upon the British consciousness. Political indifference to the fate of the Jews is best illustrated by the delegates from thirty-two countries who met in the French resort town of Évian-les-Bains in July 1938 to discuss ways to help Jewish refugees fleeing from the Nazis. Many delegates publicly professed their sympathies for the Jews, while most countries, including the USA, Great Britain, and Australia, offered excuses for why they could not accept more refugees. In opposition to allowing more refugees into the country, Herbert Morrison, the Home Secretary, was to say in 1942, 'There is considerable antisemitism under the surface in this country. If there were any substantial increase in the number of Jewish refugees ... we should be in for serious trouble.'[12]

The association of Jews with communism would later be used by Mosley's BUF to whip up anti-Semitic feelings in areas of strong Jewish settlement, such as the East End of London and certain industrial cities in the North, but it is important to understand that this simply added to the very real growth of anti-Semitism, of its own accord, in this period. Sir Arnold Wilson, MP, in a debate in the House of Commons in July 1936 about the BUF, would draw attention to the way in which 'decent men' held mistaken views and he had 'watched with alarm and anxiety' the growth of anti-Semitism. It was an irrational fear of Jews that allowed paranoia to rise to an extreme state of unreasoning exaggeration, with the Jew once more becoming the scapegoat for the economic problems of the nation.

One of the driving forces behind the rise of fascism in the years immediately after the war was a desire for the restoration of the old order based on paternalistic deference, and an undercurrent of those sentiments found voice in The Britons, an extreme anti-Semitic publishing and political pressure group that had been founded in 1919 by Henry Hamilton Beamish. This group's overriding aim was to force all the Jews in Britain to emigrate to Palestine. While membership of The Britons had remained tiny, its influence as a publisher was significant, especially its championing of the *Protocols of the Elders of Zion*, a notorious, fabricated text, first produced in Russia in 1903, that described the alleged minutes of a late-nineteenth-century meeting of Jewish leaders to discuss how to achieve global domination for the Jews. The *Protocols* were translated into Western European languages from 1919 onwards, often funded by wealthy private individuals such as the American industrialist Henry Ford, who provided the printing cost for over 500,000 copies to be distributed in the US. While this document was exposed as fraudulent as early as 1921 in Britain, it would go on to become required reading for schoolchildren in Germany when the Nazis came to power. Of greater significance, however, was the yearning for a new society that would in some way compensate for the tragedy of war, and when it was clear that politicians were failing to create what David Lloyd George had called 'a fit country for heroes to live in' and in its place were social tensions, inflation and unemployment, the real consequences of the war hit home in a mood of frustrated anger.

The Britons had common ground with the Imperial Fascist League (IFL) and the Nordic League (NL), all of which were reactionary and racially fascist movements with implicit belief in the authenticity of the *Protocols of the Elders of Zion* and exhibited a closeness to Nazi ideology that distinguished them from the Mosley fascists. All three movements, however, had miniscule membership, which consisted for the most part of intensely anti-Semitic, middle-class bourgeoisie, but their influence was significant. While The Britons as a movement lasted little more than a few years, it spawned the Britons Publishing Society, which, as a vehicle for extreme right-wing literature, would have a much longer-lasting effect on British racist thought.

Of all the fascist parties in interwar Britain, the IFL was the one most closely resembling the German Nazi Party. It had a coherent ideology of Nordic supremacy and racial anti-Semitism but there was 'an atmosphere of inspired lunacy about many of its pronouncements'.[13] The history of the IFL is inextricably bound up with the fanatical, uncompromising, and idiosyncratic Arnold Spencer Leese.[14] A quarrelsome man with a pronounced anti-authoritarian streak,[15] Leese had no time for Christian doctrine, which, in his view, preached defeatism, internationalism and universal brotherhood with its message of liberty, equality and fraternity. Instead, he advocated what he called the 'Aryan' values of honesty, justice and love of truth. His philosophy was partly based on the ideals of medieval heroic legends.[16]

Inspired by Mussolini, Leese had joined the BF in 1924 but soon veered off on an independent course of more extreme fascism with sixty others to found the National Fascisti and later the IFL, a paramilitary-style and hierarchically organisational group, in 1928 along with Major J. Bailie and Leslie H. Sherrard. Although it was Italian fascism that brought Leese onto the political stage initially, it would be his fanatical anti-Semitism that would propel him more towards the Nazis in later years. The IFL adopted the black shirt, khaki breeches, khaki puttees, black boots, black cap and an armlet showing a Union Jack to be worn on the left arm. A swastika would be superimposed on the flag after 1933. The rank-and-file membership was formed into a counter-revolutionary force of disciplined patriots primed to defend Britain and its Empire, but it attracted little more than a few hundred followers in the whole of its existence and was financed out of Leese's own personal money. It did, however, draw in some prominent personalities from the fascist and anti-Semitic fringe, including Henry Hamilton Beamish. Leese published a newsletter, *The Fascist*, headquartered on Craven Street in Bloomsbury. It called for the extermination of Jews even before the Nazi death camps became known to the general public.

The IFL advocated a Corporate State comprising an Upper House of eminent persons who had served the state with distinction, appointed by the monarch, and a Lower House made up of representatives from industry. The Upper House would become a new aristocracy of pure Aryan stock, trusted men to replace the decadent elite of the old order. All in all they would encapsulate the key principles of the old English craft guilds, with their aristocratic ideal of service and efficiency, and would eschew all concepts of liberal democracy, the universal mass franchise, the party system and parliamentary government.

Many historians claim that the public was 'blissfully unaware of [IFL] activities' and called it a 'talking shop for cranks'.[17] It did try to create a separate niche for itself on the fascist right by promoting its anti-Semitic and racial policies and in this way began to collaborate with the Nordic League, a group committed to spreading 'race-consciousness' among those in the nation of 'Nordic blood' and which saw itself at the service of 'those patriotic bodies known to be engaged in exposing and frustrating the Jewish stranglehold on our Nordic realm'. In Nazi Germany the Nordic League was seen as 'the British branch of international Nazism'.

Its membership included the Duke of Wellington, William Joyce, A.K. Chesterton, Lord Brocket and the Duke of Hamilton, all of whom would later become members of the secretive Right Club. Leese would go too far in the eyes of the law, however, in 1936 when he revived an ancient myth going back to 1255 according to which a boy had been abducted and ritually slaughtered at the Jewish Passover feast. Leese repeated this story in the IFL newspaper *The Fascist*, suggesting that the practice had been repeated over the centuries and was still going on. He was charged with seditious libel and causing a public mischief. When he refused to pay the fines imposed upon him, Leese was sentenced to six months' hard labour.

Despite its minimal following, the IFL showed itself to be relevant through its acts of physical violence against Jews during the mid-1930s, which contributed to the increase in fear, insecurity and tension within the Jewish community. In a speech delivered at an IFL meeting in 1937, Beamish is recorded as having lauded Hitler as the man who would destroy Soviet communism and so enthused the audience that they all saluted with a 'Heil Hitler' at the end.

In 1932, the IFL would be approached by Mosley's BUF with a view to amalgamation, but Leese found Mosley's 'Kosher fascism' to be insufficiently focused on the Jewish question. In 1934, the IFL amalgamated with the NL and swept up a number of smaller organisations such as the Militant Christian Patriots, the White Knight of Britain and the National Socialist League to form a militant fascist and anti-Semitic organisation based on the German *Nordischer Gesellschaft*, who had sent representatives to Britain in 1935 to encourage what the Germans saw as the English branch of International Nazism. The guiding light of the NL was Archibald Henry Maule Ramsay, the Member of Parliament for Peebles, who had also formed the Right Club. Both the NL and the Right Club were considered important enough to be penetrated by MI5 intelligence agents. Ramsay, along with Mosley, was considered to be the most significant figure on the fascist fringe of British politics. Like Leese, he was greatly influenced by the *Protocols of the Elders of Zion* and subscribed wholeheartedly to anti-Semitic conspiracy theories.

Nesta Webster, 'the grand dame of British conspiracy theory'[18], was part of a movement that elevated racial fascism to prominence through the publishing ventures of the Duke of Northumberland and the Boswell Publishing Company. Through the pages of the *Morning Post*, the *National Review* and *The Patriot*, the idea of a Jewish plot was kept before the minds of many unsuspecting readers, but the number of people who were seriously swayed by fears of a 'Judaeo-Masonic plot' was a very small percentage of the population. Webster had been on the Grand Council of the BF in 1926. For her, the *Protocols of the Elders of Zion* was a genuine document that explained all the ills of modern society as a Jewish conspiracy fomented by a cabal of secret societies. Initially it was Freemasonry that Webster attacked in books, pamphlets and speeches, but over time the focus of her venom became the German Secret Society of the Illuminati, and eventually the Jews. She was in thrall to the occult and believed herself to be the reincarnation of the Comtesse de Sabran, a character from the French Revolution that, for her, was the roots cause of all the ills in the world. From the French Revolution to the Russian Revolution, it had been the Jews, said Webster, who had undermined the national state and this theory was encapsulated in her work *Secret Societies and Subversive Movements*, which saw all plots, revolutions and attacks on society as having been caused by black magic, mass hypnosis and telepathy. This idea was of little significance in the interwar years but would find a new and enthusiastic audience in post-war Britain and the US.

By the start of the 1930s, the Die-Hards were having rather more success in pushing their agenda. Unemployment, international financial meltdown and rising worker unrest had all contributed to a much more febrile atmosphere socially and politically, and the Conservative Party experienced fierce internal strife within its rank and file membership. The rebels also had the benefit of a seasoned politician to give voice to their concerns when Churchill led a revolt ostensibly against the government's India policy, but in the end, it was not enough. Churchill had a sufficient number of detractors who were quick to label him as an 'adventurer with no fixed principles'. Lord Beaverbrook said of him that he was 'everything in every party [and] has held every view on every question'.[19]

Chapter Four

The Suffragette Movement and Fascism

Fascist movements that gained traction in Europe during the 1930s had a number of common characteristics: they had a contempt for democracy while using its conventions to climb to power; they tended to be financed by a relatively small number of wealthy individuals and institutions rather than collecting funds from a mass movement of working and middle-class people; and they had a fierce intolerance of opposition either within or without the movement. Furthermore, they favoured strong leadership, often a single person whose word was law and who would be the final arbiter of what was and was not acceptable. In this light, it might be argued that the Women's Social and Political Union (WSPU) was a proto-fascist movement. It was run by a single-minded and determined woman and embodied her personal ideas, over which nobody else was allowed to have any influence.

The WSPU was set up in Manchester as an offshoot of the Independent Labour Party by Emmeline Pankhurst in 1903 and became known as the Suffragette Movement three years later. This movement has become renowned for trailblazing in pursuit of women's voting rights but its methods were extreme. It had no compunction about inciting civil disobedience and direct action in what Emmeline called a 'reign of terror' in pursuit of its goal of 'making England and every department of English life insecure and unsafe'.[1] Its methods included bombings and arson attacks.

One of the groups that the Suffragettes saw as being in need of political enlightenment to rouse them into rebellion against the government were working-class men and women who, on the surface, seemed indifferent or outright hostile to the WSPU, and it was they who became victims of the bombing, arson and acid attacks launched by the WSPU in the two years before the start of the First World War. The use of terror against anybody who stands in the way of the leader's plans is common to all fascist movements. If the protagonists attain power, then the terror may be state sanctioned, as in Nazi Germany, otherwise individual acts of terrorism will be carried out against anybody getting in the way of the group. It is in this context that the Suffragettes' bombings and arson must be seen. Although ostensibly aimed at the government, the victims of the terrorism were in fact ordinary men and women, almost all of them belonging to the working class.

Emmeline Pankhurst had a complete disregard for the law if it stood in the way of her political ambitions. This is illustrated by her incitement of her followers to violence and subsequent denial of the right of any court to condemn them. The WSPU's policy of direct action, including sustained campaigns of property destruction, began on so-called Black Friday on 18 November 1910, when she led a deputation of around 300 women to Parliament, and resulted in long and violent clashes with the police. This eventually led to destructive action. On 1 March 1913 it was said that approximately 150 women, armed with hammers, stones and clubs, simultaneously smashed the windows of shops and offices in London's West End. Over 126 women were put on trial following the window-smashing campaign. The sentences at the trial ranged from fourteen days to six months, the harshest reserved for the working-class elements of the movement. Seventy-six women were sentenced to hard labour.

Pankhurst was brought to trial in 1913 for her part in the bombing of the house of David Lloyd George, who was then Chancellor of the Exchequer. Given an audience, especially in a court of law, Emmeline was quick to denounce corruption of the state and the threat of destruction of the English race, which was threatened by sexually transmitted diseases carried by men resulting in both infertility in women and the birth of deformed babies. The court, however, on 3 April 1913, sentenced her to three years' imprisonment for inciting terrorism. When the First World War broke out, the WSPU reached an agreement with the government under which they would end all militant activities and help the war effort if all Suffragettes in prison were released.

One of the guiding principles of fascists would be an aggressive nationalism based on the idea that their own countries were superior to others and that an empire founded by their nation would be a glorious thing. This was one of the fundamental beliefs of the early WSPU. Another important allure for many acolytes was a sense of belonging to a group whose beliefs were dictated by a wise and strong leader, leaving one no longer personally responsible for one's actions, and in this regard, again, it is no surprise to see that many suffragettes would find a home in the BUF.

The Suffragette Movement and Fascism

In his book *Suffragette Fascists: Emmeline Pankhurst and her Right-Wing Followers*, Simon Webb makes the point that 'the same general feelings and emotions which are common to religious services, sporting events, certain political demonstrations and pop concerts, both fascist rallies and suffragette gatherings offered something more, something which for a certain kind of individual is tremendously alluring ... it is not very hard to see how suffragettes could see the same attractions for a fascist movement in later years that they once felt for the WSPU.'[2] Christabel Pankhurst described her feelings of exultation and rapture at burning down a church or planting a bomb, which suggests that it was the act of terrorism itself that motivated her rather than any political changes resulting from the actions.

One significant characteristic of fascism in the years between the two world wars was anti-Semitism, which took many forms but essentially claimed that Jews were parasitic foreigners and did not really belong in the European countries in which they lived. Anti-Semitism was an important part of the Suffragette message. The two strands of anti-Semitism that were expressed by the Suffragette movement were firstly that Jews worked their way up into important positions as wealthy businessmen or politicians, and then used their influence to help enrich their fellow Jews, who would take over first the country and ultimately the entire world. Secondly, it was claimed that the country was being overrun with immigrants or undesirable types, usually Jews, who were creating unemployment, bringing down wages and also encouraging prostitution.[3]

Mary Sophia Allen, an extraordinary and outrageous woman, had been one of the first British policewomen. She had been born and brought up in Bristol, where she rebelled against the strictures of middle-class life and, in 1908, at the age of thirty, had left home to become a Suffragette. She was jailed three times for smashing windows, went on hunger strike, and was forcibly fed in Holloway Prison. When the First World War came, during which the WSPU was dissolved and Suffragette activity was suspended, her penchant for uniforms attracted her to the new Women Police Service. She soon became its leader and contributed a great deal to women's policing in Germany, Ireland, and at home, and supplied hundreds of trained women to police munitions factories. Her work was rewarded with an OBE.

The authorities, however, were dismayed to see that Mary wanted more power and influence than they were prepared to give. Her lifelong obsession with uniforms and masculine authority drew her to dictatorial men such as Hitler and Mussolini, both of whom she met on her travels, and she later became a devoted follower of Mosley and the BUF. She had tried to recapture the semi-military style of the WSPU in the woman's police reserve in the 1920s but had become detached from the feminist movement, which she regarded as a symptom of a degraded political system. Nancy Astor, the first female member of Parliament, was particularly derided as a 'sorry specimen of feminine irresponsibility' who had sold out to the traditional political parties.

Mary Raleigh Richardson is remembered best for her mutilation of the Diego Velázquez painting 'The Rokeby Venus' in London's National Gallery on 10 March 1914 on the grounds that she hated the way nude paintings were 'gloated over by men'.[4] She justified the attack on the painting as a means of drawing attention to the plight of Emmeline Pankhurst, who was on hunger strike in Holloway Prison at the time. It also led to many museums closing their doors to unaccompanied women. She described the attack thus:

> I dashed up to the painting. My first blow with the axe merely broke the protective glass. But, of course, it did more than that, for the detective rose with his newspaper still in his hand and walked round the red plush seat, staring up at the skylight which was being repaired. The sound of the glass breaking also attracted the attention of the attendant at the door who, in his frantic efforts to reach me, slipped on the highly polished floor and fell face downward. And so I was given time to get in a further four blows with my axe before I was, in turn, attacked.[5]

In her early life Richardson had studied art and then became a journalist. When she witnessed a brutal police suppression of a WSPU meeting in 1910, she joined the movement in what she described as the 'holy crusade' and soon engaged in militant activities. Her dedication to the cause and commitment may be measured by the fact that over the next few years she was arrested nine times for assaulting the police and breaking windows, serving several sentences in Holloway Prison. There she went on hunger strike and was forcibly fed. Each time she was released she immediately committed another crime and was arrested again.

When Emmeline Pankhurst authorised the WSPU to carry out arson attacks, Richardson was one of those who engaged with enthusiasm. Two failed attempts were made to burn down the houses of members of the government who opposed women having the vote, but then a house being built for David Lloyd George, at that time Chancellor of the Exchequer, was badly damaged by fire and another arson attack at The Elms, a house owned by the Countess of Carlisle, was believed to have been carried out by Richardson.

The arson campaign escalated to include railway stations, cricket pavilions, racecourse stands and golf clubhouses, where slogans in favour of women's suffrage were cut and burned into the turf. Suffragettes also cut telephone wires and destroyed letters by pouring chemicals into post boxes. After one attack, Richardson was arrested and, after being force-fed in prison, suffered poor health and was later operated on for appendicitis. Along with Flora Drummond and Elsie Bowerman, Richardson founded the Women's Guild of Empire, an organisation aimed at furthering a sense of patriotism in working-class women and defeating such socialist manifestations as strikes and lock-outs.

Richardson was with Emily Davison at Ascot Racecourse on 4 June 1913, where the Derby was being held. When the horses passed the place where they were standing, Davison ran out on the course and attempted to grab the bridle of Anmer, a horse owned by King George V. The horse hit Emily and the impact fractured her skull. She died four days later without having regaining consciousness. Richardson fled to Epsom station, where a sympathetic station master hid her in the ladies' toilet. Along with Norah Dacre Fox, Mary Allen and Mercedes Barrington, Richardson was one of the first women to join Mosley's BUF in 1932, because in that movement she saw 'the courage, the action, the loyalty, the gift of service, and the ability to serve which I had known in the suffragette movement'.[6] In April 1934, Richardson took over as head of the Women's Section of the BUF.

It was Norah Dacre Fox's skill as a speaker that had brought her to the attention of the WSPU leadership and saw her elected as General Secretary in March 1913. On 30 July 1914 she was arrested outside Buckingham Palace while attempting to deliver a letter from Emmeline Pankhurst to King George V. She was imprisoned in Holloway, where she went on hunger strike for which she received a medal with three bars from the leaders of the WSPU. At the end of the war, Fox spoke for many when she called for a clean sweep of all persons of German blood, without distinction of sex, birthplace, or nationality, to eliminate German influence. Any person in this country, she was quoted in *The Times* as saying, no matter who he was or what his position, who was suspected of protecting German influence, should be tried as a traitor, and, if necessary, shot. There must be no compromise and no discrimination.[7]

In April of that year, having changed her name to Norah Elam, Fox shared a platform with William Joyce in her West Sussex region that was described as a hub of fascist activity, and she later spoke to an audience at Littlehampton in which she gave a clear and lucid exposition of fascist policy. She was soon admitted to Mosley's inner circle. So enamoured of Hitler's new Germany was she that she sent her twelve-year-old son to live in Germany, where he joined the Hitler Youth. The British Intelligence officer Guy Liddell suspected her of being a link in a money chain from the Nazis to the BUF.

The BUF is traditionally seen as a predominantly male movement, but the evidence shows that it was highly opportunistic in exploiting minority issues, many of which were local in character. It is now clear that, unlike fascist movements in Germany and Italy, which exhibited extreme patriarchal attitudes, it actively encouraged the extensive participation of women in its activities with the appearance of gangs of militant British fascist women alongside the men and provided a striking contrast to the idea that women were prepared to return to ideals of female domesticity. It has been estimated that women comprised one quarter of the total membership.[8] They wore a black blouse, black beret, and grey skirt, but no lipstick or other make-up. In Nelson, Lancashire, some women received training in jiujitsu so that they could manhandle female communist agitators at meetings. Gottlieb says that it is clear Suffragettes from middle- and upper-class conservative backgrounds who became involved with the BUF, such as Mary Richardson, Mary Allen and Norah Elam, were every bit as racist as their male counterparts.[9] It is possible to detect a number of ideas such as extremely dangerous and unscientific concepts of racial purity and eugenics that were advanced by the WSPU and were later popular with fascists and Nazis.

The Suffragettes brought with them into the BUF a legacy of their militant feminist struggle in the pre-war period and their disillusionment with the post-war condition of the women's movement in the aftermath of female enfranchisement. In particular, they retained the militancy of their earlier Suffragette struggle, arguing that voting was pointless in a democracy that was 'a sinking ship'. In the BUF, they were welcomed with favourable publicity and went on to hold prominent positions of trust in the movement's Women's Section. For them, their journey from the WSPU to the BUF was a logical progression and their Suffragette struggle was seen as a precedent for fascist dissent.

Chapter Five

British Press Coverage of Nazi Germany in the 1930s

At the beginning of the 1930s, enthusiasm for fascist policies in Britain was limited to a few small groups who did not particularly register on the national psyche. While these groups may well have been influenced to some extent by the rise of fascism in Italy and the nascent Nazi movement in Germany, the vast majority of British opinion was governed by what people read in the newspapers and much of their content was controlled by the few powerful men who owned them. According to Adrian Bingham's *Monitoring the Popular Press: an historical perspective*, in 1930 some two thirds of the British population read a newspaper every day. Serious news reporting was dominated by *The Times* and to a lesser extent the *Daily Telegraph*, although they did not have the largest circulation. The liberal, provincial *Manchester Guardian*, whose influence greatly exceeded its modest circulation, had dismissed Hitler as a mere braggart without genuine or sustainable principles, and thought those in his party, though more aggressive, violent and barbaric, would behave as 'ordinary politicians when in office'. Right from the start, on the domestic front, the *Guardian* portrayed the BUF as a paper tiger and Mosley as a pinchbeck candidate for dictatorship.[1] *The Observer* saw Hitler as a shallow ranting fool.[2] In the Tory press, expressions of tolerance for, and, in the popular press, admiration of, the fascist regimes in Italy and Germany were commonplace at first, but the mainstream press generally regarded both with a degree of complacency, despite reservations regarding the methods used to suppress opposition.

Mosley had been a figure of interest to the press for some time before the founding of the BUF and he provided a touch of glamour that earlier manifestations of British fascism lacked, but it was with some disappointment to him that the public seemed more interested in his social life rather than his political philosophy. Even when the press started covering his meetings, its attention was on his family background, his references to the

Jews and any incidents of violence, however minor. It was rare for any newspaper to report on BUF policy or give space to its propaganda.

The Scottish travel writer Sir John Foster Fraser wrote in the *Aberdeen Press and Journal* on 8 May 1933 that the 'Nazis have stopped Berlin being the wickedest city in Europe', and alleged that many of the Berlin nightclubs were controlled by Jews, who were likened to 'pests wriggling about its heart veins'. Martin Wiesmes, writing in the *Derry Journal* in the same year, said that Hitler and his supporters had created a new moral utopia in Germany. 'There is a freshness in the air, and the hearts of the people are light once more,' he wrote. The Reverend Thomas Tiplady, after a four-day trip to Germany, wrote in the *Methodist Times* that Hitler had united Germany 'without shedding a drop of blood'.

In October the cleansing of Berlin and the rest of Germany by the Nazi Party received the passionate endorsement of Dr Arthur Cayley Headlam, the Bishop of Gloucester and chairman of the Church of England Council of Foreign Relations. In a letter to *The Times* he spoke highly of the wholesome and healthy way of life in Berlin, where the young people were now anxious for self-discipline and self-sacrifice. A few years later, in 1937, when the Lutheran Pastor Martin Niemöller was arrested and thrown into a concentration camp, Headlam, in a letter to *The Times*, said that Niemöller had been asking for trouble and had only himself to blame. A year later in 1934, Henry Wilson Harris, editor of *The Spectator*, saw a fundamentally decent, kindly people dedicated to 'wholesome family life' where 'quiet looking youths in S.A. or S.S. uniforms peacefully wandered among the pictures and statues in the Kaiser Friedrich Museum'.

When Geoffrey Dawson, born Geoffrey Robinson, left Eton and then Magdalen College, Oxford, he had joined the Colonial Office under Joseph Chamberlain and later joined the High Commission for South Africa. He left the service and became the South Africa correspondent for *The Times* in 1906, moving to London three years later to take up a permanent post with the newspaper. He got on so well with the owner, Lord Northcliffe, acquiescing to his every view and prejudice, that he was appointed editor in 1912.

The Times showed little interest in events in Germany until sales of the *Daily Telegraph* were seen to surge when it started reporting on the rise of Hitler's Nazis, but even then the pro-German views of Dawson at *The Times* meant that stories from correspondents were frequently rewritten to conform to a particular viewpoint that masked the more brutal aspects of the Nazi regime. As an early example, Norman Ebbutt, a chief *Times* correspondent in Berlin, who spoke fluent German and was well versed in German political history, complained that his reports were frequently trimmed or distorted and even rejected if they were too critical of the Nazis. Final concluding paragraphs were often cut, he said, leaving the reader without a clear idea of the main theme of the article. On one occasion, a report by Ebbutt of six deaths during a riot at a British-owned factory in Germany was cut by half and relegated to an inside page.[3]

The British press in the early 1930s was well served by knowledgeable correspondents such as Ebbutt, who had a deep understanding of the German scene having been stationed in Berlin since 1925, while another journalist, Frederick Augustus Voigt, had been the *Manchester Guardian*'s Berlin correspondent since 1920. They had a complex web of sources and contacts, had witnessed the struggles of the Weimar Republic and had seen, over an extended period, the rise of the Nazis and their methods. Coverage of Germany by the British press during the 1930s has received much attention and criticism for its blinkered attitude, but Kylie Galbraith has done extensive research and concludes that, on the whole, the British public was given extensive and detailed information about what was happening in that country, except for the issue of violent repression, murder, terror and persecution of the Jews and other minorities. While there are glaring examples of censorship in the British press, not by the government but by the newspaper management itself, it is important to take a balanced view and understand that the picture is more complicated and the pro-Nazi elements that are frequently highlighted do not distort the issue. It is notable also that criticism of press coverage also came from the readership. When *The Spectator* reported on the atmosphere of fear and repression in Germany, it was heavily criticised by its readership and printed nothing more on the subject.

The Times kept readers up to date with news of arrests and the opening of new concentration camps, but refrained from comment in its editorials. Furthermore, Dawson made excuses to not print an article that uncovered the inhuman and violent treatment of prisoners in Dachau.

The influence of Dawson at *The Times* and his policy towards Germany was clear only four weeks after Hitler had been sworn in as Chancellor when, on 27 February 1933, the home of the German parliament, the Reichstag building, burned to the ground. The Nazis claimed that it was a communist plot and the fire had been started by Marinus van der Lubbe. A Reuters report, however, claimed that van der Lubbe had been shown around the building immediately before the fire, which was started by agents of the *Sturmabteilung*. Later reports would show that van der Lubbe was arrested at the fire but had arrived after it had started. All this evidence was rejected by *The Times* editors, who had 'no belief in it', and the official Nazi explanation was allowed to prevail. Anyway, the British public were not interested, Dawson said. He was right. Until 1933, the Nazis had been just one of many extreme parties, of the right and left, on the Continent. There was little to suggest what they would later become.

There is evidence to show that the Nazis actually made great efforts to manipulate their coverage in *The Times* in particular and show themselves in a more positive light. This involved Alfred Rosenberg, the British correspondent of the Nazi Party newspaper the *Volkischer Beobachter*, acting as a propagandist and conniving with a shady character called William de Ropp to have Ebbutt moved from his Berlin posting. Rumours were spread to Nancy Astor, among others, about Ebbutt's supposed alcoholism but, despite his reservations, Dawson appreciated Ebbutt's journalistic experience and deep knowledge, and Ebbutt remained in post. Rosenberg had begun his campaign as early as 1931, when he went to London and met Dawson, among others. At that time he had described his aim as making contact with 'politicians, journalists, officers and personalities of public life [to] counteract the "horror stories" about the aims and methods of the Party, while stressing Germany's position as a front-line defence against Bolshevism'.[4]

Rosenberg became head of the Nazi Party's *Aussenpolitische Amt* (APA), the foreign policy section, a kind of foreign information service, in April 1933 and worked, uncomfortably, alongside the head of the *Auswärtiges Amt* (Foreign Ministry), Konstantin Von Neurath. The APA answered directly to Hitler and was used by him as one of the first of the many channels to try to forge relationships with other countries without having to pass through the traditional diplomatic channels.

Ebbutt refused to follow the trend and continued reporting what he saw as the true situation in Germany, but there is evidence that his personal opinions did not reflect the reality. He privately reported to the Chief Rabbi of the Jewish Board of Deputies that he thought the Nazi anti-Semitic stance was weakening due to the lessening of the paramilitary *Sturmabteilung* (SA) influence over Nazi policy. He believed that the strength of the German Army in politics and international approbation would act as a brake on the persecution of the Jews but if that failed and the Nazis achieved total power, the danger to the Jewish communities would increase significantly. The Nazis, he said, were supreme propagandists and posed a threat due to their willingness to use violence. It was his conclusion that the image of Hitler portrayed in the British press in the early 1930s that showed him as a visionary was overplayed at the expense of the threat he posed to the Jews.

After Hitler's accession to the Chancellorship, Ebbutt refused to be cowed by threats from the Nazis and said that in order to retain some self-esteem he would continue to criticise the 'official' German version of events. However, in order not to risk actual expulsion, he tended, after 1933, to restrict criticism to the Nazi persecution of the Christian Church. Any reporting of concentration camps, persecution of the Jews and other minorities was strictly censored and any attempt by journalists to write about these subjects would result in harassment and vilification as wild rumour-mongers. Ebbutt's flat in Berlin was raided by the police in early 1933 and Voigt also had his flat in Paris searched by Nazis. Robert Dell of the *Manchester Guardian* was forced to flee Germany after his reporting on the Reichstag Fire trial in late 1933. Pembroke Stephens of the *Daily Express* and G.E.R. Gedye of the *Daily Telegraph* also spoke of the dangers they faced in reporting German affairs truthfully and accurately.

One British journalist who did respond favourably to Nazi overtures was Sefton Delmer of the *Daily Express* who, in a piece printed on 3 May 1931, portrayed Hitler as a 'messianic leader ... determined to restore order out of the chaos of communist violence and democratic instability'. Soon afterwards Delmer invited Hitler to write an article himself for the newspaper, but he declined on the grounds that it might be seen as 'presumptuous'.[5] He was friendly with Ernst Röhm and knew Hitler after meeting him in 1931. Thereafter, he became a firm favourite of Hitler and was the only foreign correspondent to be invited to fly with Hitler on his private aircraft during the 1932 German presidential election campaign. He was later given an exclusive interview when Hitler became Chancellor in 1933. Delmer's articles, often sensationalised, leaned heavily towards condemnation of communism as the main threat to British democracy and other newspapers found themselves obliged to echo that sentiment in order to maintain their circulation figures.

In early February 1933, the British press had seemed prepared to give Hitler and the Nazis the benefit of the doubt but the wave of arrests that followed the Reichstag fire changed all that. *The Times, News Chronicle, Manchester Guardian*, and even the *Daily Mail*, recognised that the fire had seen the end of democracy in Germany and the start of a dictatorship.

Voigt reported that the Nazis had been able to dismantle Weimar parliamentary democracy in a mere six months. While the press reported on the destruction of German democracy, it failed to apply the same scrutiny to the campaign of terror that accompanied it. In the few articles that were published by the *Daily Express*, it downplayed the violence as a consequence of the Nazi struggle to defeat communism. The *Daily Mail* denied that a campaign of terror existed at all, claiming that it was a figment of the imagination of the foreign, especially French, press.

An official German statement in 1933 stated that 'mischievous reports on the political situation in Germany published in the foreign press [have resulted in] serious measures [being] prepared against a number of foreign correspondents'.[6] Noel Panter, the Munich correspondent for the *Daily Telegraph*, was arrested in October 1933, charged with espionage and thrown into Ettstrasse prison. He was released after nine days and expelled from the country. Suppression of accurate reporting from journalists on the spot was, in the main, successful and independent reporters outside the country found it harder to verify stories without endangering the lives of their sources within the country. The other side of the coin was that the Nazis would invite prominent journalists and opinion-formers who were much more sympathetic to Germany and entertain them with lavish hospitality. The British Conservative MP Sir Arnold Wilson actually went on German radio and spoke of hope and confidence that comradeship between nations would prevail.

After 1934, Ebbutt found his situation in Berlin becoming ever more uncomfortable. Foreign correspondents who criticised the Nazis were in constant danger of molestation or worse by the SA and many were expelled. Having risked much by writing his articles, Ebbutt was then dismayed to find that, in London, the pro-German editorial team at *The Times* repeatedly cut his articles so that 'the original meaning was distorted'.[7] Allied to the extent to which Britain and the wider world placed its trust in the accuracy of *The Times*' reporting, this manipulation of the news gravely worried Ebbutt. However, his complaints to the editorial team were brushed aside with vague promises and he was prevented from reporting on the more controversial aspects of German policy. The newspaper instead asked Philip Henry Kerr, 11th Marquess of Lothian, an 'insider' in political circles and a leading figure in the Liberal Party, to visit Hitler and write about it. Lothian was something of an arrogant know-all who thought he had all the answers to Britain's problems. He readily accepted the commission, believing that he was well placed to circumvent the normal diplomatic channels and, through personal contact, work for a better understanding with Germany. The two men met on 29 January 1935 in the presence of Joachim von Ribbentrop and Rudolf Hess, with Nazi apologist T.P. Conwell-Evans acting as interpreter. Kerr reported that, in a personal interview, Hitler ruled out the use of force against Poland and assured him that Germany had a sincere desire for peace and had no intention of interfering in 'beloved Austria' by force.

Then in early 1935, Dawson, and his deputy, Robert Barrington-Ward, actively suppressed articles warning of the dangers of German rearmament. Thereafter, Ebbutt was restricted to writing articles on subjects authorised beforehand by his editors. In a letter written by Dawson in May 1937 he said that he did his utmost 'to keep out of the paper anything that might hurt Nazi German susceptibilities'. The US journalist William Shirer, who had always found that Ebbutt took great care to write 'accurately and in detail about the excesses of the Nazis', wrote in his diary that he found Ebbutt 'extremely discouraged' by his London office not wanting to hear 'too much of the bad side of Nazi Germany'.[8] At this time, a number of *Times* journalists resigned in protest, namely A.L. Kennedy in 1936, A.L. Barker in 1937 and Godfrey Winn in 1938, but it must be said that *The Times* continued to print articles keeping readers up to date with developments in Germany, particularly the church struggle and the persecution of Jews.

Although the *Manchester Guardian* had become the most outspoken critic of the Nazi regime and its brutal methods, Voigt struggled to get his copy past his editor, W.P. Crozier, who pleaded with him to tone down his reports, which were 'dogmatic and uncompromising in the highest degree'. If reports were toned down, however, Galbraith finds no evidence that the brutal nature of the Nazi regime was obscured and careful readers of the serious press would have been left in no doubt. Galbraith is clear that both *The Times* and the *Manchester Guardian* were tireless in their coverage of German affairs in the 1930s, with articles about Germany appearing almost daily in *The Times* in 1933, and reports by Berlin correspondents were highly detailed. She notes that *The Times* has been heavily criticised for its coverage of Germany in the 1930s, but analysis shows that it reported the destruction of democracy in more depth than any other British newspaper.

Never a man who enjoyed good health at the best of times, Ebbutt fell ill in January 1936 and spent some time in the mountains of Czechoslovakia to recuperate. He was expelled from Berlin in August 1937 with fifty other foreign correspondents for reasons that were never made clear, but which coincided with a dramatic increase in Nazi censorship of news media and virulent attacks on foreign press that printed anti-Nazi articles. A week previously, Ebbutt had been the subject of an extreme attack in the German press for spreading 'lies and distortions'. He suffered a stroke and partial paralysis shortly afterwards and never worked again as a journalist.

When the British government belatedly issued a White Paper at the outbreak of war, entitled 'Papers Concerning the Treatment of German Nationals in Germany', it was particularly galling for correspondents from newspapers such as the *New Statesman and Nation* and the *Manchester Guardian*, who had worked tirelessly to uncover and report the horrors of the concentration camps ever since Dachau had opened in March 1933. The *Guardian* was incandescent, reporting that: 'The White Paper has been greeted in some quarters as though it contained "revelations" of something new.'[9]

Undoubtedly the most important press baron in the story of British fascism was Lord Rothermere, who swung his considerable weight behind Mosley's BUF in 1934 and propelled it into the mainstream. He encouraged his editors to portray the movement as relevant and necessary for the rejuvenation of British society.[10] The support of the Rothermere titles, particularly that of the *Mail*, led to a rapid increase in membership of the BUF and forced other British newspapers to take notice.

Chapter Six

Lord Rothermere

Harold Sidney Harmsworth, 1st Viscount Rothermere, inherited the Amalgamated Press empire in 1922, becoming one of the most influential men in Britain. He was owner not only of the *Daily Mail* and the *Daily Mirror*, two of the highest-circulation newspapers in the country, but also the *Sunday Pictorial*, *Sunday Dispatch* and the *London Evening News*, together with a number of magazines. He was one of the richest men in England and had been generally sympathetic to the Nazis in the early 1930s but, at the same time, was a strong proponent of rearmament in the face of a resurgent Germany. He had an uncomplicated, undemocratic and elitist approach to politics, believing that the country should be led by the upper classes and that women and working-class people in general should be barred from voting since they were incapable of understanding the issues that faced the country. His overriding preoccupation was fear of left-wing revolution. He was, said one commentator, 'very near to being unbalanced on the issue of communism'.[1] His support for Germany was based, in part, on his belief that offering Hitler a free hand to deal with the communist menace would be in Britain's best long-term interests. When Hitler was made Chancellor, Rothermere was quick to use his newspaper to register approval. It would be the only major British daily to take a consistently pro-Nazi line.[2]

Rothermere's enthusiasm for Hitler would be nurtured and exploited throughout the 1930s as a result of his relationship with an Austrian princess whom he had met in 1927. He had been in the habit of spending much of each winter in his villa, La Dragonnière, situated at Cap Martin on the Cote d'Azur, and it was here that he first met and developed a relationship with the beautiful and beguiling divorcée Julianne Stephanie Maria Veronika Richter von Hohenlohe-Waldenburg-Schillingsfürst. The two found common interest in ballet and gambling at the Monte Carlo casinos.

Stephanie Richter was born in Prague the illegitimate daughter of a Jewish woman, Ludmilla Kuranda, and a Jewish moneylender, Max

Weiner, but she would later be accepted by the Nazis as being of pure Aryan stock. She was schooled in England and by the age of twenty-one was fluent in a number of European languages. The flair she would later show for social intercourse was nurtured early in her life by her Aunt Clothilde, who owned a house in Kensington, west London, an apartment in Berlin and a villa on the shores of Lake Wannsee, near Berlin. She was well known for throwing wonderful parties, to which she invited the most famous dancers of the day like the celebrated Anna Pavlova. She also broadened Stephanie's education by taking her on her travels in Europe to places like Venice, Berlin, Paris, Kiel, Corsica and Prague; widening her knowledge, her fluency in languages and her appreciation of what it meant to move easily in aristocratic society.[3]

On 12 May 1914, Stephanie entered into a short-lived marriage with Prince Friedrich Franz von Hohenlohe-Waldenburg-Schillingsfürst, who was the chief of German propaganda and director of German espionage in Switzerland. They were divorced in 1920. Stephanie spent the next few years travelling around Europe building up an impressive list of powerful contacts, some of whom were members of the nascent Nazi Party in Germany. It was her relationship with the Crown Prince Wilhelm, the Kaiser's eldest son, that first brought her to the attention of MI5 and they began routinely intercepting her communications in 1928. A British Intelligence report claimed that she had become a 'talent spotter' for Hitler and was given the job of suggesting which of the British establishment might be inclined to become friends of Hitler and Nazi Germany.[4]

Rothermere took every opportunity to impress Stephanie, who had seen an advantage in the relationship right from the start. Her involvement with the leadership of the Nazi Party in Germany had led her to appreciate how important it would be for the party to have influential supporters in other countries. Rothermere, she realised, had already shown his sympathy for the new Germany and was one of the most powerful opinion-makers in Britain through his press ownership and one who was ideally placed to influence public opinion. She managed to persuade him that she had the contacts to give him access to many of Europe's most powerful people, and that she could open doors to almost every exclusive social circle on the Continent. He appointed her as his personal emissary in Europe with a retainer of £5,000 per year. The arrangement also allowed her to encourage Rothermere's pro-Nazi views, which strongly supported the rise of Hitler's National Socialist German Workers' Party

(NSDAP), and steer him into closer relationships with Hitler's inner circle.

When Hitler seized power in January 1933, Rothermere dismissed rumours that Stephanie was a German spy and asked her to arrange a personal meeting between him and the new Führer. By this time, she had entered into a relationship with Hitler's personal adjutant, Captain Fritz Wiedemann. She could hardly have made a more fruitful contact. Wiedemann was Hitler's trusted friend, at his side constantly attending to the Führer's private correspondence and ensuring the smooth running of his office. Acutely aware of Wiedemann's influence in Berlin, Stephanie persuaded Rothermere to send Wiedemann a gift of a gold-engraved Cartier cigarette case. Wiedemann was soon able to convince Hitler of Stephanie's value as Rothermere's personal friend, implying that she had him at her beck and call, and persuaded his boss to allocate 20,000 Reichsmarks as a maintenance allowance to ensure the princess had her hotel, restaurant bills, telephone bills and taxi and travel fares paid. In early December 1933 Stephanie had her first meeting with Hitler in Berlin, in which she impressed him to the point where he began referring to her as his '*Hochverehrte Prinzessin*', revered princess. Through Stephanie, Hitler thanked Rothermere for his 'shrewd and well directed journalistic support' of his policies.[5]

In January 1934 Rothermere published an article in the *Daily Mail* in which he praised Mosley's Blackshirts and then privately sent a personally written note to Hitler via Princess Stephanie in which he expressed his view that the Blackshirts would 'rule Britain within three years'. Three months later, Rothermere finally got the letter from Hitler inviting his 'kindred spirit' to an audience in Berlin, but it would be December before an actual meeting could be arranged. This was in spite of Rothermere privately writing to the Chancellor of the Exchequer, Neville Chamberlain, in October of that year, several months after the Night of the Long Knives, saying that the Nazis were 'the most dangerous, ruthless men who have ever been in charge of the fortunes of a people ... they will stop at nothing'.[6] His reason for maintaining close relations with Hitler, he said, was in the hope that he would be in a position to exert influence on the German leader if the need arose.

The German nation had suffered enough from 'alien elements', he wrote, and what detractors called 'Nazi atrocities' amounted to 'merely a few isolated acts of violence' that had been blown up out of all proportion.[7]

Hitler showed his appreciation by writing to Rothermere, saying that the two obviously shared a common determination to establish good and enduring relations between what Hitler called 'both great Germanic peoples'. Rothermere sent copies of the letter to all leading statesmen, but it was ignored in government circles. A copy even ended up on the desk of King George V, but he was not impressed.

Rothermere had been an enthusiastic supporter of Mosley's BUF right from the start and had offered to use his whole newspaper empire in support, but Mosley felt that such a press campaign was premature and he needed more preparation and understanding of his objectives and ambitions before launching such a high-profile campaign. By January 1934, Mosley was more confident and Rothermere started a campaign in the *Daily Mail* with an article of praise entitled 'Hurrah for the Blackshirts'. It may well have been that Rothermere's support for the Blackshirts was based not on any appreciation of the virtues of fascism, but on a desire to use the movement to pressure the Conservative Party into adopting policies more in line with Rothermere's own views. From the way his papers represented the Blackshirts, it is clear that Rothermere had a limited understanding of the fascist agenda and did not fully endorse its revolutionary potential.[8] By July, however, there was a rift. Letters between Rothermere and Mosley were printed in the *Mail*. Mosley thought that Rothermere was committed more to the Conservative Party than the BUF, whereas Rothermere condemned Mosley for his anti-Semitic rhetoric and stated aims of dismantling parliamentary institutions. He also began to face pressure from his Jewish advertisers over the *Daily Mail*'s pro-Blackshirt campaign. Important businesses were threatening to withdraw their support from his papers. None of this, however, seemed to dim Rothermere's enthusiasm for the Nazi cause, but it gave him pause for thought about what he printed.

In 1935, MI5 asked the Home Office to renew the warrant that allowed them to intercept and read Stephanie's correspondence and the Foreign Office requested that the Home Secretary restrict her visits to Britain, but the request was denied owing to the 'considerable difficulties' involved in taking such a move because of her powerful friends in the establishment who could exercise influence in her favour. Rothermere met Hitler again in September 1936, and later sent him a personal gift, via Stephanie, of a valuable Gobelin tapestry. In a letter he wrote of the 'great honour and privilege to be in correspondence with Your Excellency' and welcomed the news that the Führer was in high spirits and excellent health. Hitler replied saying that the magnificent tapestry had given him great pleasure and invited Rothermere to be his guest in January 1937 in the Obersalzberg. He sent his personal railway saloon carriage to meet Rothermere and Stephanie at the Austrian border. They arrived late in the evening and spent the night at the Berghof, a distinct privilege seldom granted to foreign visitors. Rothermere sent another gift of a jade bowl to Hitler in May 1937, expressing his heartfelt thanks for their friendship. Again Hitler replied applauding Rothermere's efforts to establish a true Anglo-German friendship with *Mail* editorials that 'contain everything that corresponds to my own thoughts as well'. After the Anschluss in 1938, Rothermere again praised Hitler in a telegram for his 'triumph', but Wiedemann warned Stephanie that 'the warmongers are now in control and war is now inevitable'. In reference to Rothermere, he added that: 'If your old fool of an English Lord still supports Hitler after this he is committing high treason.'[9]

There was another side to Rothermere, however. His apparent adulation of Hitler had not blinded him to the possibility of war between Britain and Germany and he was at pains to emphasise that it had been his main objective all along to do everything he could to avoid such a catastrophe, even at the expense of turning a blind eye to the grotesque excesses of Nazi persecutions in Germany and the annexed territories. He argued forcefully for rearmament in the face of the rapidly expanding Luftwaffe. He called for 5,000 aircraft to defend the country if Britain was not to find itself at the mercy of her European neighbour. In 1935 he had translated his views into action, funding and founding an association called the National League of Airmen, a personal effort to give wider expression to the need to start building a strong and effective air force. He invested £50,000 in his campaign, and he attracted to the league experienced pilots and supporters, aiming to convince the population, and in particular the government, of the dire need for a modern air force.

When war broke out, Rothermere feared a total breakdown of the social order that in the end would allow communists to take over in a scenario he feared even more than defeat to Hitler. His newspapers turned ultra-patriotic and whipped up a frenzy of propaganda against 'fifth columnists'. Rothermere was now afraid that his private correspondence with Hitler congratulating him on the annexation of Czechoslovakia was going to become public and that when it did the public demand for his internment and trial for treason would prove irresistible, with not even Churchill able to protect him. To avoid the scandal, he accepted the role of inspecting the aircraft industries of Canada and the US. This was, in effect, a non-position that was simply a device to get him out of the country. He became clinically depressed and moved to Bermuda, where he died on 26 November 1940.

Chapter Seven

Nazi Camp Followers

It is important to distinguish between appeasers of Nazi Germany and those whom the historian Richard Griffiths calls 'enthusiasts'. Appeasers, he says, were 'people who ... were convinced that it was essential to seek an accommodation with Germany [but] were not necessarily friendly towards Germany herself in abstract, or in favour of the Nazi regime', whereas enthusiasts were prone to give 'positive statements of approval of Germany [in which] certain aspects of that regime had to be excused, or ignored, in favour of those aspects which had attracted approval'.[1] The people who might be described as enthusiasts or apologists for the Nazi cause always reflected a minority of public opinion but were sufficiently numerous and highly placed to affect public policy.

By 1935, Ribbentrop had all but superseded Rosenberg as Hitler's personal emissary when bypassing the *Auswärtiges Amt* by making direct contact with politicians of importance. Both were very active, with Rosenberg possibly having the better contacts. He, however, had blotted his copybook very badly in May 1933 by placing a wreath of lilies and laurel leaves, draped with a band in the German imperial colours and including a black swastika, on the Cenotaph in Whitehall. While the gesture was not welcomed by the establishment, they did not intervene and it was left to a member of the public to remove it and throw it into the Thames. James Edmonds Sears was fined 40 shillings for an 'ill-mannered' act of theft and wilful damage. In Berlin the British Ambassador Sir Horace Rumbold was summoned before an irate Hitler, who demanded to know why the court had imposed such a pathetic and lenient sentence. Another swastika would be laid at the same place in January 1936 by German ex-servicemen, who were guests of the British Legion and who were photographed giving the Nazi salute, and again it was tolerated without interference.

Ribbentrop continued Rosenberg's policy of inviting leading British personalities to visit Germany and meet Hitler. Consequently, a dinner party was given by Hitler on 19 December 1934 at which the guests of honour were Lord Rothermere, Esmond Harmsworth (Rothermere's son), George Ward Price (foreign correspondent of the *Daily Mail*) and merchant banker Ernest Tennant.[2] Ribbentrop also introduced a new strategy of working through the British Legion to reach ex-servicemen who, he felt, would have a sense of comradeship with others who had fought in the First World War, even on opposing sides.

In the summer of 1934, a group of British war veterans had visited Königsberg, where the Irishman James Murphy acted as translator for speechmaker Rudolf Hess. Murphy would become the official German translator of Hitler's speeches and became employed by the Reich Ministry of Public Enlightenment and Propaganda. Murphy's translated copy of the speech was circulated widely, and leading members of the British Legion reacted enthusiastically. They asked for permission to send a delegation to Germany in 1935 and both Anthony Eden and the Prince of Wales, who was patron of the British Legion, agreed whole heartedly. The propaganda value to Germany was enormous, and it made headlines in the German press. The delegation was given an audience with Hitler and, after a visit to Dachau, were invited to a 'quiet family supper with Himmler', who impressed them as an unassuming man anxious to do his best for his country.

A few weeks after the signing of the Anglo-German Naval Agreement on 18 June 1935, two British Tory MPs attended a Congress of the Nationalist International fronted by Dr Hans Keller, its founder, at the D'Abernon Club in London. The guest list included two British Tory MPs along with Frits Clausen, the leader of a small Danish Nazi party, and Friedrich Grimm, an NSDAP member of the German Reichstag. The Nationalist International (*Internationale Arbeitsgemeinschaft der National-isten*, or IAdN) had been founded by Keller in 1934 and was secretly financed by Joseph Goebbels's Propaganda Ministry. Its aim was to spread Nazi ideology and foster international co-operation against international communism.

Keller wanted to create a counter-organisation to the British Empire which would be based on racist and *völkisch* ideas, the mutual recognition of 'organic nationalism', and a belief in the inequality of peoples. The D'Abernon Club, named after the former British ambassador to Berlin Lord D'Abernon, had been founded to promote Anglo-German relations. There were international delegates from approximately thirty countries, including the two Conservative MPs, Daniel Gerald Somerville and John Macnamara; Herbert Foster-Anderson, a journalist from the prestigious Royal Institute of International Affairs; the former diplomat Norman

Thwaites, who was also a member of the radical January Club; the Scottish businessman Archibald Crawford; and Arthur Kitson, an influential monetary theorist and ardent anti-Semite who was obsessed with the idea that 'Jewish Money Power' had infiltrated and corrupted the British capitalist system.

Keller presented the Third Reich view of itself as a guarantor of peaceful co-operation with other nations to allay fears in Britain that Germany was seeking a revisionist war. The concepts of race and white supremacy were highlighted by the Afrikaner Herman Dirk van Broekhuizen, among others, who argued that the Union of South Africa could function as a role model for international co-operation between 'White races' and across 'White civilisation'.

Liberal internationalism and the League of Nations also came under attack and was linked to the 'unjust' terms of Versailles, but Somerville objected strongly to criticism of the League and most Britons present at the London congress refused to participate in the next one held in Oslo in summer 1936. Nevertheless, the Nationalist International continued its Nazi propaganda with the help of Foster-Anderson and Margaret Bothamley. Then in April 1939, Viscount Lymington, a member of several British right-wing groups, gave a speech on 'White Nations and the Soil' as part of an IAdN lecture series in Berlin, repeating ideas of a 'Nordic race' and promoting a 'blood and soil' ideology.

E.W.D. Tennant

Ernest William Dalrymple Tennant was a merchant banker who developed extensive business interests in Germany between the wars. One of the first Allied officers to enter Berlin in January 1919, Tennant had been horrified by the famine and deprivation he saw and this above all, he said, drove his ambition to see normal relations established and maintained between Britain and Germany. Hitler would describe him as 'the determined pioneer of Anglo-German understanding'. He was a personal friend of Ribbentrop, with whom he spent a lot of time in the years 1932 to 1938 at Ribbentrop's house in Dahlem. It had been Tennant who acted as Ribbentrop's 'ideal linkman ... to introduce him to the important personages he wanted to meet'.[3] Thereafter, Tennant became a prominent pro-German propagandist, claiming that 'everything bad [about Germany] had been magnified and the good minimised', although he admitted that there had been 'deplorable excesses' especially over the

'Jewish problem' but overall he called for the British press to 'pay more attention to the constructive side of the Hitler movement'.

In November 1933, Tennant arranged a lunch meeting at his house between Ribbentrop and Stanley Baldwin who, at that time, was Lord President of the Council. On the same afternoon, Ribbentrop was also given an audience with Prime Minister Ramsay MacDonald. The following year Tennant led a trade delegation to Germany, during which initial 'hostile' opinions gave way to more sympathetic attitudes and paved the way for the formation of the Anglo-German Fellowship (AGF) in 1935. He became an apologist for Germany's early territorial claims, and even wrote to *The Times* in defence of the Rhineland occupation but later criticised the Anschluss and, in 1939, went to Germany clandestinely with the approval of the British government to try to negotiate with Ribbentrop and others in the hope of avoiding war.

Rolf Gardiner

Henry Rolf Gardiner was no politician, nor was he a powerful industrialist, but his influence on British opinion in the 1930s was more with the youth of Britain who, he believed, had kinship with the youth of Germany. He was highly articulate in a clever and superficial way, rather than truly educated or intelligent, and had spent part of his youth living in Germany where he had developed many contacts that led him to become fascinated by the Weimar Republic's myriad youth leagues and life reform movements. He was passionately involved with folk music and dance, and was developing cultural ties through youth movements in England, Germany and Scandinavia. The historian David Fowler described him as: 'An important thinker and activist in the field of youth cultures and youth movements.'

His passionate championing of rural revivalism and organic farming was allied with a belief that the 'yeomen and aristocrats of Britain [must] re-establish themselves as an élite' to lead Britain forward into a new age in which the old tired values of Christianity would be replaced by a vital paganism. The advent of the Nazis in 1933, he believed, was 'the spring storm of a new Renaissance', not only in Germany, but the whole Germanic world, which 'should have a share in the blessing of this rebirth'.[4] He believed Britain's future lay not with its doomed empire, but in ever closer union with its 'kin folk, kin tongued' neighbours in Germany, the Netherlands and Scandinavia.

Part of his world view, however, was a deep anti-Semitism aimed more at the Jews of Eastern Europe who had, in his words, come to Germany 'with the smell of Asia in their beards' and added to German Jewry 'a very unpleasant element'. He agreed with the Nazi view that they had misused German hospitality. German ambitions in Latvia and Lithuania were justified because 'what is at stake is civilisation and the preservation of the earth from the roving sand-dunes of the east'. He famously said that 'every country has the Jews that it deserves'. When the BUF began gaining supporters in rural communities, Mosley reached out to Gardiner, who rebuffed him believing that the BUF was a suburban movement that had no understanding or sympathy with rural issues.

T.P. Conwell-Evans

Thomas Pugh (Philip) Conwell-Evans was a historian, political adviser, secretary, interpreter and intelligence agent, and a 'rather shadowy figure' according to Richard Griffiths. He had been Lord Noel-Buxton's private secretary when he had been a Minister in the Labour Cabinet. Between 1932 and 1933 he spent eighteen months at the University of Königsberg, lecturing on diplomatic history, and soon afterwards came under the influence of the German Foreign Ministry propagandist Dr Margarete Gärtner, who had succeeded in building links with both main political parties in Britain, with the British press, and with most of the other organisations in Britain active at the time promoting international goodwill and understanding.[5]

He was well-connected to both Houses of Parliament through his work as secretary to the Armenian and Balkan committees and had, for a while, been a member of Baron Friedrich von der Ropp's Anglo-German Group in 1933 to promote understanding between the clergy and laity of the German and English churches. He was appointed as one of the honorary secretaries of the Anglo-German Fellowship in 1935, where he was viewed as an intellectual high priest who advised and guided Philip Henry Kerr during the latter's interactions with the Nazi regime.[6] He would later write to Kerr on 5 April 1936, soon after the remilitarisation of the Rhineland, saying that 'a German hegemony in Eastern Europe would be far less dangerous than a Russian and if the Slav conquered the Teuton, there would be an end of European civilisation'.[7]

An apologist for the Nazis, Conwell-Evans would say that it was wrong to think that the entire Nazi movement was bad and vicious since only a very small minority of its members brought it into disrepute. He wrote an article about how a new sense of nationhood had allowed the Germans to 'respect the achievement of other nations, especially young peoples like the Poles', and that the Nazis were 'not aggressively national in the sense that they desire to interfere with the independence of neighbouring countries'.[8]

In the early 1930s, Conwell-Evans had become closely associated with the British spy Malcolm Christie and Sir Robert Vansittart, who was then head of the American department at the Foreign Office and would later become Permanent Under-Secretary at the Foreign Office. They set up an informal intelligence network collaborating on German intelligence gathering. It therefore becomes difficult to correlate Conwell-Evans' outwardly pro-German attitude with his clandestine work and the latter throws doubt on what may have been seen as his sympathetic attitude towards the Nazis. While his apparent concern for friendship and peace between Britain and Germany seemed to have blinded him to other matters and made him one of Germany's most useful British contacts, there is every possibility that this was just a 'smokescreen' behind which his real work of espionage took place.

Sir Thomas Moore

During a debate in the House of Commons on 31 May 1935, Sir Thomas Cecil Russell Moore, the member for Ayr Burghs, described Germany as 'a great and gallant people [rescued] from the depths of humiliation by Hitler [and had] recovered her self-respect and her soul [despite attempts] to poison the public mind by exaggerated and inaccurate statements'.[9] An early acquaintance of Dr Gärtner, Moore visited Germany in 1933 and had a meeting with Hitler, whom he believed to have honest and sincere ambitions for peace and justice. The British press, he claimed, was anti-German and paid 'little attention to the happiness, security and hope that Hitler has brought to his followers'. In 1938, Moore was still calling Hitler 'a man of peace, a statesman and a clear-sighted administrator of his country'. Writing to *The Times* after the Anschluss, Moore said that Hitler had evolved a new and welcome technique in the practice of [bloodless] revolutions [brought about] by the will of the people affected.

George Ward Price

George Ward Price wore a monocle, hobnobbed at the dictator's courts and authored Nazi eulogies, which appeared under Rothermere's name in the *Daily Mail*.[10] Rothermere saw it as vital that Price, as his personal emissary, establish a close relationship with the Nazi leaders. Hitler quickly understood the benefits of such an arrangement and ensured that Price had privileged access to the Reich Chancellery. Price always accompanied Rothermere and Princess Stephanie when they visited Hitler and would become what the Führer called 'the only foreign journalist who reported him without prejudice'.[11] Echoing Rothermere's views, Price contrasted the virtues of dictatorship with the shortcomings of democracy. When German troops entered Vienna, Ward Price was there, standing close to Hitler as the Führer addressed the crowds.

He was a welcome guest at Göring's vast mansion, Carinhall, where in 1937 he spent a day playing with the huge miniature model railway laid out in the attics while the field marshal, as excited and enthusiastic as a child, knelt to direct the electric-powered model trains deftly around the extensive tracks. In the ceiling above the layout, a system of wires allowed model aeroplanes to fly across the room dropping miniature bombs on the railway below.

While later claiming that he simply reported Hitler's words and left his readers to make up their own minds about them, in 1937, Price wrote of Hitler's 'forceful character [and] pleasant, human character'. He described a man with 'artistic, visionary tendencies ... and tenderness in his disposition'. Ignoring the murder and terror campaigns carried out by the SS, Price told *Mail* readers that: 'To law-abiding citizens the Nazi Government brought public order, political peace [and] better living conditions.' Only the Soviets, in his reports, were capable of torture and massacre. The Germans merely 'laid a heavy hand' on those who opposed their plans and 'gross and reckless accusations' of concentration camp conditions gave the wrong impression about what Price reported as the struggle of the German people to protect themselves from the 'flood' of Jewish immigration into the country since 1919.[12]

Arthur Kenneth Chesterton

A.K. Chesterton had turned to fascism after his experiences during the First World War, but he came to it from outside the British parliamentary system and had little understanding of politics. His horrific wartime experiences as a nineteen-year-old officer at Épehy, during which he was awarded the Military Cross for capturing enemy trenches, walking back to his own lines afterwards over a mass of dead bodies, had left him deeply scarred and dependent on alcohol. Hoping for the stability and security of a centuries-long aristocratic tradition, he was strongly affected by a world that had been 'turned upside-down at a bewildering speed'.[13] For him, the positive political creed of fascism that had emerged in Germany and Italy was the solution to his search for meaning and security lost during the war. After the war he searched for a political philosophy with which he could identify and allow him to come to terms with his wartime traumas, and it was this that led him to join the BUF in November 1933. In August 1937 he was appointed editor of *The Blackshirt*, a position that gave him a platform for his virulent anti-Semitism and promotion of the *Protocols*.

Chesterton was often a guest speaker at meetings of an organisation called The White Knights of Britain or The Hooded Men, whose headquarters, shared with the Nordic League, were above a public house in Lamb's Conduit Street in London's West End. This was a fringe-lunatic body, led by Commander E.H. Cole, whose members swore an oath to 'rid the world of the merciless Jewish reign of terror'[14] and which held secret meetings in rooms festooned with swastikas where they performed strange rituals. Anti-Semitism and violent action were at the core of its creed.

Hilaire Belloc

Hilaire Belloc, poet, essayist, historian, biographer, as well as Liberal, and later Independent, MP for Salford, was a zealous Catholic, moved by a deep vein of hysterical anti-Semitism. In 1925, at age fifty-five, Belloc wrote *The Cruise of the Nona*, the closest thing to an autobiography that he ever wrote. In this book, he writes of his enthusiasm for Italian dictator Benito Mussolini and lays down a seductive programme for the regeneration of England through fascism. He went to Rome to interview him in what he described as a pilgrimage and found Mussolini to be a man with 'sense of decision, of sincerity, of serving the nation, and of serving it towards a known end with a definite will'. 'It is good to visit a society still under such an impulse, and to feel that, in one section of Europe at least, things are going well,' he wrote.[15]

Henry Williamson

The author Henry Williamson was another who was deeply affected by his wartime experiences, the first of which was not of carnage but of the Christmas fraternising between British and German troops after the first Battle of Ypres in 1914. These experiences left him with a profound sense of the futility of war that destroyed any sense of common humanity through propaganda, corruption, and war profiteering. This led him to believe that any man who had experienced the catastrophe of war at the front would never be able to contemplate being party to the creation of another. The second formative experience was Williamson's involvement in the slaughter of the Battle of the Somme on 1 July 1916, when 60,000 British soldiers were killed or wounded in a single day.

Williamson saw in National Socialism a spirit that could bring a dying Western civilisation back to its wellspring of life. He felt duty-bound to raise a voice. He was one of the first to commit himself to Mosley and the BUFs, and championed Hitler as the visionary leader of European rebirth. In *The Flax of Dreams* and *The Phoenix Generation* Williamson was to describe Hitler as 'the great man across the Rhine whose life symbol is the happy child'.

Williamson attended the 1935 Nuremberg Congress and was impressed by the economic and social achievements of Germany while the British continued to languish in poverty and unemployment. He saw a racial community based on the values of land and a revived peasantry, freed from bankers' interest, guaranteed from foreclosure, and the pioneering conservation laws and projects. Williamson saw in the faces of the German people expressiveness and confidence that looked as if they were 'breathing, extra oxygen', as he put it. In the Hitler Youth, reminiscent of his days as a Boy Scout, Williamson observed: 'the former pallid leer of hopeless slum youth transformed into the suntan, the clear eye, the broad and easy rhythm of the poised young human being'. Lest it be objected that Williamson was seeing Germany through rose-coloured glasses, very much the same description was given by the American journalist William Shirer, author of the perennially published basic anti-Nazi text *The Rise and Fall of the Third Reich*, whose hatred of Hitler is beyond doubt:

> The young in the Third Reich were growing up to have strong and healthy bodies, faith in the future of their country and in themselves and a sense of fellowship and camaraderie that shattered all class and economic and social barriers. I thought of that later, in the May days of 1940, when along the road between Aachen and Brussels one saw the contrasts between the German soldiers, bronzed and clean cut from a youth spent in the sunshine on an adequate diet, and the first British war prisoners, with their hollow chests, round shoulders, pasty complexions and bad teeth; tragic examples of the youth that England had neglected so irresponsibly in the years between the wars.[16]

To Williamson, National Socialist Germany represented '... a race that moves on poles of mystic, sensual delight. Every gesture is a gesture from the blood, every expression a symbolic utterance. Everything is of the blood, of the senses.' Williamson said, 'The spirit of the farm and what I was trying to do there, was the spirit of Oswald Mosley. It was all part of the same battle.' With characteristic descriptiveness, Williamson, writes: 'Rats, weeds, swamps, depressed markets, labourers on the dole, rotten cottages, polluted streams, political parties and class divisions controlled by the money power, wealthy banking and insurance houses getting rid of their land mortgages and investing their millions abroad (but not in the empire), this was the real England of the period of this story of a Norfolk farm.' In *The Story of a Norfolk Farm* he writes of his vision: 'One day the sewage of the cities will cease to be poured into the rivers, and will be returned to the land, to grow fine food for the people. One day salmon will leap again in the clear waters of the London River; and human work will be creative and joyful. One day the soul of man, shut in upon itself during the long centuries of economic struggle, will arise in the light of the sun of truth. And now I lay down the pen and return to the plough.'

In *The Phoenix Generation* he expresses his vision again through the autobiographical Philip Maddison, the returned soldier, his generation denied the 'land fit for heroes' that had been promised by the politicians: 'When the soil's fertility is being conserved instead of raped, when village life is a social unity, when pride of craftsmanship returns, when everyone works for the sake of adding beauty and importance to life, when every river is clean and bright, and the proud words "I serve" are in everyone's heart and purpose. Then my country will be good enough for me.'

Williamson wrote for Mosley's paper *Action*. He called for Anglo-German brotherhood, recognising that Hitler desired nothing more than peace with Britain. He saw that the result of another war would be the bringing of Asiatic Bolshevism to the heart of Europe. He sought to have his friend T.E. Lawrence (of Arabia) join with Mosley in a peace campaign. Lawrence was returning from having posted his letter to Williamson agreeing to such a campaign when he had his fatal motorbike accident.

With Mosley's rallies attracting larger audiences than ever in 1940, Williamson wrote to him to ask if he could see Hitler as a common soldier who had fraternised, on the faraway Christmas Day of 1914, with the men of his Linz battalion under Messines Hill, 'might he not be able to give him the amity he so desired from England, a country he admired ...' Williamson visited Mosley full of hope, but Mosley's reaction was that: 'I am afraid the curtain is down.' Williamson nodded, and asked

Mosley what he would do. Mosley replied that he would carry on as long as possible working for peace.

In 1940 around 1,000 Englishmen were interned without trial for opposing the war, including Mosley and 800 BUF members. Williamson was among those arrested. He was paroled on condition that he remained silent. With the defeat of Germany, Williamson said that his hopes for a regenerated Europe had been killed.

Robert Gordon-Canning

Military theorists such as Major-General John Frederick Charles Fuller and Sir Basil Henry Liddell Hart were over-represented in the membership of British fascist movements in the interwar years because they were drawn from the officer corps, a social body that was especially favourable to British fascism. Fascism warped their understanding of the role of war and pushed them to glorify violence for its supposed purifying and regenerative virtues.

Robert 'Bobbie' Gordon-Canning was born in 1888 and was commissioned into the 10th (Prince of Wales's Own) Hussars serving in South Africa, India and in France during the First World War. A popular officer, he won the respect of his men and brother officers and received the Military Cross for 'conspicuous gallantry and devotion to duty'. After the war he wrote stirring poetic ballads that decried modern liberalism and capitalism, which he saw as the perceived enslavement of humanity by modernity. His works were suffused with virulent anti-Semitism and called for a return to the higher ideals of a bygone age.

In late 1925, he became a military adviser and supplier of illicit arms to Abd el-Krim, the political and military leader of the Rif rebellion in Morocco. He would later try to fashion himself into something of a freelance diplomat and peacemaker in the Middle East and North Africa and allied himself with the Arab cause in Palestine. His ultimate failure to influence British policy had the effect of turning his latent anti-Semitism into a much more rabid and virulent form of hatred. He blamed the lack of foresight of the British government on the Palestine question on a cabal of international Jewish financiers.

In January 1934, he returned to Britain and met Oswald Mosley, with whom he established an immediate rapport by sharing the concept of fascism as a means of rejuvenating an old nation and lifting it out of the morass of spiritual decay and class warfare into a new era of unity and peace. Through Mosley, Gordon-Canning acquired influence and found himself welcomed into Mosley's inner circle, becoming his confidante and a trusted agent to liaise with international partners, namely the Italian fascists and the German National Socialists, whom he visited often to study the methods of fascism.

He was seen as the ideal type of candidate for a movement that was anchored on an ethos of action, modernity and elitism; privately educated, a regular Army officer with a High Tory outlook on life and a distinguished service record. From a privileged social background, this sort of person considered themselves part of an elite that would provide a new ruling class for the new century, composed of 'modern' men, who were both physically and intellectually superior and who would break free of the social and moral norms of the previous era. They would become the pioneers of a new political age that would see a 'higher echelon in the evolutionary development of society'[17] and hark back to a mythical golden age where Britain ruled unopposed over much of the world.

A military background was seen as essential for leaders of the BUF because they would not be shocked by the militaristic nature of the movement. Their patriotism and sense of duty would naturally attract them to a new crusade against the materialistic ideology that, they argued, had robbed the British people of their moral strength. This warrior cult was a rallying cry for many disenfranchised officers, who sought to re-appropriate the 'spirit of the trenches' to apply it to the political struggle for the rejuvenation of Britain. Military officers were also drawn to the BUF because it aligned with their preconceived notions of masculinity, a concept central to the ethos of the BUF. The link between British revival through fascism and the creation of the empire in the previous century was a key feature of the BUF's propaganda. Officers who were closely associated with the BUF embraced apocalyptic visions of future war in the sense of it ushering in a new era, quite different from the reality of the previous one. It focused on rebirth and radical transformation into a new world. BUF ideology was based on the idea of war as the ultimate arbitrator in international relations and the crucible through which nations could fortify and purify themselves.

The fascists wanted to create a new scientific ideology for a new scientific age and provide universal solutions to tackle the cultural malaise of the time. In this sense it was not only a political movement but an 'attitude towards life based upon a national mystique' that appealed to both middle-class sensibilities and youthful ambition.[18] The League of Nations had failed to abolish war through liberal internationalism, leaving fascists to embrace the concept of international relations as a struggle for survival by annihilation of enemies before they could strike first in a conflict where only the strongest nations survived and the capacity to wage war became the embodiment of the national will to survive.

Gordon-Canning was one of the few among the BUF leadership who took an interest in military matters. Mosley was no great strategic thinker and therefore relied heavily on Gordon-Canning for the development of a foreign and defence policy for his movement which inevitably followed his own political and intellectual development. His concern for the fate of the Empire required the country to be optimised for the purpose of warfare to prevent its break-up and piecemeal annihilation by the combined forces of Bolshevism and international Jewry. His main area of concern was the Middle East, whose fate was the keystone of the Empire. He was the architect of BUF anti-Semitic and pan-Islamic policy. In the guise of peacemaker between Arab and Jews, Gordon-Canning tried to return to Palestine in 1936 to set up a Blackshirt movement among the Arabs and British security forces stationed there, but was thwarted by the Home Office and the security services, who denied him access to the region due to his reputation for trouble-making.

His war record and reputation, alongside his considerable knowledge of foreign and imperial affairs, gave Gordon-Canning a status that others in the leadership lacked and enabled him to speak with authority on a variety of topics. In this way he became instrumental in the development of apocalyptic visions of future war that defined the defence policies of the BUF and fed into the perception of war by officers who were inclined towards fascism. Rearmament on a massive scale, along with huge industrial and agricultural projects, were essential and the whole effort should be centralised in the hands of a few technocrats in a newly created Ministry of Defence. The lines of communications within the Empire were to be secured by expanding the Navy and the Air Force under a new political system where the corporate state would replace the parliamentary system that had failed to accept the new realities and had allowed the Empire to fall into disarray. This completely flew in the face of what had become the political consensus of the day among the majority of parliamentarians, which was for an international approach to global governance relying on the principle of collective security embodied in the League of Nations and a gradual decolonisation.

In September 1935, Gordon-Canning attended the Nuremberg rally as an official envoy of the BUF and met Nazi Party officials, including Ribbentrop, with whom he established friendly relations, and even met

Hitler, whose opinion of him as someone with neither intellect nor heart would not have pleased Gordon-Canning. He was lavishly treated, installed in luxury accommodation and driven everywhere by a stormtrooper chauffeur. During the next two years he visited Germany on a number of occasions and cultivated close relationships with the Nazi leadership while also maintaining contact with several Nazi and Italian fascist operatives in Britain.

In May 1938, Gordon-Canning, along with William Joyce, fell out with Mosley over the way the leadership of the BUF was becoming over-centralised under the militaristic influence of Neil Francis Hawkins and disagreed with Mosley's decision to purge from the movement the fanatic National Socialists, who wanted a broader alliance with hard-core anti-Semitic elements. Threats of legal action to recover money that Gordon-Canning had spent building up the BUF further soured the relationship with Mosley beyond repair.

There is no doubt that Gordon-Canning's separation from mainstream Mosley philosophy was the result of his obsessive embrace of an apocalyptic vision of racial war and his obsession with the 'Jewish Question'. Only through war against Judeo-Bolshevik ancestral enemies, he said, could there be a new mystical rebirth of the Aryan race built on a foundation of spiritual supremacy. This vision was based on the idea of war as the ultimate struggle for survival between competing racial blocks, with the 'Aryan' world made up of European peoples on one side and the racialised 'hordes' who were controlled by international communism and Jewry on the other. Light against darkness; good versus evil. Mosley found this vision too extreme and unlikely to be embraced by the general electorate.

Working outside the BUF, in 1939, Gordon-Canning joined the Council for Christian Settlement in Europe, a fascist group devoted to pressuring the British government to strike a negotiated peace with Hitler. When interviewed by the Home Office Advisory Committee on 18B Detainees, Gordon-Canning argued that his peace campaign was meant to save Britain from impending doom but his defence was undermined by the numerous occasions on which he is said to have expressed treacherous views, leading agents who had worked on his case to become convinced that he was a security risk. Regulation 18B was a sub-section of the Emergency Powers (Defence) Act 1939. It made associating with a member of an organisation that was associating with the government of an enemy power a clear criminal activity, and allowed the government to intern individuals suspected of being Nazi sympathisers, suspending their right to habeas corpus. Gordon-Canning's peace campaign was labelled as treasonous by the British establishment and he was interned under Regulation 18B and spent the better part of the war in Brixton prison with other Nazi sympathisers. While in detention, his anti-Semitism further hardened with deranged diatribes against Jewish infiltration of the Home Office.

Arthur Headlam

On the whole, British churches were appalled by the anti-Semitism and general anti-Christian policies of the Nazis, but there were a few exceptions. The reverend Arthur Cayley Headlam, Bishop of Gloucester, was one who saw communism as a greater evil and argued that Germany was not getting enough credit for having crushed the communists there and said they were standing up as a bulwark to the Soviets in the east. He lauded German youth, saying 'the great body of the young Nazis [are] the best element in the country, anxious for self-discipline and sacrifice'.[19]

In 1933, Headlam had irked Church leaders by writing to *The Times* saying that all sorts of 'sinister and untrue' rumours were being spread about the removal of leaders of the German Christian churches for challenging the Nazis. All sorts of false and one-sided views of Germany were being presented by 'Jews [who have] an excessive influence on the press of Europe'.[20]

On 22 June 1937, Headlam wrote a preface to a Church Assembly report on the affairs of Continental Churches in which he offered a 'true judgement on the significance of what is recorded and a right sense of proportion' over Germany. 'Nazism,' he said, 'was based upon orthodox Christianity and is the greatest moral and spiritual force in Germany.'[21] Headlam's letter was published widely in German papers. For this he was subjected to very violent criticism from those who feared that the pronouncements of a churchman as prominent as Headlam could be misrepresented as the opinion of the Church Council itself and that Headlam represented a far greater authority than he actually did. When pressed, Headlam reacted with some force, asserting the 'rightness' of his attitude, having taken the time and trouble to 'learn about things', and calling his detractors 'intolerant bigots'. The bishops of Chichester and Durham, he said, were exactly copying the policies of the National Socialists.

As pre-war Chairman of the Church of England Council for Foreign Relations, Headlam was obliged to respond to the arrest and incarceration by the Nazis of Pastor Martin Niemöller in February 1938. Niemöller came to stand for all men of faith who became victims of the Nazis and his imprisonment in Sachsenhausen concentration camp became a defining feature of the Nazi attack on the Christian churches. Headlam was sent on a fact-finding mission to Germany a couple of months later when he discussed the fate of German churches with leading Nazis and returned convinced that Niemöller had somehow engineered his own downfall by getting too involved in politics and the Nazis were justified in arresting him. To *The Times* he wrote, in a letter that has been described as 'the most lamentable letter ever written by an Anglican Bishop to a newspaper', that German churches were oppressed by only minor regulations and interference and that Niemöller was a 'troublesome clergyman' who would be released if he promised to keep out of politics.

The Duke of Buccleuch

Walter John Montagu Douglas Scott, Eighth Duke of Buccleuch and Lord Steward of the Royal Household, was one of a party of British dignitaries who attended a parade of 40,000 Nazi troops comprising infantry and cavalry regiments, naval units, SS, armoured cars and tanks along Unter den Linden in Berlin on 20 April 1939, while 162 Luftwaffe aircraft flew overhead. It was the occasion of Hitler's 50th birthday. Alongside Buccleuch were Arthur Ronald Nall-Cain, the Second Baron Brocket, and Major General John Fuller, who had described the Jews as 'the cancer of Europe'.[22] All three were enthusiastic admirers of Hitler. They were there as personal guests of the Führer and their presence was the culmination of years of Nazi attempts to cultivate a strong relationship with influential figures in British society. Buccleuch had previously entertained Ribbentrop at his estates in Scotland and his presence at the parade was particularly embarrassing for the royal family, who tried desperately to distance themselves from his action.

Even after war had been declared, Buccleuch continued to expound his pro-Nazi views and pointed the finger at Churchill, whom he saw as the main obstacle to peace in Europe. During the early part of 1940, he and Brocket had personally financed James Lonsdale Bryans, who attempted to communicate directly with Hitler to negotiate peace terms that, given the circumstances, would have marked Bryans down as a traitor. However, his sponsors ensured that nobody connected with the scheme was even questioned. In June 1940, King George relieved Buccleuch of his royal duties and effectively banished him to spend the rest of the war on his Scottish estates.

Lord Tavistock

Hastings William Sackville Russell was one of the richest men in Britain and enjoyed the courtesy title of Lord Tavistock. On the death of his father on 27 August 1940, he would become the 12th Duke of Bedford. During his twenties, Tavistock 'fell into the hands of every kind of crank and eccentric', which led to an estrangement with his father.[23] His emotional instability is evident in his early courting of socialism and even communism before turning to the politics of the extreme right, which brought him into contact with John Becket. It was in collusion with Beckett, Benjamin Greene and Robert Gordon-Canning that he created and funded the British People's Party (BPP) in the summer of 1939 that was ostensibly committed to social reform at home and peace abroad. On the outbreak of war, the BPP was subsumed into a new organisation, the British Council for Christian Settlement in Europe (BCCSE), also bankrolled by Tavistock, with offices at 13 John Street. It also brought him to the attention of MI5, who began monitoring his communications in October 1939.

Tavistock felt that he was above the law, specifically Regulation 18B, and prepared to go to Dublin to meet a delegation of Germans to discuss peace proposals. MI5 became aware of the plan through informants inside the BCCSE but they did not know that the mission had the unofficial backing of the Foreign Secretary, Lord Halifax, at this time still looking for ways to avoid a shooting war. When the mission was exposed in the House of Commons, the Home Secretary, Sir John Anderson, said that: 'While [such] activities ... are to be deplored' he did not think that the incident 'afforded sufficient grounds for the imposition of ... penal restrictions'.[24] Tavistock offered a defence of his actions as necessary due to 'the failure of the British Government ... to display the slightest intelligence'. Accusations of German atrocities against the Jews were disingenuously brushed aside by him saying that his critics should make themselves better acquainted with British atrocities in Palestine. It became a matter of acute embarrassment for the government, who were too craven to bring to justice a man of such wealth and status.

Henry Channon

The US-born Henry (Chips) Channon arrived in England at the age of twenty-three in 1920 to study at Christ Church, Oxford, for 'social rather than academic purposes' and there he was introduced to the English aristocracy and to European royalty.[25] He rapidly integrated into British society and rejected his US heritage. A strident social climber, he was, according to the *Oxford Dictionary of National Biography*, in thrall to 'society, privilege, rank and wealth', but Simon Heffer would later describe him as 'trivial, snobbish, shallow and profoundly lacking in judgement ... a toady to the rich ... vile and spiteful'.[26] In 1933, he married the brewing heiress Lady Honor Guinness. At their house in Belgrave Square they hosted fabulous parties attended by such luminaries as King Edward VIII and Joachim von Ribbentrop. Fifteen years after arriving in the country he was elected as Conservative Member of Parliament for Southend and served as Parliamentary Private Secretary to Rab Butler at the Foreign Office.

When it came to Germany, Channon was 'impressed by the glamour and excitement of the new régime, and shallowly unconcerned by the realities behind it'.[27] His susceptibility to the Third Reich went far beyond naïve delusion. Whenever Ribbentrop was in London, he would often dine with the Channons and it was during one such evening when, perhaps overcome with bonhomie and champagne, Ribbentrop invited all the guests to the Olympic Games as personal guests of Hitler. In Berlin, Channon, an inveterate diarist, wrote that: 'One was conscious of the effort the Germans were making to show the world the grandeur, the permanency and the respectability of the new régime. On seeing Hitler, he wrote that: 'One felt one was in the presence of some semi-divine creature.' A visit to Dachau left him with an impression that: 'England could learn many a lesson from Nazi Germany.' As for persecution of the Jews,' he wrote: 'Who cares?'[28]

When Chamberlain resigned on 10 May 1940, Channon wrote that: 'England in her darkest hour has surrendered her destiny to the greatest opportunist and political adventurer alive.' In despair he drank champagne with Butler, Alec Dunglass (Alec Douglas Home as he would become), and Jock Colville, toasting 'the king over the water (Chamberlain)'.

William Joyce

The American-born William Brooke Joyce was described as a frightening figure, 'diminutive, chain-smoking, dressed in a grubby raincoat, his face disfigured by a razor-slash'.[29] The scar, which stretched from his right ear lobe to the corner of his mouth, was the result of an attack on him by communists during a violent political meeting and left him with a deep hatred of left-wing politics. He was a brilliant orator who rivalled Mosley in his eloquence.[30]

His family had moved to Galway, Ireland, and Joyce grew up there. In 1921, during the Irish War of Independence, as a fourteen-year-old schoolboy, he was recruited by British Army Intelligence as a courier and was almost assassinated by the IRA. He started working with the Black and Tans, a group of former British soldiers who had a reputation as a terrorist group noted for extrajudicial killings, arson, and police brutality. Joyce was linked to the murder of a twenty-eight-year-old Irish priest Michael Griffin, but never charged. With Partition in 1922, Joyce's parents took refuge from expected retribution from Irish nationalists and moved to England. He read English Language and Literature and History at Birkbeck College, gaining a first-class honours degree in 1927.

He had joined the British Fascisti in 1923 and then, in 1932, joined Mosley's BUF, distinguishing himself as a brilliant speaker and becoming Director of Propaganda in 1934. Along with Chesterton, he had been associated with the Nordic League and later founded the National Socialist League (NSL) with John Becket, which broke away from the BUF in 1937 when Mosley saw Joyce's anti-Semitism as too vitriolic and forced him out with accusations of financial irregularities. Becket, whom MI5 called 'an utterly unscrupulous political intriguer [who had a liking for] subversive and violent methods' reacted by saying that Mosley's 'powers of self-delusion had finally conquered his sanity'.[31] The violently anti-Semitic NSL distanced itself from Mosley but, while expressing huge enthusiasm for Hitler, retained a strong sense of Britishness. At the same time, Joyce founded the Carlyle Club as a more respectable front for the NSL. Both he, as vice-president, and Chesterton then briefly joined the British Council against European Commitments at the height of the Czech crisis.

Together with Chesterton and the eugenicist George Lane-Fox Pitt-Rivers, Joyce published the *New Pioneer* magazine in 1939, which was filled with pro-German and anti-Semitic articles. The virulence of Joyce's rhetoric is clearly seen in a speech he delivered to the Nordic League in which he referred to the 'lying, Jew-corrupted press' and called Churchill, Duff-Cooper and Eden 'that slobbering, bastardised mendacious triumvirate'.[32]

Joyce joined Ramsay's Right Club in June 1939, then during the last days of peace, in August, he, Frances Eckersley and Margaret Bothamley left Britain for Germany and began broadcasting to Britain. Eckersley had gone first with her teenage son and found work for Joyce at a radio station in Berlin. Eckersley and her son, who would go on to read the nightly news bulletin from Germany that preceded Lord Haw-Haw's broadcasts, later ended up in concentration camps and returned to England, where they were arrested in 1945. She was sentenced to a year's hard labour. Bothamley was also put on trial in 1946, when no mention was made of her pre-war anti-Semitic and pro-Nazi activities. Her defence portrayed her as a rather harmless old lady who, all the time she was in Germany during the war, had hung on her wall a picture of the King and Queen. She was sentenced to a year in prison.

Joyce and his wife, Margaret, left Britain for Berlin on 26 August after a tip-off from a contact in MI5, rumoured to have been Maxwell Knight, telling him that he was at risk of arrest. When he arrived in Germany, Joyce found work as a translator in the German Foreign Office and then with the *Reichsrundfunk* (German Radio Corporation's External Service) as an English-language broadcaster. He took out German citizenship and his initial broadcasts were focused on inciting distrust within the British public towards their government. A German colleague of Joyce's would assume the role of Schmidt, while Joyce would portray Smith, an Englishman. The two would then engage in discussions about Britain, with Joyce continuing his previous pattern of degrading and attacking the British government, people, and way of life. During one broadcast, Joyce exclaimed: '[British democracy] is an elaborate system of make-believe, under which you may have the illusion that you are choosing your own government, but which in reality simply ensures that the same privileged class, the same wealthy people, shall rule England under different names.'

His broadcasts went out under the heading of 'Germany calling' and were generally well-received by a British audience of some 6 million regular listeners who found them amusing. The British press christened Joyce Lord Haw-Haw. However, after Germany invaded France in May 1940, Joyce's propaganda became even more violent, emphasising Germany's military might and urging Britain to surrender. Audiences now turned away from his constant sarcasm about Britain and took his propaganda less seriously. He continued broadcasting from Germany throughout the war until his final rambling, drunken address on 30 April 1945, warning of the menace of the Soviet Union and castigating Great Britain for pursuing war against Germany. Unhinged and defiant, Lord Haw-Haw signed off on his final broadcast with 'Heil Hitler and farewell'.

Joyce and his wife then fled to Kuffermuille, a small village just on the border with Denmark, near Flensburg.

He was discovered by British forces on 28 May 1945 and, although unarmed, he was shot and wounded in the leg during his arrest. The government argued that sine he carried a British passport he was subject to British law and was subsequently put on trial. He was found guilty of high treason and was hanged in Wandsworth Prison on 3 January 1946. His body was buried in an unmarked grave in the prison grounds. In 1976, at the request of his daughter, it was exhumed and reburied in Galway.

Chapter Eight

The Mitford Sisters

Probably two of the best-known upper-class supporters of fascism were the Mitford sisters, Diana and Unity, both of whom rebelled strongly against their aristocratic upbringing and Conservative background. The Mitford sisters were raised in a family that found itself struggling to define itself in the early twentieth century. Their father had lost most of his wealth through unwise investments and this gave the two sisters a grudge against the inefficiency and downright incompetence of their class and a distrust of the political system. Both Unity and Diana initially tried to live within their traditional constraints. Diana, who was considered to be extraordinarily beautiful, dined at Chartwell with 'Cousin Winston', who delighted her by not treating her as a child. In 1927 she travelled to Paris with Churchill, who was on his way to meet Mussolini in Rome.

She came out as a debutante when she was eighteen and became secretly engaged in 1929 to Bryan Guinness, son of a wealthy Conservative MP and heir to one of the greatest fortunes in the country. Both at the time were part of the Bright Young Things social group of Bohemian young aristocrats and socialites in 1920s London. They married in 1929 and, being rich, young, intelligent and beautiful, became the acknowledged leaders of London society. When their first son, Jonathan, was born in 1930, Diana proved to be a natural mother but, at only twenty, had not lost her youthful desire for gaiety and fun. There was entertainment nightly, dinner, dance or fancy dress. A second son, Desmond, was born eighteen months after Jonathan and the family had moved into Biddesden near Andover, where they entertained an eclectic circle of friends from the worlds of politics, literature, art and science.

Gradually she fell under the spell of Oswald Mosley, whom she met at a garden party at the home of Emerald Cunard in 1932. Although she was not especially impressed with him that evening, she found what he had to say interesting.[1] 'He knew what to do to solve the economic disaster we were living through,' Diana wrote, 'he was certain he could cure unemployment. [He was] lucid, logical, forceful and persuasive, he soon convinced me, as he did thousands of others.'² This was at a time when Mosley was just about to launch his fascist movement, which at the time seemed to Diana to be the only dynamic movement led by the only politician in England who combined the experience, the force, the intellect and all the other essential qualities of leadership to make possible the difficult task of shifting the dead weight of conventional politics, which was smothering the country with inertia and complacency. They began to cross paths frequently and not by accident. They sought out each other's company at every opportunity, trying to suppress their feelings but unable to draw back from the delicious thrill of being together.³ To Diana, Mosley was the best of companions; he had every gift, being handsome, generous, intelligent and full of wonderful gaiety and joie de vivre.

Diana began to look upon her marriage to Bryan as a mistake and came to believe that she had married him in haste simply to escape the boredom and claustrophobia of her family home. At the same time, she became conscious of social deprivation in many parts of the country and began to question her own position of wealth and privilege. Unwilling, however, to accept that her class had to make sacrifices to help the poor, she looked for another way to resolve the problem and it was Mosley's fascist ideas of totalitarian government, freedom for the individual within complete state control and a democratically elected government headed by an authoritarian leader that seemed to offer a solution.

Diana and Bryan made plans to spend the summer months touring southern Europe and the Mosleys had made similar plans. Diana and Mosley hoped to meet secretly along the way but in the end were able only to write, which Diana did almost daily. The two families did, however, meet in Venice along with others of their set including Randolph Churchill, Bob Boothby and Emerald Cunard. It was soon clear to Bryan that Diana and Mosley were now more than just good friends. Mosley was an inveterate philanderer, which was something Diana found difficult to deal with, but nevertheless in the end she decided, at the age of twenty-two, that she had to leave her family and live openly as the lover of a man in public life who had a wife and three young children, even though Mosley made it clear that he had no intention of leaving his wife for her.

She moved out of the family home, leaving her two young sons with Bryan, and moved into a flat at 2 Eaton Square just around the corner from Mosley's home. The scandal of divorce hung over both the Guinness and Mosley families. Bryan offered to fake evidence of his own infidelity to facilitate a divorce, but it was a dangerous game. If there was any suspicion that the divorce was 'arranged' the courts would deny the petition and could invalidate the divorce if evidence of collusion came out at a later date.

Tragedy struck in May 1933 when Mosley's wife, Cynthia, was rushed to hospital with a perforated appendix. After an operation, peritonitis set in and she died on the 16th. Mosley appeared devastated by the death of his wife, and public opinion, sympathetic to Cynthia, shifted against Diana, who became something of a pariah. The two, however, continued to meet but Mosley decided to take an extended holiday on the Continent with Lady Alexandra Curzon, who was now married to Major Edward Dudley (Fruity) Metcalfe. Alexandra was no stranger to infidelity either and would, in her time, have affairs with several men including Jock Whitney, the US Ambassador to the UK, Lord Halifax and the Italian ambassador, Dino Grandi. Mosley would now begin an extended affair with Alexandra.

During much of the 1930s, the pretty young ladies of the great houses of England were sent off to Germany for 'finishing'; a combination of art, music, balls, and husband hunting. Even as late as 1939, the tours were still taking place: Lady Elizabeth Montagu Douglas Scott, the daughter of the Duke of Buccleuch, who later married the Duke of Northumberland, spent two months right before the Second World War in Munich. With Mosley away, Diana now chose to visit Bavaria, along with her sister Unity, and it became a critical turning point in her younger sister's life. Already showing interest in the BUF but by no means committed to fascism, Unity's experiences in Germany at this time were described by Diana as harnessing 'the streak of obsessive behaviour in Unity's character, which might have made her ultra-religious had she leaned towards the Church [and turned it] instead on Nazism'.[4]

Earlier in the year, Diana had met a German called Putzi Hanfstaengl, the US-educated son of a rich Munich family. Hanfstaengl had been part of Hitler's Beer Hall Putsch in 1923 and was later involved in raising funds to finance Hitler's rise to power. He was now a senior public relations adviser for the Nazi Party. When Diana and Unity went to Germany they made contact with Hanfstaengl and met him in Munich. At the end of August 1933, he took them to the four-day Nuremberg Rally that drew hundreds of thousands of Nazi Party members and spectators, including hundreds of foreign journalists, and included rousing speeches by Hitler. Diana described the event as 'a fantastic sight [with] hundreds of thousands of men in party uniforms [and] flags in all the windows ...

A feeling of excited triumph was in the air, and when Hitler appeared an almost electric shock passed through the multitude.'[5]

Later in the year, the sisters and Mosley all returned to England, where Diana and Mosley revived their affair and, early the next year, left for Provence, where they lived together near Grasse. In the autumn, Diana and Unity went again to the Nuremberg Rally, which was now an annual event. Diana was eager to learn to speak German and, for a short while, moved into a flat just off the Ludwigstrasse in Munich with Unity. Hanfstaengl got Diana a press pass, which allowed both girls to get into meetings where Hitler spoke. At the time, while the darker elements of the Nazi regime were eliminating political opposition and laying the foundations for repression and persecution, Hitler was still able to portray himself to the world as a statesman with a new and radical form of government that appeared to be working well.

Diana and Unity again attended the Nuremberg Rally in autumn 1935, during which time they met Hitler at the opera and found themselves seated next to Hitler's mistress, Eva Braun. By now the British press was becoming interested in the Nazis and printed many photographs of the sisters flanked by Nazi banners and against a backdrop of marching stormtroopers. At the rally observers recorded Nazi hierarchy bowing and scraping to Unity and kissing her hand.

All throughout this time, Mosley continued his relationship with Alexandra Curzon and other women. Outwardly, Diana tended to treat these affairs as no more than a 'tiresome silliness' that he somehow could not help but privately admitted to suffering 'agonies of jealousy'.[6] Despite this, early in 1936, Diana and Mosley decided to marry, but Mosley wanted it kept a secret until after the event. They were going to live at Wootton Lodge, called 'one of the most beautiful houses in England', in Staffordshire, where they would bring together all the children of both their marriages. Bryan Guinness had continued to support Diana after their divorce and made her a generous settlement to furnish and modernise the house.

Diana and Unity went to Cologne for the German elections on 29 March 1936. Lunching at the Dom Hotel where they were staying, they were surprised to see Hitler enter the dining room. He immediately invited them to join him at his table and further invited them to be his personal guests at the Berlin Olympic Games due to be held that summer and the Wagner Festival at Bayreuth to be held soon after. At the games, the sisters stayed at Goebbels' country house, *Schwanenwerder*, and were driven each day to the stadium by limousine. At Beyreuth, Diana told Hitler that she had not enjoyed *Parsifal* but Hitler replied that she would come to appreciate it more as she grew older. Unity would also criticise Hitler's appointment of Ribbentrop, whom she referred to as 'brickendrop', as ambassador to Britain to the Führer's face, much to the discomfort of other guests, but Hitler did not take offence. In fact they spent time together occasionally, sometimes watching a film and sometimes just talking. Diana found Hitler to be 'quick and clever' in conversation and he saw Diana as good company. It was no hardship for him to spend time with a sophisticated and beautiful woman who happened to share his taste in art and music.[7] Upon her return to England, Diana was then invited to lunch with Winston Churchill, who was eager to hear about her meeting with Hitler. It is interesting to note that Diana was one of the very few people who knew both Hitler and Churchill on a personal level.

Diana became a close friend of Magda Goebbels and they compared notes since they were both partnered with notorious philanderers. Magda had appealed to Hitler to allow her to divorce Goebbels but he refused permission. Magda invited Diana to hold her forthcoming marriage ceremony to Mosley at her home in Berlin. Hitler fully supported the idea and invited himself to be guest of honour, but insisted that the German press must not be allowed to know about it. The couple were married on 6 October 1936. Diana wrote: 'The ceremony was short; the Registrar said a few words, we exchanged rings, signed our names and the deed was done.' The Goebbels gave Diana a leather-bound twenty-two-volume edition of Goethe's works inscribed to 'Liebe Diana' and Hitler gave her a photograph of himself in an eagle-topped silver frame, which had pride of place in their bedroom at Wootton.[8] The witnesses were Bill Allen, at the time probably an MI5 agent, and Robert Gordon-Canning. Magda invited the guests to lunch at *Schwanenwerder*, where Unity and Diana distinguished themselves by giving the Nazi salute on every possible occasion. The party went back to the Reichskanzlei [Reich Chancellery] for a dinner hosted by Hitler, during which the new Lady Mosley gave Goebbels the inside story of the affair between Edward VIII and Mrs Simpson.

Mosley had for some time been working on the idea of establishing a radio station based in Germany that could broadcast to Britain to deliver his political message and also raise finance through advertising. Goebbels was entirely against the idea of having a radio station in Germany over which he did not have personal control and for a time the project faltered. Diana used her influence with Hitler, however, and he eventually he agreed to look at the matter. In June 1937, he approved the setting up of a joint venture, Air Time Ltd, based in Heligoland. It was a remarkable achievement and says much about Hitler's relationship with Diana.

Diana was unable to attend the Nuremberg Rally in 1938 owing to the fact that she was pregnant with Mosley's child, who was born in November and christened Alexander. After the birth, the Mosleys were obliged to make their marriage public. When the news broke it was a sensation. Many reports said that Hitler had acted as Mosley's best man and all the stories about Diana's divorce from Bryan came out. It was only at this time that Mosley's family, including his mother, became aware of the marriage and it was also the first that Alexandra Metcalfe had heard about it. Incredibly, her affair with Mosley had continued after his marriage to Diana.

In July 1939, Unity and Diana attended the Bayreuth Festival at Hitler's personal invitation. On 2 August, the final day of the Wagner Festival and a day before they were due to leave Bayreuth, the sisters lunched with Hitler, who told Diana that he believed Britain was determined on war and warned her that if Mosley continued to campaign for peace he risked assassination. Diana, pregnant again, returned to Wootton, where she displayed a huge autographed photograph of Hitler that he had presented the couple on their wedding day.

Many years later, Diana would claim that her support of fascism was less through political activism and more because of her devotion to Mosley. She became fascinated by his fascist ideas and her relationship with him was less of an ideological dependency and more as a result of being with the man she loved. Later in life she admitted that she could not 'regret [her friendship with Hitler], it was so interesting and fascinating'.

The younger sister, Unity Valkyrie, came to fascism by a more direct route. She met Mosley through Diana but, far from any ideological motivation, she was initially attracted to the fascist movement simply because it 'sounded like great fun to her,'[9] and a way to shock her family. However, she would soon identify deeply with fascist ideology. It gave her a chance to break from the constraints of her class, which she believed to be doomed and she saw no reason for her to go down with it.

It may well have been that Unity's embracing of fascism and Nazi ideology was a way to assert her individuality. One of six sisters, all very bright with strong characters, she created for herself a persona that rebelled against everything and tried to shock. As a teenager she developed a 'scowling discontent' and displayed all the symptoms of someone who was 'quite simply, bored stiff',[10] but her sister Jessica described her as 'a huge bright glittering personality [with] a sort of huge boldness and funniness and generosity – a unique character that is hard to explain to anybody who did not know her in those days. She was tremendous fun to be with. She wasn't at all interested in politics.'[11] Unity, however, was a very difficult child. She was expelled from St Margaret's boarding school in Bushey at the end of 1930 for being 'remorselessly naughty' and showing 'a fine disregard for the rules of the school'.

She first met Oswald Mosley in July 1932 and, greatly impressed by him, quickly developed a fascination for his personality and a keen interest in his fascist ideas. By the following year, Unity had joined the BUF and became active in promoting its philosophy. Although not yet totally committed to the BUF, she was anxious to expand her knowledge of the Nazi regime in Germany and, at the age of nineteen, went with her sister Diana to Bavaria on a trip that 'unquestionably changed her life'.[12] On her return to England, Unity took to attending BUF rallies dressed in her black shirt and wearing her special BUF badge given to her personally by Mosley.

She now urged her parents to let her spend some time living in Germany to learn the language. They agreed and Unity went to Munich to attend Baroness Laroche's finishing school, where she habitually wore her black shirt and BUF badge, which were not seen as anything out of the ordinary there. In June 1933, a friend of Unity, Derek Hill, was visiting Munich and sitting in the Carlton tearooms one evening when Hitler entered with his entourage of acolytes and bodyguards. Hill immediately phoned Unity, who quickly came down and sat at her friend's table and, according to Hill, trembled violently with excitement to be in the same room as Hitler.

Three weeks later the Nazis launched the Night of the Long Knives, a series of political extrajudicial executions carried out by the Gestapo, primarily against Ernst Röhm's *Sturmabteilung*, intended to consolidate Hitler's grip on power. This ruthless purge saw several hundred of his opponents murdered and more than 1,000 arrested. Unity's reaction to the event shows just how far she had travelled politically and the extent to which she was now in Hitler's thrall. 'I am terribly sorry for the Führer ... it must have been so dreadful for [him] when he arrested Röhm ... Poor Hitler,' she wrote to Diana.[13] To her mother she wrote: 'Aren't the English newspapers absolutely nauseating. All this absurd and lying outcry about "brutality" at Olympia only goes to show the urgent necessity for getting rid of disgusting Jewish influence in all walks of English life.'[14]

Unity got into the habit of eating at the Osteria restaurant, where she knew Hitler occasionally had lunch. On the occasions that Hitler turned up, Unity would make some attempt to get noticed by him and eventually, after several months, succeeded when he sent the owner with a message asking her to join him. During the following weeks, Unity managed to engineer a number of 'casual' meetings at the Osteria and Carlton when Hitler would often invite her to his table. He also invited her to a luncheon party, which she was surprised to find was in honour of Oswald Mosley who was visiting Germany at the time. On 10 April 1935, Unity accompanied Hitler to Hermann Göring's wedding. Hitler began to see more and more of his fair-haired English companion, much to the annoyance of his 'official' girlfriend, Eva Braun. In public, he was observed to be much more relaxed and affable in Unity's company than he was with any others of his inner circle.

This close relationship with the Nazi leadership encouraged Unity to give vent to her anti-Semitism. She got along particularly well with Julius Streicher, publisher of the vitriolic anti-Semitic newspaper *Der Stürmer*. Writing to him she said: 'The English have no notion of the Jewish danger ... We think with joy of the day when we shall be able to say with might and authority: England for the English! Out with the Jews! With German greeting, Heil Hitler! I want everyone to know that I am a Jew hater.'[15] This letter was widely reported in the British press, causing a great furore but some reaction supported her sentiments. Undaunted, back in London, Unity was quite unapologetic. This caused great discomfort to her parents, who were quite unable to cope with her behaviour but were unable to prevent her return to Munich. While the first concentration camps were being set up around them, and Jews and dissidents were being persecuted, Unity sunbathed naked in the English Garden [Englischer Garten], went to the cinema and drove her black MG convertible with a Danish mastiff on the passenger seat to go sailing on Lake Chiemsee.

Unity returned to England for the coronation of George VI but her friendship with Hitler became stronger. Often he would invite her back to his flat, where they would talk for hours, but she was never to witness his periods of aggressive outbursts, megalomania or cruel humour. Only on one occasion did she see him lose his temper and found it 'wonderful' the way that his outburst silenced the room. She went with him to the opera and later to the Bayreuth Festival, sending his long, black Mercedes to collect Diana and her. They were there for ten days and returned on Hitler's special train, watching delightedly as loyal Germans lined the track waving swastika flags and saluting Hitler.

At this time Unity became intensely jealous of Stephanie von Hohenlohe, whom she feared was rising above her in Hitler's affections. For her part, Stephanie was irked by the fact that it was she who had encouraged Unity to seek out Hitler's company in the first place by looking out for him at the Osteria Bavaria. Unity was not slow to show a very vindictive side by playing on Hitler's anti-Semitism, but by now it was widely understood that Stephanie's usefulness as a go-between with Rothermere and other prominent people far outweighed prejudice.

On 10 June 1938 Stephanie had an extraordinary audience lasting several hours in the Reich Chancellery when Hitler solemnly pinned on her dress the Nazi Party's Gold Medal of Honour, elevating her to the level of 'Nazi royalty'. The honour was normally reserved for a small group of people, mainly long-standing Nazi Party members who had given outstanding service to the National Socialist movement. Stephanie, born a full-blooded Jew, was now *de facto* a member of the Nazi Party and 'an honorary Aryan', as Heinrich Himmler declared her.

Even Himmler was much more favourably disposed towards Stephanie than he was to Unity, whom, it was said, he could not stand. In fact Unity was being closely watched by the SS as well as by the British secret services, who called her 'More Nazi that the Nazis'. According to MI5 files, Stephanie had 'wormed her way' into British society circles, mixing with Lady Oxford and Lady Cunard and constantly speaking favourably of the present regime in Germany. She was clearly part of a larger scheme to act as a 'talent spotter' and worked towards inviting influential people in England to meet Hitler personally.[16]

At this point Unity considered becoming a German citizen and the press was rife with rumours that Hitler planned to marry her. One day in April 1938, she was passing Hyde Park Corner while the MP Sir Stafford Cripps was making a speech. A fight broke out and it was noticed that Unity was wearing a swastika badge. Some of the crowd tried to attack her but she was only slightly hurt and was sent home on a bus by the police. The press did not report the incident favourably calling her 'Hitler's Nordic Beauty'. Later in Prague, while Hitler was making his bloodcurdling threats against Czechoslovakia, Unity walked the streets, attracting much attention with her two swastika badges. As a known Nazi, she had been advised not to enter the country for fear of causing a disturbance but ignored the warning and was immediately recognised. She accompanied Hitler to Breslau and sat behind him as 150,000 Sudetens marched past. However, she had been ill for some days and when the party returned to Bayreuth, she collapsed with pneumonia and was admitted to a private hospital.

When she had recovered, Unity moved into a flat in Schwabing, which had been found for her on Hitler's personal orders. It actually belonged to a young Jewish couple who were 'going abroad'.[17] She could hardly have failed to see the reality behind the euphemism. Diana, in an interview, would later say that: 'It is impossible to defend Unity ... she condemned herself out of her own mouth.'[18] Towards the end of August, Unity was instructed by the British consul to return to England otherwise he could not guarantee her safety if war broke out. Unity refused but became somewhat isolated as British journalists and other British subjects left the country. Furthermore, with Hitler totally preoccupied with his war plans, he had little time for her.

When Britain declared war on Germany on 3 September 1939, Unity's resolve collapsed. At first she feared that she might be interned as an enemy alien, but then fell into despair and wrote a suicide note saying that she was unable to bear the thought of a war between England and her beloved Germany. She left a sealed letter for Hitler, a signed framed photograph of him and her special Party badge and drove off to one of her favourite places, the Englischer Garten, the beautiful park beside the River Isar. Once there, she took her pearl-handled pistol and shot herself in the head. Passers-by alerted a nearby military base and Unity was whisked away to hospital in a Luftwaffe car. The bullet was lodged near the back of her skull. She was alive but in a coma and was not expected to survive. Surgeons decided against trying to remove the bullet. While she was unconscious, Hitler visited her and later, when she had regained consciousness, spoke to her briefly on the phone.

Her action to take her own life was kept quiet and plans were laid to have her removed to a hospital in Switzerland, but by November she was still in Munich when her parents heard through the US embassy that their daughter was recovering from an attempted suicide. Soon the British press knew the story and were printing all sorts of speculative articles, mostly saying that she was dead. At Christmas, however, the family were able to speak to her on the telephone from a hospital in Bern, Switzerland, to which she had now been moved, with all medical bills being paid for by Hitler. Unity's youngest sister, Deborah, and their mother rushed to her bedside and found her propped up in a sitting position looking frail and very thin with her eyes seeming enormous in her yellowy white face with its sunken cheeks. Her hair was short and matted and her teeth were yellow; they had not been brushed since the shooting. She had an odd vacant expression and was a 'most pathetic sight'.[19]

Arrangements were made to have Unity returned to England in an ambulance railway carriage. Waiting at Calais for a ferry, the party was suddenly descended upon by the press eager for the truth of what had happened. Eventually Unity was settled in a cottage in High Wycombe and, under police protection, was allowed to recuperate in relative peace. However, she made little progress physically and remained 'childlike' for the rest of her life.[20]

Unity Mitford was taken seriously ill on a visit to the family-owned island of Inch Kenneth and was taken to hospital in Oban. She died on 28 May 1948. Her death certificate stated that she had died from meningitis caused by the cerebral swelling around the bullet.

Chapter Nine

The Cliveden Set

Cliveden (rhymes with lived-in) is a house in the Italianate style at Taplow on the Thames, 5 miles upstream from Windsor Castle and readily accessible from the centre of political power. It was owned by an American couple, William Waldorf Astor, one of the world's richest men, and his wife, the somewhat unstable Lady Nancy Astor. George Bernard Shaw, who knew her well, said of her that she could not think consecutively for more than sixty seconds. She was 'diminutive of stature – at 5ft 2in – slender of build and of fair complexion, she had aquiline features set off by a firm chin, a strong, finely shaped nose, blue eyes and a high forehead'.[1] After her husband succeeded to the peerage and entered the House of Lords, as Lord Waldorf, Nancy entered politics as a member of the Conservative Party and won her husband's former seat of Plymouth Sutton in 1919, becoming the first woman to sit as an MP in the House of Commons. She would later be referred to as 'the honourable member for Berlin'. She embodied many of the prejudices of the time, common among American and British upper-class society, including a deep loathing for communists and Jews. She also had a deep personal dislike of Catholics. In 1914, she had come across Mary Baker Eddy's Christian Science Movement and in it claims to have found 'the answer to all my questions', although it was observed that when it came down to its tenets, she exhibited 'a certain originality of [interpretation]'.[2]

Cliveden, with its forty bedrooms, became renowned for its weekend parties that attracted some of the most prominent people of the day, spanning the widest spectrum of opinion and taste and refusing to conform to any rigid social-political mould.[3] The young people who were invited to Cliveden were among the most vivacious and intelligent of their age, who took out boats on the river or played tennis and were waited on hand and foot by some thirty household servants supervised by the legendary Edwin Lee. As an example of what the guests were presented with, footmen were dressed in livery with their yellow silk stockings, knee breeches and buckled shoes. The Archduke Franz Ferdinand and his escort, the

Countess Sophie, had come to Cliveden shortly before they were assassinated in Sarajevo in 1914.

After the First World War, the Astors found themselves at the centre of London social life that also gravitated around Lady Cunard, Mrs Neville and Lady Colfax. Neither Cunard nor Colfax were favourites of Nancy. The competition, however, could not keep up with the Astors. Cliveden was opened up after the years of austerity, the gardens were restored with the views and vistas set off by great groups of delphiniums and tuberoses and great bowers of oleander, and the weekend house parties resumed. Every Friday the household would be moved 'lock, stock, and barrel' from the Astors' London home in St James's Square to Cliveden.

Altogether a classic country house atmosphere prevailed with the great expanse of grounds tended by an army of gardeners, football and cricket against local teams, chimes of the clock tower and an enormous log fire in the Great Hall. The stable boys and housemaids would be up before dawn and be finished and out of sight before the first guests emerged. Breakfast was at nine o'clock but the highlight was five o'clock tea in the Great Hall. At these weekend parties politics was forever at the forefront of conversation and the frequent consensus was that Parliament was hopeless at sorting out the nation's problems.

In summer 1931, Joseph Stalin invited George Bernard Shaw to visit Moscow to celebrate his seventy-fifth birthday. Unwilling to travel alone, Shaw asked Nancy and William Astor to go with him as part of a larger party. They were in the Soviet Union for nine days, during which time they had a meeting with Stalin on 31 July. Nancy famously called out the Soviet despot for his brutal Tsarist methods in suppression of political dissent, but Stalin responded by recounting similar episodes of British history such as Cromwell's crushing of the Irish. Upon their return, the Astors were met coolly with accusations of having sold out to the left by going to Moscow in the first place.

The elevation of Hitler to the Chancellorship of Germany in 1933 saw a significant increase in overt anti-Semitic violence in Germany and anti-Semitic rhetoric in Britain. The Astor family had historical family roots in Waldorf in southern Germany and Lord Astor's two newspapers, *The Times* and *The Observer*, promoted Hitler as someone of 'moderate outlook' beneath the uncouth exterior. *The Observer* portrayed Hitler's anti-Semitism as a mere 'blot' on his 'Christian ideals', while *The Times* referred to Nazi violence as 'a manifestation of ... discipline'[4] and an example of Hitler's 'moderation and common sense' as he advanced towards his goal of ruling Germany.⁵ While attending a dinner at the Savoy Hotel in 1934, Nancy asked the League of Nations' High Commissioner for Refugees whether he believed 'that there must be something in the Jews themselves that had brought them persecution throughout the ages'.

Those on the guest list at Cliveden in the 1930s generally had benevolent views of Nazi Germany. It included Consuelo Vanderbilt, Duchess of Marlborough; Consuelo Yznaga de Valle, Duchess of Manchester; Mary (May) Goelet, Duchess of Roxburghe; Joseph Kennedy; the aviator Charles Lindbergh; Lord Lothian; Lord Halifax, British Foreign Secretary between 1938 and 1940; Geoffrey Dawson, editor of *The Times*; Sir Samuel Hoare, British Foreign Secretary in 1935; Neville Henderson, the British ambassador to Berlin; former Prime Minister David Lloyd George; and the Duke of Kent. German guests included Ribbentrop; Princess Stephanie von Hohenlohe; and Charles Edward (Carl Eduard), Duke of Saxe-Coburg and Gotha. Ribbentrop was a frequent guest at the Astor home in Sandwich.

By October 1937, the guest list at Cliveden had expanded to include Anthony Eden, Sir Alexander Cadogan, the Rt. Hon. Edward Algernon Fitzroy and Lord Lothian. Discussion centred on the German question. Lothian, in particular, argued that Germany had taken only those measures to defend itself as any other rational nation would have done. Britain and France were the ones blocking a reasonable settlement and pursuing their traditional policy of encirclement of Germany. Germany had to be given equality by agreement, otherwise it would come about by illegal rearmament. More than anything, an Anglo-German dialogue must be revived. Britain had no fundamental interests in eastern Europe and to be dragged into a conflict over events there would be fatal for the unity of the Empire. Nancy saw no flaws in Lothian's arguments. 'In twenty years,' she said, 'I've never known [Lothian] to be wrong on foreign politics.'⁶ Dawson was very much in favour of a direct Anglo-German dialogue to arrive at a European settlement before Britain distanced itself from irrelevant conflicts.

Following an invitation for Lord Halifax, now Foreign Secretary, to visit Hitler in Berlin, *The Week* published an article by Claud Cockburn on 17 November 1937 claiming that a 'queer Anglo-American gathering [of] a little knot of expatriate Americans and super-nationally minded Englishmen' was exercising a 'powerful an influence on [British foreign policy]'. The concept of the 'Cliveden Group', or *Astorgruppe* as Ribbentrop called it, emerged. It was perceived by some to be so powerful that the British popular press characterised the group as a shadow government and the Astors as Germany's most powerful supporters in England, seen as having immense influence and political power. The *Washington Post* characterised the Cliveden Set as 'the real centre of British foreign policy, challenging the constitutional structure of British Democracy'.[7]

The Week intensified its attack weeks later by referring to the 'Cliveden Set' as 'friends of the Third Reich' and insinuated that Neville Chamberlain was unduly persuaded by the 'vast influences emanating from Cliveden', which was described as' Britain's other Foreign Office'.[8] The rest of the British press now piled in with attacks on the Astors, who were alleged to have engineered the replacement of Eden by Halifax as Foreign Secretary. Having been a talking shop for prominent members of society, the Cliveden house parties were now demonised as secret gatherings where plots were hatched against the government. This was exacerbated by a lunch at the Astors' St James's Square house, where Prime Minister Chamberlain was said to have briefed American journalists about the framework of a German–Italian–Franco–British pact to be aimed, eventually, at the Soviet Union. The meeting was duly reported in the US, with the result that the British were seen by many there as fascists in disguise.

The Astors and their friends were now attacked from all quarters. Nancy called it mischievous rubbish published by a communist rag. She was, she firmly declared, 'a true believer in democracy and parliamentary government and opposed all forms of dictatorship, whether fascist, Nazi or Communist'. Her husband called the whole idea of a Cliveden Set a myth at a time when the house on the river was starting to be referred to as 'Schloss Cliveden'. It is true that Nancy was instrumental in petitioning Ribbentrop to release Dr Solomon Frankfurter, who had been arrested in Vienna just after the Anschluss, and while Frankfurter's US relatives were grateful, they could not refrain from criticising the political philosophy associated with Cliveden and Nancy's wholesale condemnation of the Jews, which they saw as undermining the common decencies of civilisation. Nancy's anti-Semitic position, however, was not moderated.[9]

The Munich Crisis sharpened debate at Cliveden. Twice Chamberlain met Hitler to discuss the Nazis' threat to incorporate Czechoslovakia into the German Reich, by force if necessary. The threat of war hung over Europe but only Germany was close to being militarily ready and it was this fact above all others that exercised the minds of political leaders in

Britain and France while their armed forces desperately tried to make up for lost time by rearmament. Lothian spoke for the Cliveden group when he condemned the Czechs for intransigence and the French for encouraging them to continue in that vein. Waldorf called Czechoslovakia 'a festering sore in the middle of Europe'. When he went to the US at the end of 1938, he was shocked to find that US opinion saw the Cliveden Set as 'aristocrats and financiers ... selling out democracy ... because they want to preserve their own property and privileges'.[10]

Breaking away from his pro-appeasement stance, Lothian now began to harden his attitude to Hitler, calling him a fanatical gangster, which brought a swift response from Nancy, who concluded that he had never really understood Hitler in the first place. However, when Hitler tore up the Munich Agreement by annexing Bohemia and Moravia, even she was driven to condemn Germany's actions in the House of Commons. When the blame game started, Anthony Eden was quick to point the finger at the Astors, who were castigated as Nazi fellow-travellers who had held back the British government from taking a stronger line against Hitler.

By the summer of 1939, only Dawson of the Cliveden Set held out for further appeasement. A meeting at Cliveden in June was attended by Lothian, Halifax, Dawson, Brand, Sir Thomas Inskip and thirty others, who politely listened to Adam von Trott zu Solz, a member of the German Foreign Ministry although in this instance acting independently, lay out plans for a Europe led by but not dominated by Germany. This idea, however, had little appeal for the vast majority of his audience and the last great meeting at Cliveden came to an end. Lothian took up an appointment as ambassador to Washington, where he set about harnessing US support for Britain's war effort.

Emeline Pankhurst being arrested outside Buckingham Palace in 1914.

Rotha Lintorn-Orman, founder of the British Fascisti.

Arnold Spencer Leese was sentenced to six months' hard labour for seditious libel.

Flag of the Imperial Fascist League.
(*Wiener Holocaust Library Collections*)

German ex-servicemen parading through Whitehall on 21 January 1936.

Lord Rothermere and Adolf Hitler at Berchtesgarten in 1937.

Diana Mitford and Bryan Guinness on their honeymoon in Taormina, Italy, 1929.

Daily Mail headline on 15 January 1934.

Hurrah for the Blackshirts!

By VISCOUNT ROTHERMERE

BECAUSE Fascism comes from Italy, shortsighted people in this country think they show a sturdy national spirit by deriding it.

If their ancestors had been equally stupid, Britain would have had no banking system, no Roman law, nor even any football, since all of these are of Italian invention.

✦ ✦ ✦ ✦

THE Socialists, especially, who jeer at the principles and uniform of the Blackshirts as being of foreign origin, forget that the founder and High Priest of their own creed was the German Jew Karl Marx.

Though the name and form of Fascism originated in Italy, that movement is not now peculiar to any nation. **It stands in every country for the Party of Youth.**

It represents the effort of the young... generation to put new life into out-of-date political systems.

That alone is enough to make it a factor of im- and disgusted by the incompetence of their elders in dealing with the depression that has followed on it. The other is made up of men too young to remember the war but ready to put all their ardour and energy at the service of a cause which offers them a vigorous constructive policy in place of the drift and indecision of the old political parties.

Blackshirts proclaim a fact which politicians dating from pre-war days will never face—that the new age requires new methods and new men. They base their contention on the simple truth that parliamentary gov- views" were an effective substitute in human affairs for action, the National Government would be the best that Britain has ever had. But the experience of the past two years has proved that these futile and time-wasting devices are no more than a screen for inertia and indecision.

✦ ✦ ✦ ✦

THE huge majority obtained by the present Government at the general election of 1931 was the last vote of confidence that the nation will ever give to Old Gang politicians. Two years from now another general election will be almost due. The whole future of Britain will depend upon its issue.

A prolongation of the present régime may be regarded, in the country's present mood, as out of the question. There will be a pronounced swing either to Right or Left.

If the inflated, impulsive, and largely

Crazy News Reel

Presented by
D. B. WYNDHAM LEWIS

OLD soldiers will note, with grati fication, one of the Morlands "The Soldier's Return," a cottag group, at the British Art Exhibition.

The handsome, even foppish, youn soldier, wearing an expensive ruffle shirt and a natty velvet neckband, and looking like Squire Thornhill, is evidently telling his humble and astonished relatives how became quartermaster-sergeant, and how is now going to buy the village. His age father waggishly holds out to him a po mug of rum. He ignores it. Rum interest him henceforth only in bulk.

✦ ✦ ✦ ✦

I looked in vain for the companion picture, "The Sailor's Farewell," depicting honest tar taking leave of his creditors. is not on exhibition, possibly owing to t Censor.

WOMAN THROUGH THE AGES
"One woman burst into tears whe she was told she could not land fiv cases of Scotch whisky."
—New York cable.

Crowds giving Mosley a rapturous reception at Olympia in June 1934.

Mosley receiving the adoration of his followers.

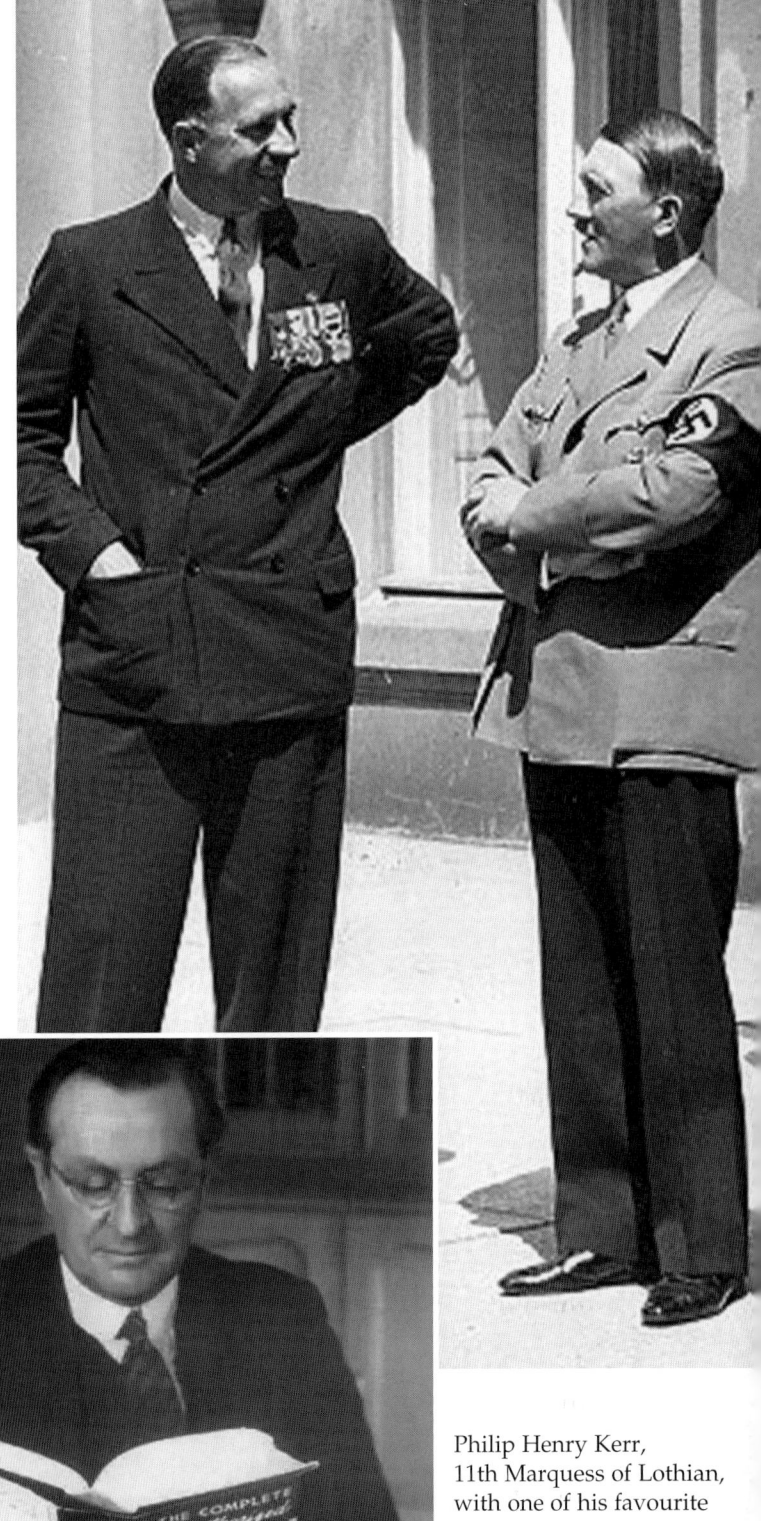

The British Legion chairman, Major Francis Fetherston-Godley, meeting Hitler in July 1935.

Philip Henry Kerr, 11th Marquess of Lothian, with one of his favourite books.

Mosley being pelted by an angry crowd in Liverpool on 10 October 1937.

Edward VIII and Wallis Simpson.

Boca do Inferno, where the Windsors stayed in Portugal.

A wounded William Joyce after his arrest on 29 May 1945.

Chapter Ten

Oswald Mosley and the British Union of Fascists

It was Thomas Carlyle's ideas of authoritarian leadership and the heroic aristocratic leader-figure that excited fascist activists such as William Joyce. Such a charismatic leader would revive the old values of duty, responsibility and service, which contrasted with the mediocrities that currently sat in high offices of the state. Radical right-wing activists thought they had found the ideal leader in Oswald Mosley.

Oswald Ernald Mosley came from a broken home and was educated at Winchester College, where his skill at boxing ensured that he avoided being bullied even though his fellow pupils found him 'strange' and he had few friends. He was an obdurate youth and resented authority. After becoming an officer cadet at Sandhurst, he served during the First World War in the 16th Queen's Lancers before transferring to the Royal Flying Corps as an observer. Having trained to become a pilot, he was involved in an accident while demonstrating an aircraft in front of his mother that left him with a permanent limp. He returned to the trenches at the battle of Loos in 1915 but then spent the rest of the war in the Ministry of Munitions and the Foreign Office. His experience of war left him with a keen sense of responsibility towards those who had served in the war and he promoted himself as a spokesman for that 'lost generation', both in a drive to ensure that their sacrifice would not be forgotten and that the survivors should live in a better world. He saw the British system of party politics as an impediment to the sort of radical social change that was required to reverse Britain's decline as a world power.

Mosley won the Harrow seat in the 1918 General Election for the Conservative Party, campaigning on a ticket of 'socialistic imperialism'. He distinguished himself as an orator and political player, one marked by extreme self-confidence, and made a point of speaking in the House of Commons without notes. He became the youngest member to take his seat in the House of Commons but he soon fell out with his party over his criticism of the Black and Tans' operations against Irish civilians during the Irish War of Independence (1919–21). His admiration for Lloyd George's premiership (1917–22), especially his ability to overcome red tape and tackle problems head-on, was tempered by his anger at the failure of the government to tackle unemployment and its futile attempt to restore the gold standard to pre-war parity as the foundation of economic policy. This led him to cross the floor of the Commons and sit as an independent after 1920.

In 1919 he met Cynthia Blanche 'Cimmie' Curzon, the second daughter of Lord Curzon, and they married in an extravagant society wedding on 11 May 1920. Cimmie was a strong, emancipated woman ready to serve her husband as well as the interests of the national community and someone who was able to give support and guidance to her husband during his erratic political career. During their marriage, she was constantly loyal to Mosley and endured with dignity the social ostracism of virtually all her former society acquaintances, who saw her as a socialist turncoat, but she always maintained that she and her husband worked for 'a better and happier England'.[1] After the 1929 General Election, she took her seat as the member for Stoke-on-Trent and for two years sat in the Commons alongside her husband.

His rhetorical skills earned Mosley a reputation as the most polished literary speaker in the Commons and he easily held his seat during ensuing elections. Lesley Hore-Belisha described him as 'dark, aquiline, flashing: tall, thin, assured [with] defiance in his eye [and] contempt in his forward chin'. A.J. Spender, in the Liberal *Westminster Gazette* wrote that Mosley was 'the most polished literary speaker in the Commons, words flow from him in graceful epigrammatic phrases that have a sting in them for the government and the conservatives. To listen to him is an education in the English language, also in the art of delicate but deadly repartee. He has human sympathies, courage and brains.'[2]

By 1924 he had joined the Independent Labour Party, the left-wing pressure group, for which he stood against and narrowly lost to Neville Chamberlain in Birmingham Ladywood. He now began to study economic theory, especially that of John Maynard Keynes, and his political speeches began to contain radical ideas of economic reform. His first target was the banking system, which, in a speech to the Independent Labour Party conference at Gloucester in 1925, he called a 'combination of private interests and public plunders'. He called for wage rises to stimulate the economy by creating demand, and venues for his public meetings were regularly packed beyond capacity.

When he was selected to stand in a by-election in Smethwick, the right-wing press was quick to characterise him as a wolf in sheep's clothing. On 8 December 1926, the *Daily Telegraph* accused him of 'preaching socialism in a Saville Row suit'. Despite attacks all round, including criticism from his own father who, in the same newspaper, described him as having lived off the fat of the land and never having done a day's work in his life, Mosley won comfortably. In his victory speech he proclaimed a new era for British democracy.

The General Election of May 1929 was held against a background of industrial unrest and unemployment. Mosley became a vitally important figure for Labour in the run-up to the vote. In Birmingham on 15 May he told his audience that the 'realities of the present age' were unemployment, wages, rents, suffering, squalor and starvation, struggle for existence in our streets and the threat of world catastrophe in another war. Bias in the electoral system saw the Labour Party win the most seats despite having lost the popular vote, but no radical economic policies followed. It was not that new ideas were unappealing, said Keynes, but that it was so difficult to abandon the old ones. Mosley was denied high office and given the Chancellorship of the Duchy of Lancaster, a position that gave him a seat in Cabinet but little responsibility. There was a sense, as one Labour politician put it, that he had had a fatal flaw in his character, one of overwhelming arrogance and an unshakable conviction that he was born to rule. Clement Atlee said Mosley was in the habit of speaking to his colleagues as though he were a feudal landlord abusing tenants who are in arrears with their rent.

Unemployment continued to rise, which led Mosley to propose a radical solution in what became known as the Mosley Memorandum. This called for an overhaul of the machinery of government and a public works programme to reduce unemployment that would require mobilisation of national resources on a huge scale. Specifically, he advocated the provision of old-age pensions at sixty, the raising of the school-leaving age and an expansion in public works programmes. In macroeconomic areas he went against the orthodox views of the Manchester School and rejected limits on public expenditure, preferring instead to increase credit levels and allow the government to create a deliberate budgetary deficit. The increase in consumer spending that this would stimulate would serve to revitalise manufacturing and service industries. When his ideas were, unsurprisingly, rejected by the ultra-orthodox Chancellor Philip Snowden on the grounds that they would 'plunge the country into ruin', he resigned on 20 May 1930.

The only way to get his ideas across, Mosley now believed, was to form his own political party, which he called the New Party, and he got support for this from the motor manufacturer Sir William Morris, who made a donation of £50,000 as start-up capital. Other industrialists followed Morris's example. With three other members of Parliament who resigned with him, Mosley set up the New Party on 1 March 1931 and they held their first meeting on 14 May. One of the things agreed at the meeting was to form a group of young men to provide protection at political meetings from other political groups such as the communists, who had challenged fascist movements abroad. Meetings were marred by disorder and violence, which drove some members to object to the way things were going – believing that rallies smacked of Nazi *Sturmabteilung* (SA) tactics – and much moderate support quickly fell away.

Mosley's wife, Cimmie, was one of those worried by Mosley's apparent lurch to the right and threatened to publicly dissociate herself from him and his new politics. At the Ashton-under-Lyne by-election of April 1931, however, she campaigned vigorously for the New Party candidate Allan Young. Mosley got out of his sick bed to canvas. In his rousing speeches, during which Harold Nicolson described him as 'striding up and down the rather frail platform with great panther steps and gesticulating with a pointing, and occasionally a stabbing finger', he generated huge enthusiasm, but after the vote Young emerged a poor third. Harold Nicolson had joined the New Party at its inception but quickly became disillusioned with Mosley and in a letter of 20 May 1932 distanced himself from a strategy that risked 'the violent and untruthful methods which the fascists have adopted in Italy'.

The defeat convinced Mosley to adopt new tactics. He became convinced that he could not count on support from the left and held meetings with David Lloyd George and Winston Churchill with a view to creating with them a new political entity. He even had fruitless conversations with Neville Chamberlain, but then suffered a setback when Nicolson and Allan abruptly jumped ship fearing that the movement was about to 'subordinate intelligence to muscular bands of young men'.

During the General Election of October 1931, Mosley toured the country making rousing speeches to large open meetings wherever he went, making it clear to his audiences that he was done with socialism. He stood in Stoke-on-Trent but despite getting over 10,000 votes, came last. The New Party was a dismal failure at the polls, having fielded twenty-five candidates and collected only half the total number of votes the communists received. With such a disappointing result there was little enthusiasm to continue and the New Party was wound up on 5 April, just thirteen months after it had been formed. Mosley admitted that his party had been 'swept away in a hurricane of sentiment' but, undaunted, he insisted that 'our time is yet to come'.[3] His analysis was that he had been too cautious with his political message and the party had not been sufficiently fascist in character, even though there had been undertones in the way it had embraced a cult of physical fitness and had encouraged violence as a political tool.

Up to this point, Rothermere's newspapers had been hostile to Mosley but a change occurred in December of 1931 when he met Mosley and discussed moving forward with a new fascist movement that would have the full backing of the whole Harmsworth press. Rothermere's conditions were that any new party would actively seek the support of the working classes to weaken the other left-wing parties and work in favour of the Conservatives.

In January, Mosley went to Italy with Nicolson and William E. Allen where they had a meeting with Mussolini, whom he found to represent the first emergence of 'the modern man' to power. This inspired him to launch the British Union of Fascists on 1 October 1932 with an initial membership of thirty-two, who were called upon to 'dedicate their lives to building in the country a movement of the modern age'. Numbers rose quickly and Mosley decided that members, when representing the party in public, should wear black shirts, similar to the Italian fascists, as the 'outward and visible sign of an inward and spiritual grace'. The uniform, he said, would enable his stewards to recognise each other in a fight against those trying to disrupt BUF meetings. Uniformed BUF members were henceforth referred to as Blackshirts.

The BUF headquarters were established in the Whitelands Teachers' Training College in Chelsea, which was renamed the Black House, and to celebrate, Mosley organised the first large BUF march in June 1933, when a thousand Blackshirts marched. The BUF set up its northern headquarters at 17 Northumberland Street, Higher Broughton in Manchester, where it expanded its membership rapidly. There was fighting in the streets when BUF members marched through Strangeways along Bury

New Road as a provocation to the Jewish population, which greatly boosted membership of the Communist Party of Great Britain (CPGB), especially in Jewish areas like Cheetham Hill. Opposition to the BUF in Manchester came not only from Jews and communists but also from the police. The Manchester police chief, John Maxwell, refused to tolerate uniformed BUF members stewarding public meetings, which he saw as a purely police role. Maxwell particularly objected to the wearing of black shirts by the BUF at such meetings, which, when so many were massed together, he saw as intimidation and a direct provocation. On 23 November 1933 the decision was taken at a conference in the Home Office that the BUF should be subjected to systematic surveillance by local constabularies, the Metropolitan Police, Special Branch and MI5.

The message of the BUF was still the same on the economic front. A consumer boom would flow from new injections of capital into an economy in which industry would be powered by developments in modern science. Trade would be restricted to countries within the Empire where reciprocal trade agreements would be drawn up so that all benefits of the new prosperity would be shared equally and not dissipated through trade with countries outside such as Germany, Japan and the US. On the political side, Mosley began testing public opinion on radical topics such as the replacement of parliamentary democracy by a small executive body.

Julie Gottlieb discusses the way that the BUF projected its image to the public after 'the shattering of male identity caused by the war experience'.[4] Ideals of manliness exemplified by physical fitness and paramilitary organisation of the gang proved to be important ideas around which dislocated young men could rally. One BUF supporter wrote of 'untold numbers of desperate men in England' who had 'lost all hope' after being 'brutally treated by those to whom money is everything and human life next to nothing'.[5] The Blackshirts evoked codes of manliness and behaviour of an imperial age that was becoming a distant memory. Having said that, the BUF was much less obsessed with male supremacy that the New Party had been. The BUF was notable among fascist movements for high levels of female support and consistently claimed that it adhered to the principle of the equality of the sexes and was the ideal home for the patriotic but independent and active woman.[6]

The value of women members was readily accepted and they became a common sight during marches, when they were not allowed to wear any make-up. It is interesting to note that, as a result of BUF branch activities such as dances, summer camps, marches, and rallies, a large number of marriages took place within the organisation. Marriage, however, was not uppermost on the minds of some members. By 1934 there were allegations of sexual licentiousness at the Brixton Branch, where it was reported to the landlord that men and women fascists were habitually sleeping there together. 'Loose women appear to be plentiful,' cried the local Labour Party, who suggested putting a red light above the door. Significantly, while four women were expelled from the movement because of their 'immoral conduct', the men, who must by necessity have acted as accessories to their offences against propriety, were not expelled.

While the headquarters of the BUF had been set up at 233 Regent Street, the Women's Section established itself at 12 Lower Grosvenor Place and began publishing a fortnightly paper, *The Woman Fascist*, described as an 'enterprising little paper which will deal with news and problems peculiar to women members'.[7] There were few activities from which women were excluded but there were areas in which their expertise was considered of particular usefulness. In public, women acted as Blackshirts and stewards, were involved in violent confrontations, spoke at meetings, raised funds, sold newspapers, marched, canvassed, and stood as candidates in elections the BUF contested. Their uniform was a black blouse, black beret and a grey skirt. Despite describing herself as 'no believer in fascism', the first leader of the Women's Section was Esther, Lady Makgill, who was soon removed from office having been found embezzling funds. She would later be jailed for similar offences with a different employer. She was replaced by the ex-Suffragette Mary Richardson, who herself had a long criminal record. It must be said that the Lady Makgill incident left the women's section weakened and it was never thereafter able to boast strong female leadership. Eventually a man, Neil Francis Hawkins, assumed control and its independence was eroded, never again to occupy anything other than a subservient position in the movement. Even so, at the 1935 General Election, a full 10 per cent of BUF parliamentary candidates would be women, which was higher than any of the mainstream parties.

The general health of the British nation was poor, especially among the working classes, and unemployment was high. Mosley saw this as something the BUF could remedy within its own organisation at least. They directed much of its efforts to recruiting young members, using sport, the excitement and seething violence of the Blackshirt movement, and various displays of male camaraderie and bonding, couched in hyper-nationalist, anti-communist, and patriotic rhetoric, to attract young men to its ranks.

Summer camps were organised at Selsey, and fascist sports leagues and exchange trips to Italy and Germany through which Mosley hoped to generate a spiritual rebirth and national renaissance. This, of course, was designed to emulate the youth movements in Germany and Italy, where, from an early age, young men and women were encouraged to give their allegiance to the movement above all else.

Thurlow characterises the BUF as Janus-faced, with one face representing a movement that was 'intellectually the most coherent and rational of all the fascist parties of Europe in the early years', while the other face showed an 'aggressive style [that] attracted political violence'.[8] It was, however, the New Party that had tried and failed to amalgamate both muscle and brain in the movement. Nicolson had tried to recruit intellectuals but the majority of the young recruits were more interested in uniforms, marching, saluting and physical activity, sport and self-defence with the introduction of the 'Biff Boys', whose role was protection and security of premises and meetings. Carefully posed images of proud, lean, angular, well-tailored Blackshirts giving the fascist salute were commonly printed in newspapers such as the *Daily Mail*. Fascist youth were trained in physical fitness not for its own sake but as a rehearsal for conflict.[9] Those, who found that distasteful were not only rejected but often beaten as punishment before being thrown out.

Mosley had been on the wrong end of violence at a New Party meeting in Glasgow in December 1931 when he was hit on the head by a stone. This had led him to believe that violence was becoming a serious threat at public meetings and encouraged him in his move to create a youth movement, Nupa, which became a defence force and personal bodyguard. Despite later deploring Mosley's tactics, Nicolson at this stage was supportive of Nupa and even suggested its uniform might be grey trousers and grey shirt.

At this stage it is worth looking at the debate surrounding BUF violence. Fascism has been seen by some as a uniquely violent form of politics but the BUF were far from being alone in this respect and were often rather less adept than their opponents. Mosley always claimed that any violence that his men were involved in was purely defensive. Later in 1933, he was quoted as saying that when the communist revolutionaries finally take to the streets, 'we will be there ... with fascist machine guns to meet them'.[10] He said that it was his experience of violent, organised, left-wing opposition to his New Party in 1931 that led him to create the

Blackshirt movement. In particular, he frequently cited the violent disruption of the NP's Birmingham Rag Market meeting as the key event.

The meeting had started to get out of hand when the loudspeaker system failed, possibly as the result of sabotage. The crowd of some 15,000 people became restless and a group of Labour and communist supporters at the back of the hall started heckling and hurling abuse at Mosley. A whistle was sounded and New Party stewards who had been located throughout the hall, led as always by the stocky figure of Ted 'Kid' Lewis, marched to the front, then moved into the crowd with Mosley jumping down from the stage, climbing over the rail, and following in their wake. All across the hall, fights broke out between New Party stewards and sections of the crowd as Mosley and his comrades battled their way back to the stage under a hail of fists, chairs and bottles. Missiles continued to be thrown and the stage rushed before the police finally moved in to disperse the crowd and convince Mosley of the need to return to his hotel under escort. That, he claimed, was why he had to organise the Blackshirts to prevent the communists from curbing his right to free speech. There is some justification for that in Special Branch and MI5 files, which indicate that the BUF was primarily the victim of offensive political violence rather than its prime instigator. However, the anti- Semitic commentary of various BUF speakers, especially in east London, along with the BUF's marches in areas of east London with large Jewish populations and high degrees of support for communism, raises the issue of provocation and the question of what constitutes a legitimate reaction to such provocation.[11] Home Office files show that 64 per cent of all BUF meetings in the London Metropolitan District in 1934 were interrupted by violence, but police reports indicate that only about a fifth of these disturbances were as the result of organised communist opposition. However, where the CPGB organised attacks on the BUF they were particularly violent and effective.

The BUF, of course, was guilty of instigating violence, as when thugs attacked BF headquarters in 22 Stanhope Gardens in July 1933 when, according to the police report, they caused a considerable amount of damage and slightly injured a number of BF members. Later that year BUF members attacked a meeting of Arnold Leese's IFL in Trinity Hall, Great Portland Street when both sides weighed in with truncheons, knuckledusters and broken chairs.

As a central tenet of the BUF creed, Mosley turned again to promoting the idea of the Corporate State in which all citizens were encouraged to join interest groups who would than send delegates to participate in the process of national policymaking. The government would preside over corporations formed from the employers, trade unions and consumer interests. Within the guidelines of a national plan, these corporations would work out a policy for wages, prices, conditions of employment, investment and terms of competition. Government would intervene only to settle deadlocks between unions and employers. Strikes would be made illegal. In such a state there would be no need for parties or politicians. This would give the ruling elite considerable control over the economy through its control of the interest groups. Again he used the argument of raising the level of wages to stimulate industrial production, which should be protected from foreign competition.

Other right-wing groups were encouraged to amalgamate with the BUF. Rotha Lintorn-Orman's British Fascisti (BF) voted to reject the idea but that did not stop many of its committee members leaving and signing up with the BUF anyway. This left the BF with what Mosley contemptuously called 'three old ladies and a couple of office boys'.[12] When some BF rank and file shouted abuse at a BUF rally in Hyde Park on 23 July, some fifty BUF rowdies attacked the BF headquarters and wrecked it. More violence ensued when IFL leader Arnold Leese, who Mosley thought of as an anti-Semitic crank, threatened to become a rival for leadership of the radical right in Britain. Leese had no intention of becoming subservient to Mosley in any shape or form. Whether under Mosley's direct orders or not, BUF members broke up an IFL rally in November 1933 using truncheons and smashed chairs. They ripped up IFL banners and caused physical injury to Leese among others. Mosley himself was no stranger to violence. In 1936 at a meeting in Prestwich, he launched himself from the stage and laid into some hecklers, knocking three of them unconscious, and then a year later was on the receiving end when he spoke to an open-air meeting on Queen's Drive in Liverpool. He had just jumped onto the top of a van and was giving the fascist salute when he was pelted with stones and one hit him on the head. Reports state that he fell semi-conscious and was taken to Walton Hospital, where he remained for a week before being released. At the same meeting a woman fascist was felled by a stone that struck her on the head, causing a wound requiring nine stitches.

After a visit to Italy with her husband, during which they were photographed giving fascist salutes on the balcony of the Palazzo Venezia, Cimmie became ill and after an operation to remove her appendix she died of peritonitis. Mosley was very badly affected by the death of his wife but dedicated himself to the cause of fascism in her memory. This was ironic in that although Cimmie had generally supported her husband's political career, she had never been a believer in fascism.

The question of Mosley's personal relationships with the women of his family and his class is important when assessing the development of his sexual politics in terms of feminine fascism and the way in which his renowned sex appeal attracted women to his cause in the sexually charged atmosphere in which British fascism flourished during the 1930s. After Cimmie's death at the age of thirty-four, Mosley changed his approach to women in politics. This is partly due to his belief that the stress of bringing up a young family at the same time as having a political career, when she had been subjected to 'the most blackguardly abuse from some sections of the press',[13] had contributed to her death. He apparently accepted no personal blame for his wife's stressful life, even though he was serially unfaithful to her.

Mosley reiterated the fascist philosophy in a speech made in March 1933 when he described fascist principles as private freedom and public service that required a certain discipline and a certain restraint. He argued strongly for public organisation to bring some order out of the economic chaos that existed in the world, and that such public organisation could only be secured by the methods of authority and of discipline which were inherent in fascism. Parliament, he said, had destroyed the means of government, first by breaking the feudal Monarchy, then the Church and finally it had broken the aristocracy. This had left the country at the mercy of private commercial capitalists and landowners, employers and financiers of all nations and races. We see here the first inklings of anti-Semitism creeping in. Anyone, he claimed, who had ambitions to buck the trend might arrive at Westminster roaring like a lion only to find their vitality and fighting power blunted, leaving the warrior of the platform a few months later the lap-dog of the lobbies.

There was much discussion about how to present the BUF to the population, who, if they wholeheartedly supported the party, would effectively destroy Parliament and rob them of the franchise. Clearly a softer face needed to front the organisation. It was this requirement that led to the formation in late 1933 of the January Club, led by Sir John Collings Squire, who invited membership from all those who were 'in sympathy with the fascist movement'. The objectives of this new organisation were stated to be bringing together men who were interested in modern methods of government; providing a platform for leaders of fascist and Corporate

State philosophy and widening the debate and listening to the voices of those who might not be supporters of fascism. Interestingly, the January Club membership included a number of prominent Jewish political figures.

Rothermere, a member of the January Club, was true to his promise and lauded BUF doctrine in his newspapers as sound, commonplace, Conservative doctrine inspired by loyalty to the throne and love of country. Its popularity naturally led to MI5 taking a close interest in its activities, and they were to conclude that it became a powerhouse for the development of fascist culture and brought fascism to the notice of large numbers of people who would have considered it much less favourably otherwise. During this first phase of the movement, Mosley had successfully laid the foundations on which to build a mass movement. He had limited but vocal support in government circles as well as friends in the press and all he needed was a crisis to exploit, but British society proved itself to be particularly resilient and unresponsive to perceived threats. The economic crisis he had warned about and had hoped would propel him onto the political centre stage was seeming less likely now that the government had managed to engineer a minor upturn in the economy that took much of the wind out of the BUF sails. The road to power was not going to be precipitous and would now boil down to a protracted battle with the democratic parties and require a new, revitalised message. There was little sign of mass defections to the BUF from the Conservative Party.

Membership of the BUF peaked in 1934 with around 10,000 active members and two or three times that many passive ones. The intelligence services, who were by now reporting to the Home Office twice monthly, were becoming increasingly concerned. A memorandum to the Home Office in 1934 said:

> Superficially, at any rate, the British Union of fascists follows Nazi methods very closely. There is the same massing of banners, the same spot-light on the leader, the same defence force, the same facile promise of relief from economic stress, the same kind of excessive simplicity of thought wholly at variance with the complexities of life and the infinite variety of scientific facts. There can be no doubt [that] they lead up to the same conclusion: the capture of power at a general election followed by the suppression of all opinion opposed to the policy of the fascist government.[14]

The organisation set up a Foreign Relations and Overseas Department under George A. Pfister, who ran the Reliance Translation Bureau from

177–178 Fleet Street. Members of the BUF who wanted to communicate with the German National Socialist Party were instructed to do so through that department. Pfister tried to act as an intermediary between Mosley and Hitler in July of that year by going to the Nazi Party headquarters in London, but Otto Bene, the local group leader of the *Orstgruppe* NSDAP, who thought Mosley to be a political adventurer worthy of no serious consideration, denied the request, calling him 'a person of little importance'.[15] The BUF, however, was making 'somewhat crude attempts to establish sympathetic relations with fascist movements all over the world' and this gave it some significance to the Nazi propaganda magazine *Der Stürmer*, whose editorials urged extreme anti-Semitism. Its publisher, Julius Streicher, warmly greeted Mosley for 'valued advice in the midst of our hard struggle' to destroy Jewish corruption in all countries to achieve peace and justice.[16] Bene, however, was distancing his *Orstgruppe* from the BUF and forbade any of its members from attending BUF meetings. Mosley reacted to this by closing down Pfister's department and suspending him without pay for six weeks, but still the Nazis gave little encouragement to the BUF.

In Germany, meanwhile, the BUF had set up branches in Berlin and Cologne, which came to the notice of British diplomats by commemorating the Nazi Putsch of 1923. The leader in Cologne, one Captain Levi, called it a 'sacred day' when Germany's warriors bravely fought and died for their country. He rounded off his speech by calling for a 'hearty cheer' for Adolf Hitler and Oswald Mosley. The British consul encountered Levi and some of his followers a few days later at a wreath-laying ceremony at the War Memorial and found them to be 'men of little intelligence [who] sooner or later may do something to cause friction with the local authorities'.[17]

Chapter Eleven

Olympia

The willingness of the CPGB to organise premeditated and violent attacks on the BUF is supported by specific reports, often from Special Branch sources, on violent incidents nationwide such as the Olympia meeting of 7 June 1934. It is clear that the communists made well-organised plans to assault fascists and break up the meeting, while the fascists used excessive force in resisting this attack on one of their set-piece events. A Special Branch report noted that:

> Two or three leading members of the Communist Party have made a tour of inspection of the neighbourhood of Olympia W. in order to obtain a good idea of the exact situation of the building etc. They have reported that there are many old bricks, of which use could be made, lying about near a large hoarding close to a railway bridge adjacent to Olympia.[1]

The same report also noted that the CPGB was planning to get mileage out of the use of organised violence by making 'every effort to bring off a spectacular coup against the fascists, in order to counteract the loss of prestige the CPGB has suffered at recent by-elections'.

The BUF rally held at Olympia in June 1934 was planned along the lines of Hitler's Nuremberg rallies and Mosley set out to make it the largest, most spectacular public gathering in the history of British politics. Fifteen thousand gathered to hear Mosley speak, including young men and women in evening dress, middle-class family parties with small children, a large gathering of workers in their working clothes and, by some accounts, about 150 Members of Parliament.[2] The proceedings were carefully stage managed on an impressively theatrical level, but instead of swastikas there was a profusion of Blackshirt banners bearing the 'bolt of lightning' symbol and Union Jacks fluttered everywhere.

The *Manchester Guardian* reported that:

> It is not easy to apportion the blame for the disturbance. For when the anti-Mosleyites – Communists, pacifists, and Left-wing members

of the Labour party and the I.L.P. – arrived at Olympia with their placards and pamphlets a couple of hours before the meeting was due to begin it was to encounter massed groups of Blackshirts and a strong force of police, not only on foot but mounted, and it is an odd fact that of all the emblems of authority which drew booing and catcalls from a crowd of British Communists and Left-wingers the mounted policeman seems to be regarded as the most provocative.

Proceedings were delayed for about half an hour by violent protests outside the building but when Mosley eventually arrived the lights of the hall flickered, and a spotlight swung round from the platform to illuminate him arriving to a fanfare. Some people raised their arms in a fascist salute but above the cheers could be heard the unmistakable sound of booing. Flanked by his bodyguards and preceded by a procession of uniformed BUF members bearing fascist banners, Mosley walked down the central aisle of Olympia towards a raised platform at the end of the hall. Collin Brooks, the former editor of Rothermere's *Sunday Dispatch*, reported that 'searchlights were directed to the far end, the Blackshirts lined the centre corridor – and trumpets brayed as a great mass of Union Jacks surmounted by Roman plates passed towards the platform'. Mosley gave the fascist salute and began to speak but the sound amplification system malfunctioned and his words were unintelligible. Immediately, a well-organised campaign of disruption began. Agitators shouted slogans, leading to chaos in the hall. The Blackshirt stewards swiftly and brutally attacked the first hecklers. Despite the presence of 1,000 police officers, fights broke out all over the arena. For close to two hours the meeting dragged on like that, interruption following interruption and ejection. Outside the auditorium, 200 Blackshirts patrolled the corridors, beating up those already ejected from the main hall. Of the hundreds who suffered injuries, some fifty needed hospital treatment and five were detained there as a result of the beatings they received.

Mosley continued to speak even though nobody could make out what he was saying as the venue continue to empty. Outside, communists such as Phil Piratin were waiting to attack BUF supporters. 'Some of them paid for what they had done that night.'[3] Then, inside the arena, a voice sounded high up in the rafters shouting 'down with fascism!' Balanced 150ft above the crowd, in a scene that would have graced any adventure cinema screening, a man was seen clambering across the girders pursued from each side by Blackshirts. All the men then were lost in the darkness and there came the sound of breaking glass. Chaos ensued.

Olympia

It was the bloody rally at Olympia that was the catalyst for the 1936 Public Order Act that banned the wearing of uniforms during political rallies and marches and required police consent to be obtained for any political marches to take place. Nevertheless, the *Daily Mail*'s Ward Price, who regarded Mosley as a more eloquent and persuasive speaker than Hitler, Mussolini or Goebbels, chose to put a different gloss on the rally in the next day's paper: 'If the Black shirt movement had any need of justification, the Red Hooligans who savagely and systematically tried to wreck Sir Oswald Mosley's huge and magnificently successful meeting at Olympia last night would have supplied it. They got what they deserved. Olympia has been the scene of many assemblies and many great fights (the sporting version) but never had it offered the spectacle of so many fights mixed up with a meeting.'

The gratuitous display of brutality with large numbers of Blackshirts seizing and beating hecklers, it is argued, successfully alienated respectable opinion and irredeemably associated the BUF with thuggery.[4] Thurlow writes that after Olympia public opinion began to harden against the BUF and that the event was a watershed in BUF fortunes, after which membership started to fall dramatically and it 'almost collapsed as a national force'.[5] The movement has gone down in history as a political failure and much has been written about the causes of that failure, but the reality is more complex. Mosley was delighted with the reaction to Olympia. A Commons' debate immediately after the event on 14 June saw eight of the fifteen government supporters who spoke defend the BUF's actions and heaped blame for the riot on the communists, who were acting against the interests of free speech, and in any case, reports of violence had been overblown. 'Where are the bodies?' Mosley asked. Michael Beaumont suggested that reports of violence had been greatly exaggerated and the BUF was attracting 'respectable, reasonable and intelligent people'. T.F. Howard called them 'the best elements in this country'. There was a widespread sympathy for Mosley in the ruling Conservative Party and a feeling that, on the economic front, he was offering to do what the government had promised but failed to deliver. He was in fact a convenient stick with which to beat Prime Minister Baldwin. When Sir Thomas Moore called for concord and agreement between the old historic Conservative Party and this 'new virile offshoot' he spoke for many and the events of Olympia did nothing to dampen their enthusiasm.

Olympia is often cited as the moment when Rothermere began to distance himself from the BUF, but press reaction was as mixed as that in

Parliament. During the seven months leading up to Olympia, Rothermere's newspapers had given enormous and highly flattering coverage to the fascists. The *Sunday Dispatch*, for example, offered regular features on 'What the Blackshirts are doing', 'Who's who of leading fascists', and £1 prizes for readers' letters in response to the question 'Why I like the Blackshirts'. In early July, the *Mail* was still carrying enthusiastic articles about BUF meetings that were carried off quite peacefully, implying that violence at Olympia had been exaggerated or, at best, an anomaly. However, there was a change in late July when Rothermere felt the need, for whatever reason, to distance himself from fascist ideology but he still promised Mosley his cooperation and assistance to 'defeat the forces of Socialism'. Rothermere had not been disturbed by BUF violence at Olympia and approved a *Sunday Dispatch* editorial on 14 June that said where necessary the Blackshirts should be ready to meet violence with violence. It was noted by Thurlow, however, that the links that were starting to be made between BUF rallies and meetings and the much more extreme actions of the Nazis in Germany were starting to play on Rothermere's mind. Essentially, though, it was the risk of the BUF creaming off Conservative votes at the next election, risking allowing a socialist government to take power, and threats from his Jewish advertisers to close their accounts that was the real motivation behind Rothermere's cooling of support for Mosley.

While the Beaverbrook press had reported Olympia in an even-handed way, it continued to treat the BUF as a sideshow and gave it little publicity or criticism. The left-wing press – the *Guardian*, the *News Chronicle* and the *Daily Herald* – had been hostile to Mosley long before Olympia and used that event to shine a light on its methods. On 8 June, the *Chronicle* simply reiterated its antipathy towards the BUF by calling Olympia 'a complete failure except as an exhibition of violence'. *The Times* had, up to this point reported Mosley's speeches fairly comprehensively but had generally retained an aloof and disdainful attitude. The *Morning Post* saw no need for 'private armies marching about in exotic costumes and under exotic names', but in general reporting by both papers was sympathetic and laid the blame for the violence on the communists. During the following months, their editorials actually softened and they reported on BUF meetings fairly comprehensively and without bias either way. Letter pages indicated a large measure of readers' support for the BUF and 'disgust' at the 'un-British' behaviour of the communist mobs. Overall it must be said that Olympia did not signify any turning point in the opinions expressed by the newspapers. It seemed to simply confirm both hostile and sympathetic views of the movement.

It has been said by some commentators that the violence seen at Olympia had a marked effect on the lawmakers, but there was no immediate reaction. The Home Secretary may well have considered banning uniforms at public meetings and there were mutterings about extending police powers to control meetings but it was another three years before the Public Order Act came into force. Clearly the Conservative government was reluctant to make too much of a fuss because of the sharp divisions within its ranks over the BUF and also because it was felt by some that elevating the debate to prominence would only add the oxygen of publicity to the fascist cause and an outright ban would simply drive the movement underground, where it would be much more difficult to monitor. There was no shortage of arguments for doing nothing. How could you ban uniforms without alienating the Boy Scout movement and the Salvation Army?

There were dangers inherent in this approach. If no action was taken the BUF would most likely increase its paramilitary units along Nazi lines, which in turn would lead to more violent reaction from the left and result in an escalation of violence. On the other hand, some pointed out that in Germany fascism had not lost its appeal and was going from strength to strength. The same could happen in Britain with the BUF gaining more support and respectability. The government was fearful of public reaction at a time when the public mood was difficult to read. The BUF was certainly a topic of conversation but it was not necessarily seen as a threat in much the same way that the Nazis, in 1934, were considered to be of minor concern and little more than a sideshow in European politics.

For the BUF, Olympia proved to be a catalyst for recruitment. There were queues outside its Chelsea headquarters as people of all classes waited to sign up as members but, in a worrying sign in terms of public safety, the communists saw a sudden rise in their membership also. Fortunately, there was no escalation in violence as BUF meetings continued to be held without disruption, but that was not because the left retreated. Significantly, anti-fascist demonstrations deterred outdoor gatherings of the BUF and in some cases caused cancellation of rallies, and indoor meetings were controlled by allocation of tickets and strict police controls.

Chapter Twelve

Mosley after Olympia

When he launched the BUF, Mosley seriously considered incorporating a Nazi-like note of anti-Semitism into his programme by highlighting what he saw as the conspiracy of international Jewish bankers, and only decided against it because of opposition from Harold Nicolson. Mosley, however, never abandoned the theme and remained ambivalent about restraining what was no more than a reflection of the pervasive public anti-Semitic sentiments of the time up until October 1934, when he appeared to make a public declaration of his conversion to the anti-Semitic cause first at Belle Vue Gardens, Manchester, in September 1934 and then at the Albert Hall a month later. It has been suggested that this was an act of political expediency given the less than favourable reaction in some places to Olympia, but it did leave the way open for anti-Semites in the BUF to attack the Jewish community.[1]

Mosley, in what John Newsinger calls a 'fatal error of judgement', appeared to be constructing a rationale for the failure of the BUF to make the sort of progress that was essential to maintain momentum on the road to power and blamed the Jews for this. At the Albert Hall, Mosley told his audience: 'I have encountered things in this country which, quite frankly, I did not believe existed. And one of these is the power of organised Jewry, which is today mobilised against Fascism.' He went on to say that 'there is no [part of the economy] which was not dominated by the Jew'. What was required was a 'crusade against Jewry', which as a force had burst upon the scene, and anti-Semitism was now the one great issue that could arouse the passions of an audience.[2] Chesterton tells us that the BUF now proposed expelling the majority of Jews from the country and stripping those who remained of British citizenship.[3]

It is generally accepted that the BUF did not adopt an official anti-Jewish policy until October 1934 but there had been signs of a latent anti-Semitism before this time. There had been significant prejudice against Jews since before the First World War and there was no shortage of conspiracy theories linking Jews with everything from communism to control of international banking. Despite strong denials that it was anti-Semitic, however, the BUF had attracted opposition from sections of the Anglo-Jewish community even though there had been little BUF activity in the Jewish districts in the East End of London before 1935. As early as 1933, where the BUF had been active in London's West End the police noted that the Blackshirts were coming into contact with Jews who often congregated around Coventry Street on Sundays. Many Jews were concerned that the BUF was disseminating Nazi propaganda and their concern that events in Germany were being copied in London caused tension to boil over on 30 April when a crowd of 1,000 Jews chased and surrounded a group of Blackshirts and beat them up.

The first East End rally was held on 7 June 1936 in Bethnal Green and two weeks later, when Mosley tried to address a meeting in Finsbury Park, he was shouted down by a large crowd of protesters. By now, anti-Semitism was central to the BUF message. Mosley said: 'Up to three years ago anti-Semitism was unknown as a strong force in Britain. Today, in any audience, the strongest passion that can be aroused is the passion against the corruption of Jewish power.'[4]

In the East End, communist action was channelled through the International Labour Defence (ILD), which had organised a demonstration at Liverpool Street Station in May 1933 against the visit of Hitler's emissary, Alfred Rosenberg. By 1934, the communists were working alongside the Jews to confront the BUF in the East End. At the Hyde Park rally of September 1934, the communists distributed leaflets written in Hebrew calling on Jews to oppose the BUF. This they did in the form of the Jewish Labour Council (JLC) and the non-sectarian New World Fellowship (NWF). These organisations held weekly meetings that were well attended and distributed propaganda leaflets widely. These led to the formation of the British Union of Democrats (BUD) in the East End in February 1935, who carried out an intensive campaign against Mosley's Blackshirts in the summer of 1936. The BUD later merged with other anti-fascist organisations, the British Democratic Association and the Legion of Blue and White Shirts, to become the Federation of Democrats.

Mosley had been challenged by British Jewish organisations to declare his position concerning Jews ever since the days of the New Party. Repeated assertions that the BUF was not an anti-Semitic organisation were undermined by visits of BUF delegates to Nuremberg as guests of the Nazis and a refusal of BUF officials to distance themselves from the blatant anti-Semitic rhetoric espoused in a public meeting at Chiswick

Town Hall by William Joyce. Then, at the Albert Hall meeting in October 1934, it became clear that a racial element had become an intrinsic part of BUF dogma. Even the Italian press condemned any idea of 'the domination of one race over another' as not being a part of 'true Fascism'.[5]

From 1935 onwards, the BUF began to focus its activities on the East End of London, where the highest concentration of Jews in Britain, often relatively poor, first- or second-generation immigrants, was to be found. This prompted a more active response from Jewish organisations by the creation of a Coordinating Committee (CoC) to work with the police and Home Office to prevent attacks on their community. It was a cornerstone of Mosley's message that the cycle of violence between the fascists and their opponents was as the result of anti-fascist activity, and so anti-fascist protests were discouraged so as not to draw attention or give publicity to the BUF.

The extent to which anti-fascism became a mass movement in response to the rise of the BUF is exemplified by the crowd of 100,000 people who gathered in Hyde Park on 9 September 1934 to demonstrate against the BUF, and this surge in popularity requires an examination of the way in which the police related to both extremes of political activism. Evidence suggests that the BUF was never subjected to the same level of harassment as the communists. While some such as the police commissioner, Sir Philip Game, clearly saw the BUF as a threat to public order, lower ranks seem to have shown some sympathy and more partiality towards the Blackshirts. Mosley was insistent that his followers avoid direct confrontation with the forces of law and order, not least because he relied on them for protection at BUF meetings and rallies. Home Office guidelines actually encouraged the police to intervene to assist stewards in the face of 'organised interruptions' even if there was no breach of the peace.

Once Mosley had made his declaration concerning what he called Jewish opposition to fascism at Belle Vue Gardens in September, the way was open for anti-Semites in the BUF to confront the Jewish community, especially once the movement had entered east London, but they were not going to be allowed to march with impunity. Initially news of plans to hold a march had been greeted with disdain by the Jewish establishment, who had called upon people to ignore Mosley, but local left-wing activists were determined to stop it, arguing that to ignore it would give Mosley and his Blackshirts a propaganda victory. The march through Stepney, they decided, was to be stopped at any cost, and the place where the march would eventually be stopped would be Cable Street, an impoverished area densely populated with mostly Jewish families and packed with houses described at the time as little more than slums.

The BUF planned the march with precision. It would be the first time that Mosley would publicly wear the uniform of black military-cut jacket, grey riding breeches and jackboots, which he topped with a black peaked military hat and a red arm band. He would first inspect a Blackshirt parade in Royal Mint Street. The 5,000 marchers would then divide into four columns marching towards Limehouse, Shoreditch and Bow. A major rally organised by the Communist Youth League had been planned for the same day in Trafalgar Square but was cancelled so that its members could be diverted to confront the BUF march. Train loads of communists, Jewish ex-servicemen from Manchester and Leeds, veterans of war, tough men used to taking orders, flowed into Stepney.

On 4 October 1936, between 100,000 and 300,000 people comprising Jews, Irish dockers, trade unionists, socialists and communists, gathered in the East End of London. Barricades, including a bus and a tram, were used to block Cable Street, Leman Street, Gardiners Corner in Aldgate, and St George's in Wapping. Improvised weaponry, including sticks, rocks, chair legs, rubbish, rotten vegetables and the contents of chamber pots, were readied, and children were deployed to roll marbles under the hooves of the police horses. It was really the large numbers of Irish labourers and dockers who came out onto the streets that really made sure Mosley did not get through. The Mayor of Stepney, Mrs H. Roberts, told a reporter that she had never seen the people of the East End so thoroughly roused and angry.

Time and time again, the police charged the crowd to try to make way for the marchers to get through, The windows of neighbouring shops went in as people were pushed through them. Anti-fascist attackers pushed the police back up the street and pelted them with stones, and as the violence escalated, protesters were injured and arrested as police waded into them with truncheons. Horses trampled over bodies as they lay on the ground and charge after charge continued, neither side giving way.[6] Mosley had arrived in a Bentley to inspect the marchers before they set off but his car had its windscreen smashed by protesters and as he got out, Mosley was pelted by stones. He eventually made it to the parade, being driven along the procession in another car escorted by Blackshirts on motorcycles and surrounded by 1,000 policemen. Then he got out and proceeded on foot. Despite baton charges and strenuous attempts by the 6,000 police, many on horseback, they could not clear protesters from the streets and

Mosley could only reach Tower Hill before a message was passed through to him and he turned into a side street. There, Sir Philip Game told him that his march was being diverted down Great Tower Street and Queen Victoria Street towards the Victoria Embankment. Blackshirts reconvened in Aske Street, where they hoped to hear Mosley speak. However, he had retired to Great Smith Street headquarters, where he addressed a crowd from an upstairs window, telling them that the BUF would 'triumph over the parties of corruption [and] light the world'.[7] The day ended with Blackshirts rioting in Roman Road, where they smashed the windows of Jewish businesses.

Many left-wing and Jewish protesters who had battled with the police were arrested and taken to Leman Street Police Station. There had been many police casualties and those arrested were subjected to brutal beatings. Eyewitness accounts tell of one man being carried by four policemen, who used his head as a battering ram to open some swing doors, while a woman, one of eight arrested, whose blouse had been ripped, was called a 'Jewish bitch'.[8]

This humiliation for Mosley has been seen by many as the real turning point for the BUF, but the reality is that the confrontation was not between the BUF and its opponents but between the police and the antifascists. In addition, Cable Street did not, by any means, end BUF activity in the East End. Mosley had backed off from a confrontation because he was scheduled to be in Berlin on the following day to secretly marry Diana Mitford at the home of Joseph Goebbels. One month later, Parliament passed the 1936 Public Order Act, which banned the wearing of political uniforms in public and controlled parades. An order was passed that had to be renewed every three months prohibiting marches in the East End.

The BUF portrayed themselves as the innocent party whose rights to free speech had been denied by communist-Jewish violence and employed a useful piece of misleading propaganda by claiming that the police had openly surrendered to alien mobs. In fact, police reports seem to show that the BUF was far more the victim than the perpetrator of offensive political violence, especially outside east London. Similarly, the use of weapons by members of the BUF was a relatively rare occurrence. In contrast, anti-fascist attacks on BUF meetings were far more frequent, and there is much evidence to suggest that the CPGB was an organising force behind many, often violent, attempts to disrupt BUF events. CPGB involvement was such that we may be able to talk about the party having some strategy of political violence that operated nationally.[9] It appears that the BUF was not using violence for political gain, unlike the CPGB, which appears to have used Jewish fears about fascism, and its own willingness to employ violence against the fascists, as both a recruiting tool and a way of discrediting the BUF. Yet the BUF was still part of this violent equation. Too many of its speakers, especially in east London, attacked the Jewish community, stirring up racial tensions that long pre-dated the BUF, and convincing many communists and Jews of the correctness of their violent attacks on the fascists.

Very powerful speakers such as William Joyce, Mick Clarke and Richard Alister 'Jock' Houston, all of whom might be described as 'doctrinal fascists',[10] had much personal support in east London but Houston's verbal abuse of Jews was too much even for the BUF. This 31-year-old 'street-level fascist activist and notoriously violently anti-Semitic rabble-rouser' who 'fizzed with energy [and was] never more at home than on a soap box ranting at a crowd,'[11] was eventually arrested, not for inciting violence but for burglary, and was shown to have a long criminal record, at which point the BUF ditched him. His legacy, however, was to encourage other BUF speakers in east London to introduce more anti-Jewish commentary into their meetings. Mick Clarke immediately threatened that 'the British people of the East End [should know] that London's pogrom is not very far away now'. The police were criticised for not arresting blatantly abusive anti-Semitic speakers, but Sir Philip Game admitted speakers' tactics kept mostly within the law, which was vague and difficult to enforce. While Mosley had never adopted an official anti-Semitic policy, he had allowed his supporters to exploit public prejudices for political gain. However, the utterances of Joyce, Houston and others, which were widely reported in the press, were starting to create in the public mind a strong link between the BUF and Nazism. This had the two-fold effect of energising the hard-line fascists at the same time as encouraging opposition from Jews, left-wingers and Catholics.

The historian Daniel Tilles believes that the primary consequence of the Cable Street violence was to make life significantly worse for Jews in the East End and ushered in the most intensive phase of anti-Semitic activity in modern British history. Mosley held a series of large rallies across the East End and, according to Special Branch reports, membership in the capital jumped by 2,000. On the weekend after the Cable Street violence, there took place what was probably the worst incident of anti-Jewish violence in Britain during the interwar period. On Saturday, 10 October, an estimated 10,000 people gathered in Tower Hill and occupied the streets where the Blackshirts had intended to march. When this crowd spilled over into Grove Road, hostile women and teenage girls lined up on the pavements gesturing and shouting anti-Semitic slogans. At the corner of Bethnal Green and Roman Road, a double wall of police held back hundreds of young men and women, who were hurling abuse at the marchers. When the procession reached the gates of Victoria Park, the fascist hecklers chanted 'we are the boys of the bulldog breed' and spat on the marchers.

After the march had stopped in Victoria Park to listen to speeches, the crowds started walking back to Tower Hill, at which point the verbal abuse tipped over, first into fist fights and then into more violent attacks using weapons. At the same time as the police were preoccupied with the march towards Tower Hill, other fascist teenagers set out to attack local Jewish businesses in Clinton Road, smashing the windows and looting all the Jewish-owned shops in their way. Shopkeepers were attacked with stones and wooden planks. There was a razor slashing and one Jew, Samuel Jelen, who owned a hair salon on Mile End Road, was hurled through a shop window together with a four-year-old girl. Another Jewish man had his car flipped over and set ablaze. Though less serious, attacks on Jews were also reported in Manchester and Leeds.

The Women's Section of the BUF held its own rallies and marches. Anne Brock Griggs, Doreen Bell, Olive Hawks, Mrs Carruthers and Miss Good were all credited with having a 'stimulating effect upon massed audiences' and were as liberal as their male counterparts with anti-Semitic rhetoric, although by now they, like the men, were required to avoid the word Jew and use appropriate euphemisms.[12] The East End was also the setting for the first ever Women's Propaganda March in May 1936, led by Olga Shore, and followed a route from Bethnal Green to Victoria Park.

While the BUF had been liberally funded from within Britain initially, it also received money from abroad. In October 1933, Mussolini authorised his foreign ministry to subsidise the BUF to the tune of £5,000 a month 'in the easiest way for [Mosley] to withdraw it secretly'. On 21 October £1,900 in notes, $7,150 and 25,000 Swiss francs were duly dispatched.[13] In return, Mussolini expected Mosley to 'render the Italians all support in their power should [Britain] attempt to interfere over the question of Abyssinia'.[14] It was this cash injection that had allowed the BUF to move into new headquarters in the Whitelands Teacher Training College at 232 Battersea Park Road. By 1935, MI5 reported that the BUF was now 'for all practical purposes dependent on foreign funds' and

Mussolini was becoming concerned about the value of his investment with no sign of the strict disciplinarian, authoritarian, centralised mass movements he had hoped to see emerging in Britain. He lost patience in 1935 and reduced the subsidy in February. The organisation was only able to continue because of private donations such as one of £35,000 from oil magnate Henri Deterding. All appeals to the Nazis for financial support had been shunned up to this point. Mosley flew to Rome to plead with Mussolini to resume his financial support, which he did but imposed strict conditions that would have to be met if the BUF ever attained political power.

Mussolini again cut the subsidy in January 1936 when Mosley had made a visit to Berlin and was beginning to employ anti-Semitism in his campaign to a much greater degree, and this prompted another visit to Rome. Mussolini had taken umbrage at Mosley's refusal to attend a meeting set up by Italy in Montreux to discuss international fascism, which Mosley had seen as no more than a propaganda exercise to promote Italian leadership of an international fascist movement. He tried to convince the Italian leader that the BUF was making inroads in the East End of London and was on the verge of a breakthrough in the municipal elections to be held in the following March. When there was no breakthrough, however, Mussolini shocked Mosley by once and for all cancelling the subsidy. Both German and Italian governments were convinced that, despite assurances to the contrary, membership of the BUF was falling and its prospects of becoming a serious player in the British political game were receding. The decision may well have also been precipitated by news reaching Rome of Mosley's wedding in Berlin, which prompted the Italian leader to take umbrage, catch a diplomatic cold and refuse to meet Mosley when he visited Rome. The loss of the subsidy, which had amounted to £234,730 over the years, plunged the BUF into a series of internal crises from which it never really recovered. Headquarters staff was cut from 143 to 30. Joyce was one of those to leave under acrimonious circumstances. When others defended Joyce, Mosley called him a traitor and 'a small man' who had tried to create a revolt in the party and angrily vowed that he would never rest until he had 'broken him and rolled him in blood'.[15] Joyce sued for wrongful dismissal, won an out-of-court settlement and went on to form the NSL, committed to a pro-Nazi racial nationalist ideology.

Mosley had managed to offend the Nazis by not sending official BUF congratulations after the return of the Saar to the Reich on 1 March.

Relations were cooling rapidly but Ribbentrop intervened and arranged a personal meeting between Mosley and Hitler in Munich. The Nazis appear to have considered changing their mind about financing the BUF in 1937, as shown by an entry in Goebbels' diary for 19 June of that year. Mosley, he wrote, had asked for £100,000 and again a month later Diana Mosley had made a similar appeal. Only £2,000 had been allocated, wrote Goebbels, but he promised to speak to Hitler about it.[16] There is evidence that the BUF received a further £4,000 but, in the end, although they continued to hope that the BUF would promote a pro-German agenda, the Nazis, always short of foreign currency, made no further financial contributions to BUF funds.

There was little to choose between much of government policy towards Germany and the BUF position in 1937 and, for that matter, the view of much of the population. All had sizeable sections who held favourable views of both the German and Italian dictators and were enthusiastic about appeasement, but this was against a background that was changing fast. Britain had launched its programme of rearmament and Hitler was reassessing his approach to Britain. Chamberlain replaced Baldwin as Prime Minister and seemed determined to end the policy of drift and actively engage in improving diplomatic channels with the Nazi leadership. It was becoming increasingly obvious to Ribbentrop that power in Britain did not lie with the aristocracy with whom he had spent so much time cultivating relations. He was no longer popular among London's socialites and was now convinced that Britain would not be an ally to Nazi ambitions.

The BUF's reversal of fortune after 1936 can be viewed within the context of a recovery of the British economy with wages rising, reducing the attraction of the movement, whose stated ambition had been to rescue the country from an economic crisis that was appearing less likely by the day. With no immediate crisis in sight, the party lost direction and purpose. The prospect of a guerrilla war against the communists, which had enthused so many recruits, was for many becoming a fading dream, while fascist aggressions became inwardly focused against internal enemies. Mosley could no longer capture public attention with warnings of economic collapse and it became vital to identify a new threat around which to refocus the attention of his increasingly undisciplined members. An alleged Jewish conspiracy was just such a crisis. A BUF survey in autumn 1934 had revealed a surfeit of unmotivated and bored members who had been allowed to settle within its ranks due primarily to the lack of efficient administration as Mosley concentrated on his speechmaking. Financially, the BUF was a complete disaster. Expenditure was now at twice the level of income and, because of inadequate control, corruption and embezzlement were rife. The party clearly lacked the bureaucratic structure necessary to support a nationwide organisation. Radical measures were required to rein in the troublemakers and find a new message.

Mosley had banned Jewish entry into the BUF in the spring of 1934, but there had been no overt anti-Jewish rhetoric until the autumn of 1934, when Joyce and Chesterton among others exploited the lack of direction the party had found itself confronting by ramping up their anti-Semitic venom, especially after Olympia. While this new approach paid dividends in London and parts of the north-west, overall BUF support was diminishing if sales of the *Blackshirt* newspaper were anything to go by. Within a month they had dropped by a sixth. The January Club also saw a dropping off in meetings and overall activity, suggesting that the establishment figures who had filled its ranks were cooling their interest. The public image of the Blackshirts was becoming counter-productive as there was more awareness of the excesses being perpetrated by the Nazis. Rather than coalescing around a single strategy, however, the party split into factions.

One faction wanted the BUF to lose its paramilitary image, cut out any anti-Semitic rhetoric, become a more mainstream party, build up a strong electoral administration and fight to win seats in Parliament. Predictably, another faction proposed a diametrically opposite strategy of increased militarisation, more parades and rallies and direct action against the communists. Another proposed a similar plan but for them the enemy was not the communists but the Jews. A fourth group proposed a middle way of preparing to contest elections while maintaining its paramilitary anti-communis and anti-Jewish image. Mosley had the task of maintaining unity, which as someone who had given little thought to how the party should be run, was a very tall order. He compromised by splitting the party into two sections; the Blackshirts on the one hand would remain as a security force and, on the other, a political wing would be formed to prepare the party for elections.

Rothermere had continued to give the BUF the support of his newspapers after Olympia but it was not enough to bring in new membership in Lancashire, traditionally a good recruiting ground for the party, where Mosley had made a great effort in the spring of 1935 to increase his support. The problem here was that the BUF message had not been sufficiently nuanced so as to appeal to both the working class and the middle classes. Neither was comfortable being associated with the other. The party in the north-west could not decide between projecting itself as a socialist organisation or one that could be trusted by business.

On an organisational level, new instructions were issued. These give a clear indication of what had been going on inside the party and why it was languishing so badly. The new regulations covering the following areas were not universally well received:

- No gambling
- No private telephone calls
- No criticising officials
- Premises to be kept clean and tidy
- Uniform to be worn
- Smoking and drinking on the premises to be restricted

Factional in-fighting continued between the moderates and extremists, many of whom, impressed by Leese's anti-Semitism, had started drifting away into the ranks of the IFL. BUF support was ebbing and Mosley's popularity both within the party and with the public was definitely on the wane. It was only by cutting the price of the *Blackshirt* in half that sales were increased, but they remained well below peak circulation levels.

Mosley was realistic enough to see that the party was in no condition to fight a General Election but he planned to increase the number of meetings and contest selected by-elections to bring the party up to speed before the contest expected in 1937. However, with its finances in crisis, he was planning to move into cheaper premises at Sanctuary Buildings in Westminster, and Joyce, much to Mosley's annoyance, planned to cut back on expenditure by reducing the number of meetings and rallies.

The plan for separating the paramilitary and the administration had foundered, with the political side failing miserably to make any headway in reforming the party structure and thus leaving the Blackshirts effectively in control. However, acrimonious internecine squabbles continued to affect morale and create a feeling of instability. Things came to a head when Mosley set up a tribunal to settle a dispute between Joyce on the paramilitary wing and F.M. Box, Mosley's 'ablest political mind'. These two might be said to have been the leaders of rival factions who had diverged over the elevation of anti-Semitism to a much higher position on the BUF agenda. Joyce came out on top and Box resigned from the party soon afterwards. This was something of a relief to Mosley, who had never been comfortable with Box's hard-headed, realistic assessments of BUF prospects that did not correspond to other sycophantic opinions, and neither did they reflect Mosley's self-image as an internationally important personage. Box's departure, however, robbed Mosley of a wise counsellor, who had done much to improve the efficiency of BUF administration, and left him more at the mercy of the ultra-right wingers.

Mosley again turned to Italy for inspiration and travelled there in August 1936. On his return he planned three large meetings in London, Birmingham and Manchester, where fascist propaganda would be reduced to a minimum with all speeches concentrating on the growing international crisis. Against a background of rapidly cooling Italian support, the meetings would be used to justify Italian ambitions in 'the plagued area' of Abyssinia, but the British public were not impressed by Mosley's cosying up to Mussolini.

Neil Francis-Hawkins had been made head of the Blackshirt Organisation in July 1935 and immediately proceeded to impose his agenda on the whole BUF administration. He planned to raise the profile of the paramilitary Blackshirts and won the support of Mosley, who by this time was advocating the same military-style shift in emphasis possibly as a result of the failure to project himself as a statesman over the Abyssinian affair. The East End was an area characterised by a deep division between its Jewish and non-Jewish population, with much native anti-Semitism, and this had been exploited by Houston and Clarke, which proved that the party could attract significant backing there. Much to the delight of Joyce and Chesterton, Mosley went along with this by adjusting the Blackshirt uniform to one more closely resembling the SS and he changed the name of his organisation in April 1936 to the British Union of Fascists and National Socialists, which was usually shortened to the British Union (BU), in a move toward giving it a more domestic appeal.

At the same time, Mosley was steering his party into more of a peace organisation. On 22 March 1936, he again spoke to a meeting at the Albert Hall, telling his audience that the 'best hope of peace in Europe and the world is the closest possible association between Britain and Germany',[17] but he went on to sustain his attack on the Jews by saying, somewhat disingenuously, that anti-Semitism was not an issue for Britain before the rioting in the East End. He did, however, resist taking large donations from people such as A.C. Scrimgeour, whose conditions were that meetings would be heavily focused on the Jews. Demonstrators outside the Albert Hall rally were charged by police on horseback, who were accused of favouring the fascists, but while this was not necessarily true, it was the case that the forces of law and order were certainly not prepared to sanction violence by the far left, which was probably seen at the time as marginally more of a threat to public order. Certainly the police suffered more injuries at the hands of the anti-fascists than they did from Mosley's men.

At Holbeck Moor, Leeds, in September 1936, Mosley addressed a crowd of some 50,000 and police reports make it clear that the communists were the organisers of a ferocious, unprovoked attack on the meeting. Mosley was pelted by stones as he spoke from the top of a van and anti-fascist demonstrators fought with the police, with one police horse suffering so many razor cuts that it had to be destroyed.[18] The police reported that: 'The fascists were not to blame as nothing was said or done to provoke the crowd. They did not interfere with anyone until bricks and other missiles were thrown. Owing to the violence of the crowd it was impossible to take anyone into custody. At no time [was] any action on the part of the Blackshirts likely to provoke the crowd into the way in which it acted.'[19] CPGB opposition in Sheffield, too, was well organised, as indicated by one speaker exhorting the members to attend a BU meeting in Firth Park and 'smash them up [and] drive them off the streets'.[20] For a BU meeting scheduled to take place in Oxford at the Carfax Assembly Rooms in May 1936, the CPGB made thorough preparations. Their intentions were to break up the gathering and a speaker urged all workers and communists to keep Mosley out and give him such a time that he would not forget it for the rest of his life. The Public Order Bill had the effect of reducing the number of incidents of violence at meetings but it did not eliminate it entirely. Extra police presence at BUF meetings was also instrumental in forcing speakers to tone down the anti-Semitic rhetoric, which in turn reduced the incidences of violence.

At the London County Council elections of March 1937, the BU put up six candidates in Bethnal Green, Shoreditch and Limehouse, none of whom were elected. Recriminations rocked the BU leadership, with factions blaming each other for the debacle. At the same time, the Italian subsidies were terminated, resulting in massive staff redundancies and a major downturn of activity. Things went from bad to worse when the party failed to make any inroads in the November Metropolitan Borough Council elections. Membership was plummeting and money was running out. Chesterton resigned, calling what remained of the BUF a 'circus'.[21]

In spring 1937, Mosley had dipped into his own fortune and bailed the BU out to the tune of £100,000 but that was not going to last long. Desperately he looked round for other ways of raising finance and hit on the idea of establishing a commercial radio station. None of the stations currently transmitting to Britain, the BBC, Radio Normandie and Radio Luxembourg, would give the BU airtime. The big incentive for Mosley was that the last two stations that transmitted to English audiences from abroad were reputed to take paid advertising to the tune of £400,000 annually. To achieve this goal, Mosley recruited three helpers. Peter Eckersley had worked for the BBC, and was familiar with technical issues. William Allen was an advertising executive and Leonard Frank Plugge, who had founded Radio Normandie, understood the process of acquiring licences.

The first option looked at was to contact Colin Beaumont on the tiny island of Sark in the British Channel Islands. He was known to be a fascist sympathiser, although not a member of the BU, and agreed to a thirty-year contract in the spring of 1937. However, he stipulated that his mother, the Dame of Sark, must know nothing of his involvement in the enterprise. Other stations were planned in Ireland to broadcast to the west of the country and in Belgium for the east. The BBC blocked the Sark licence under a 1934 Act that forbade transmission from the island, despite Mosley arguing that the Channel Islands were not bound by British law.

The next idea was for a station in Belgium but when the British authorities became aware of the plan, the ensuing publicity, which centred on the rumour that the station was being financed by Germany, ensured that the Belgians would back out of the deal and Mosley had to abandon the plan. However, that still left Germany itself as a potential base for the radio station. Eckersley went to Germany to negotiate but the Germans were not willing to allocate any of the medium-wave frequencies, which they coveted for their own use. However, after the Anschluss, Goebbels decided that he would allocate one of the Austrian wavelengths to the BU. Hitler had been petitioned personally by Diana Mosley to support the idea and he readily gave his approval. A joint German-BU venture, Gemona AG, was proposed for a radio station to be set up in Heligoland, an island in the North Sea some 60km off the German coast. A company, Radio Variety, would sell advertising while Air Time Limited would act as the holding company to obscure BU involvement. The Germans agreed to finance construction of the station and meet all operating costs for a return of a 55 per cent share in the profits, which, crucially, would come in the form of foreign currency. British authorities cleared the way for sponsored broadcasts in English from foreign stations provided that they did not contain anything that could be construed as political propaganda. Mosley was entirely happy about that since his aim was to maximise his audience for financial gain, not to alienate them. The Germans, however, were less than happy. The war, of course, prevented any possibility of the scheme ever coming to fruition.

Hitler had boosted BU morale in a roundabout way. In March 1938 his annexation of Austria darkened European skies with war clouds and the British public reacted with trepidation. Mosley saw his chance and ramped up his anti-war message, which led to an upturn in BU membership. This was welcome since the BU, like all British fascist organisations, had failed to make the transition from a hardcore of activists into a mass movement. Mosley's ambition had been underpinned throughout the mid-1930s by a conviction that the rise of Nazism was about to be replicated in Britain, but social and economic conditions that precipitated crises in Germany, such as unemployment and social disintegration, were never as acute in Britain. As a result, the BU found itself operating in circumstances of limited economic recovery and falling unemployment, a situation that guaranteed failure for such a movement. Mosley, however, remained 'convinced that crisis would eventually return in aggravated form ... on which [he] rested [his] whole action' but the crisis that he and the country would be faced with was war itself and with war looming it was natural that the government would become concerned about the activities of fascist organisations in the country.[22]

In early 1939, Mosley accepted that his popular appeal was fading and so he sanctioned a campaign of disruption at meetings of mainstream politicians in east London at Limehouse, Hackney, Shoreditch and Bethnal Green, where prominent politicians were confronted by organised interruption, including missiles and physical assault. When Chamberlain gave his guarantee to Poland, Mosley ramped up his anti-war rhetoric. 'The jackals of Jewish finance are again in full cry for war,' he said on 25 March and saw membership, especially in London, begin to rise again.[23] He hit a note that resonated with many when he said that 'any Englishman who will not fight for Britain is a coward; any Englishman who wants to fight for Poland is a fool'.[24] While he continued to hold well-attended outdoor meetings, most large indoor venues were closed to Mosley, who was now being ignored by both the radio and the press. The government, however, was getting nervous and closed down the AGF but Ramsay continued to distribute German propaganda through the Nordic League, which was being closely monitored by MI5.

The role of women after 1938 took on a more important aspect when the BU increasingly became an anti-war movement. With the virtual disintegration of the leadership structure due to the desertion of leading figures, women members began taking over a number of roles from the men and established an all-female pressure group with a decidedly more revolutionary message. They planned to undermine national morale through a National Campaign for Peace, calling for 'resistance to false [nauseating] sentimentality' and claiming that 'Mosley and the BU alone had been consistent in their work for peace'.[25] The first large-scale indoor meeting to be organised, addressed, and stewarded entirely by women was held at Holborn Hall on 28 February 1940.

Mosley was now concentrating more and more on projecting the BU as a party of peace, which seemed to find a positive response from the public, but his ideas of appeasement were quite different from those of the government. He was comfortable with the idea of Hitler expanding his influence in the east, militarily or otherwise, but Chamberlain was restrained by international commitments and alliances and could not be so generous, even if he had wanted to. On 16 July 1939, after a last-minute cancellation, Mosley was able to book Earls Court Exhibition Centre for a meeting that was attended by as many as 20,000 people.

The rally opened with a fanfare of trumpets and a parade of massed flags and honour standards of hundreds of branches. Mosley, in a dark suit, black shirt and tie, entered to a roll of drums and, picked out by searchlight all the way, marched down the centre aisle to a rising chorus of cheers that reached a deafening crescendo. Mosley gave the fascist salute and began to speak. John Charnley, a member of the BUF organisation called it 'the finest speech he ever delivered. At many points he had to stop speaking because of the wave of applause.'[26]

On 1 September 1939, the day Germany invaded Poland, Defence Regulation 18B was issued via an Order in Council, which gave the Home Secretary the authority to detain people he suspected could carry out acts 'prejudicial to public safety or to the defence of the realm'. Then, in May 1940, the new Prime Minister, Winston Churchill, concerned about a possible fifth column threat, argued for the large-scale arrest of suspect persons and enemy aliens in Britain. However, no case could be brought against Mosley, who had ordered his followers to be loyal to the nation.

Mosley was far from being the only peace activist on the radical right. The BU held talks in September 1939 with other fascist, anti-Semitic, and pro-German organisations, such as the Right Club, the Nordic League, and the Link, with the aim of forming a united front against the war but one that remained on the safe side of treason. Meetings were held in secret at the home of Margaret Bothamley. On 26 July the Mosleys gave a dinner party for sympathetic MPs, pro-Nazi journalists and prominent figures connected with the Anglo-German Fellowship, the Link and the Nordic League. Mosley saw that this was the only way for the BU to survive but he was uncomfortable with the more aggressive anti-Semitic views of Ramsay and Chesterton. It was his connection to Ramsay, in particular, that would be his undoing.

Anna Wolkoff was the daughter of Admiral Nicolai Wolkoff, who had been the Tsar's naval attaché in London before the Bolshevik revolution and had remained in England ever since, opening the Russian Tea Room that became a meeting place for Russian émigrés. In February 1940, she met Tyler Kent, a cypher clerk from the American Embassy in London who had previously worked in a similar capacity in Moscow, where he had passed confidential information to the Nazis. He had arrived in London in the company of a known Nazi agent, Ludwig Matthias, at which point MI5 opened a file on him. His sympathy for White Russian émigrés soon brought him to the Russian Tea Room, where he met Wolkoff and members of the Right Club, including Ramsay.

As part of MI5 surveillance on the Right Club, agent-runner Maxwell Knight had infiltrated Joan Miller, whose real name was Joanna Phipps, into the Right Club with the specific task of gaining Anna Wolkoff's confidence. Miller had a special relationship with Knight, whom she found to possess 'charm of a rare and formidable order'.[27] She had, in fact, lived with Knight for a number of years but he was widely believed to be homosexual and there was never any suggestion of a sexual relationship between the two. He was also a drummer and clarinettist, often playing with a jazz band at the Hammersmith Palais, a writer of thriller novels and an antique gun enthusiast.

Wolkoff was a woman who was known to be fiercely suspicious of others. Miller, however, was able to break down barriers and convince Wolkoff that she was totally opposed to Britain's involvement in the war and was a strong supporter of the fascist cause. She invented a pre-war romance with a Nazi officer to account for these views. Miller later changed to counter-espionage work against communists and spent her time looking into innumerable reports from people who suspected others of being Fifth Columnists. She then worked in Holloway Prison interviewing suspect enemy aliens, a role that left her feeling guilty when she realised how unwarranted were the detentions of many of those she interviewed.

Miller inevitably came across Kent, whom she immediately considered to be 'pro-fascist' in outlook and kept a close eye on him whenever he came to the Tea Room. When Kent offered to show Wolkoff and Ramsay copies of secret correspondence between Churchill and US President Roosevelt concerning US commitments to come to the aid of France if it was attacked by Germany, she and another of Knight's infiltrated agents, Marjorie Amor, reported it to Knight. Amor then convinced Wolkoff that she could get copies of these documents to Germany via the Italian diplomatic bag. They would, she claimed, be handed over to Duco del Monte, Assistant Naval Attaché at the Italian Embassy, who would then pass them on to Wilhelm Canaris, head of the Abwehr, the German military intelligence service.

On 20 May 1940, the Special Branch raided Kent's flat, where they found almost 2,000 classified documents and a copy of Ramsay's Red Book, which listed the names of all Right Club members. The next day Churchill was told, and the Home Secretary was advised that 'dangerous elements [Wolkoff, Kent and Ramsay] should be interned without further delay'. Wolkoff and Kent were arrested and charged under the Official Secrets Act. Despite Wolkoff's documents never having left the country, her attempt to send them was the vital piece of evidence of 'communicating with the enemy' that got her ten years imprisonment at her secret trial on 7 November 1940. Kent, because he was an American citizen, was treated less harshly and received only seven years. He would later argue that his motivation was for Ramsay to somehow get these copies to American politicians hostile to Roosevelt. Mosley was now fatally implicated through his association with Ramsay. His safe was broken into and its contents showed the extent to which the BUF had attempted to set up a radio station in Germany. MI5 wanted Mosley to be interned and used the Tyler affair as an argument.

MI5 still had no evidence that the BU was involved in Fifth Column activities, which meant that action was impossible under existing regulation, so Chamberlain, Halifax, Attlee and Greenwood agreed to authorise new powers and do whatever was needed 'to cripple the organisation'.[28] Defence Regulation 18B was amended on 22 May by Privy Council regulation to cover organisations that the Secretary of State was satisfied was 'subject to foreign influence or control', or persons controlling the organisation 'have or have had associations with persons concerned in the government of, or sympathies with the system of government of, any power with which His Majesty is at war'.

On 23 May, as Boulogne fell to the Germans and the British Expeditionary Force was in full retreat from the German panzers at Dunkirk, the government decided that Mosley's liberty was 'a luxury [it] could no longer afford'.[29] With invasion staring to look like a distinct possibility, MI5 asserted that Mosley was the only person with whom Hitler would be prepared to talk peace and that the BU would be likely to assist the Nazis in the event of invasion. Mosley was arrested at his flat in Dolphin Square and a search of the premises uncovered a forty-four-page typed list of officers, agents, contacts and speakers, corrected up to 25 January 1940, three handguns and two rifles. His wife, Diana, was arrested on 29 June when police burst in and interrupted her dinner at Savay Farm in Denham, Buckinghamshire. The Mosleys were held in Brixton, then in Holloway. On 15 August Lord Newton, addressing the House of Lords, was appalled that the Advisory Committee had spent a whole day discussing Mosley's appeal to be released, calling him 'a national infliction' who should be 'deported to some colony'.[30] For a time, the Mosleys were allowed to live together in a little house inside Holloway Prison, where they were allowed to cook their own meals and be visited by their son Nicholas, who could stay talking long into the night. They were given a small garden, where they could sunbathe and grow their own vegetables. They were even allowed to employ fellow prisoners as servants.

A total of some 800 Blackshirts were also swept up in the internment frenzy and put in prison, but many prominent members of the BU remained at liberty. Norah Elam was the only ex-Suffragette to be interned in Britain as part of the first group of BU officials to be arrested. The prominent fascists Viscountess Downe, former lady-in-waiting to Queen Mary, and her friend Lady Pearson, were arrested but immediately released. Lady Dunn, who attended the secret meetings of the Right Club, escaped detention, unlike her butler, Howard Hall, who was arrested. In fact, few Right Club members were arrested. The Home Office thought it wrong to punish those 'simple-minded' MPs and Peers who were unaware of their leader's pro-German activities, but the lower classes apparently were ironically considered to be much smarter and were not given the same benefit of the doubt.[31]

The writer D.S. Lewis believes that the BUF was not so much a revolutionary party as a movement that grew out of the 'authoritarian centre' with elements taken from both extreme left and right, and it was Mosley's failure to reconcile one with the other that led to its downfall. Lewis also draws attention to Mosley's weakness as a leader who failed miserably to establish an efficient party administration and whose focus on his public image allowed internal power struggles to eat away at morale. Had there been a significant crisis in Britain during the early to mid-1930s to galvanise the movement and give it direction then things might have been different but the crisis, when it came after Munich, was too big and too late for the BUF and overwhelmed it. Robert Benewick believes that the BU creed too closely resembled the German fascist model, which became ever more brutal and oppressive. Where once there had been tacit admiration for the German economic transformation that seemed to be binding the country together in a bright future, there grew within British minds a fear of its ambitions and disgust at its methods. Mosley failed to see that his BU, by projecting its image in the Nazi fashion, was incrementally distancing the movement from the fundamental traditional British sense of decency and tolerance, which is why its appeal remained limited to a fringe mentality that thrived on violence and prejudice. When the real enemy revealed itself after the annexation of Czechoslovakia, Mosley was cast adrift without a compass on an ocean of anti-German fervour.

On 30 May the BU was disbanded and its publications banned. An anonymous security memorandum dated 10 July 1940 told Churchill that the executive of the Special Warfare Executive were keen to deport overseas certain leaders of the BU, including Mosley and his wife. It went on to say that BU members were being held in jails where the warders and police were unarmed, which seemed to be an undue risk when 'these people are just nasty gangsters who will stick at nothing'. The law, however, did not have provision for the deportation of British citizens, although the Home Office was asked to look at ways of amending that law.

Chapter Thirteen

The British Legion

Despite warnings from Permanent Under-Secretary of State Robert Vansittart that the Nazis would use them for propaganda, on 14 July 1935, a high-ranking delegation from the British Legion led by its chairman, Francis Fetherston-Godley, arrived in Berlin to be met by Ribbentrop and representatives of three major German veteran's organisations. A welcoming message called for 'mutual trust, mutual respect and the firm belief [in] honourable comradeship of the people'.[1] This was far from being the first contact between ex-servicemen's organisations of the two nations after the end of the First World War. A little over a year earlier, the then chairman, Sir John Brown, had accepted an invitation from Baron Hans von Redwitz to make an informal visit to Munich. Brown consulted the Foreign Office and was told that they had no objections as long as the party went as individuals and not representatives of the British Legion.

Right from the end of the First World War, veterans on both sides of the conflict had worked towards reconciliation. The British Legion, which had been formed on 15 May 1921 with the stated aim of providing support for members and veterans of the British armed services, proposed inviting Germans to join in an international organisation but were prevented by opposition from the French and Belgians. The idea was revived in 1933 when the Nazis came to power in Germany as a way of defusing incipient fears of future conflict. However, events soon showed that the political agenda would not be set by ex-servicemen motivated by memories of the horrors of trench warfare but by a Nazi movement hell-bent on creating a new European landscape on the back of rearmament and military might. Hitler, though, had not included war with the British Empire as part of his megalomaniacal plans and saw merit in encouraging close ties with the British Legion to create a closer bond between the two nations.

Brown was disturbed to find that, as part of the delegation, von Redwitz had also extended an invitation to Graham Seton Hutchison, who had been one of the founders of the British Legion, and two others who were all known to be zealous, ultra-right, anti-Semites. Brown privately considered Hutchison to be 'a second Hitler' and even von Neurath, the German Foreign Minister, thought him 'unbalanced'.[2] Brown's fears were realised when Hutchison, on their arrival in Munich on 28 March 1934, started making distinctly pro-Nazi statements to the German press and considerably heightened Brown's distress when he laid a wreath at a German War Memorial commemorating Hitler's abortive 1923 Munich Beerhall Putsch. The delegation was feted by leading Nazis such as Rudolf Hess and Hutchison responded by heaping praise on the Nazi movement, which, he said, had many admirers in Britain. 'I have never heard such violent attacks on the Jews or praise for the Germans,' said H.M. Bateman, who had gone along as a member of Brown's delegation.[3]

The following year, Hutchison proposed that another delegation go to Germany, this time led by him. However, aware of the adverse publicity Hutchison's previous trip had generated within the British establishment, Hitler turned down his request but was still enthusiastic about rapprochement between French, British and German veterans through official channels. It was Ribbentrop who made the next approach to the British Legion and the Foreign Office in February 1935 by proposing an official visit, an idea that was debated at the British Legion annual conference in June. It was addressed by Edward, Prince of Wales, who supported the visit saying that 'representative members of the Legion' were the ideal people to 'stretch forth the hand of friendship to the Germans'. Neither the Palace nor the Foreign Office was pleased by Edward's intervention but, writing in *The Times*, Ribbentrop was effusive in his praise of a move that supported government endeavours 'definitely to establish peace and cooperation in Europe'.[4] The Foreign Office warned the British Legion that they were deluded in thinking that there existed an equivalent organisation in Germany outside Nazi control. What existed were the *Kyffhäuserbund*, the *Nationalsozialistischer Deutscher Frontkämferbund* and the *Kriegsopferversorgung*, all of which sent delegates to welcome Fetherston-Godley and his party in July 1935 along with Ribbentrop's personal representative.

The delegation were astounded to find that a meeting had been arranged with Hitler himself at the Chancellery on the day after their arrival. They talked for two hours exchanging memories of the war, in which they had all taken part. This had a profound effect on the visitors but Hitler's translator, Paul Schmidt, noticed that over the following days, their attitude changed to one more critical of what they found. Ribbentrop then met them and spoke of 'international reconciliation and a spirit of

The British Legion

comradeship that would bring the two nations together'. However, the sense of camaraderie was crumbling and took a sudden downturn when the delegation laid a wreath at the Munich War Memorial, which was fine, but then they were asked to lay another wreath at the Beer Hall Putsch Memorial as well. They declined on the grounds that such a gesture was too political and not in keeping with the spirit of their mission.

The delegation went on to visit a Hitler Youth holiday camp before being received at the home of the Aviation Minister, Hermann Göring. Some days later, they were treated to a guided tour of the Dachau concentration camp. On returning to England, Fetherston-Godley described the camp's pleasing appearance with trees, shrubs and flowers separating the dormitories but was dismayed by the 'low types of humanity' who were incarcerated there. Other members later spoke of the camp's ambition to 'reform [miscreants] by healthy exercise, good food, and work'. They had been reliably informed that the whole staff were out solely to help the inmates 'make the best of themselves'. Clearly the delegates were being fooled and fell for it hook, line and sinker. Immediately after the Dachau visit, they were the guests of Heinrich Himmler, whom they found to be 'an unassuming man' with 'a great sense of humour'.[5]

Not all were convinced by the testimony of the delegation and four weeks later another unofficial party went to Germany and came back with a different story of constant surveillance and officials who restricted their visits to museums and cathedrals and such. It is likely that Ribbentrop had been made aware that this second delegation would be much more sceptical and so they were kept under close control. Requests to interview political prisoners were denied. The Foreign Office knew full well that Fetherston-Godley had been duped but was in no mood to see Anglo-German relations disturbed so soon after the signing of the Anglo-German Naval Agreement and publicly went along with the German conclusion that this second party had been motivated by communist sympathies.

Fetherston-Godley's visit had also stirred up a debate about the role of Jewish veterans in the British Legion. The Jewish Ex-Servicemen's Legion (or JEXL) had opposed the July visit right from the start, but small Jewish veterans' groups that joined branches of the British Legion often found themselves isolated with no status. Less than two months after the Legion's visit to Germany, the Nuremburg Laws were passed, stripping Jews of German citizenship rights, after which British national newspapers, who by and large had voiced support for Fetherston-Godley's visit, became more openly critical as the persecution of German Jews accelerated. Withering scorn was poured on the remarks of the Chairman of the Legion that he was satisfied with German assurances following the Nuremburg Laws that the persecution of the Jews would be 'modified in due course'.

Groups like the British Legion had attempted to operate within a space free from party politics and sectarian strife but that meant pursuing a programme of inclusivity. Major J.B. Brunel Cohen, the Honorary Treasurer of the Legion for most of the interwar period, defended the Legion's visit to Germany, arguing that while he deplored the Nazis' 'abominable anti-Jewish policy' the Legion was acting 'purely in the interests of peace'. That summer Fetherston-Godley was knighted for services to the Legion.

The British Legion seemed unaffected by this criticism and was heartened by the Prince of Wales's plan to host a delegation of German veterans in September. Thereafter they would formally accept German veterans into FIDAC (*Fédération Interalliée Des Anciens Combattants*), the existing international organisation of allied ex-servicemen. However, growing opposition at home and an increased awareness of the level of persecutions taking place inside Germany gave Fetherston-Godley pause for thought and he wrote to Ribbentrop saying that mutual friendship was doomed to failure if 'events in Germany do not very soon become more tranquil'.[6] The German visit lay in the balance for weeks but eventually an eleven-man delegation led by Ribbentrop's special representative, Heinrich Georg Stalmer, arrived on British soil on 19 January 1936. When they laid a swastika-bedecked wreath on the Cenotaph there was no disturbance and a series of dinners and receptions followed.

Just before the Czech crisis broke at the end of 1938, an eighty-eight-strong delegation led by the Duke of Saxe-Coburg-Gotha made a final visit to England as guests of the British Legion. As a result, the Legion offered to send a body of men to Czechoslovakia to act as a neutral police force in the immediate aftermath of the Munich Agreement. They amassed 17,000 volunteers and, amazingly, were encouraged by the Foreign Office and Downing Street, but after giving the matter some consideration, it was Hitler who rejected it on 13 October.

Chapter Fourteen

Edward VIII and Mrs Simpson

The British royal family has a long association with fascism, as evinced by Queen Elizabeth II's husband, Prince Philip, who had four sisters who were ensconced in Nazi Germany, some serving as conduits of the Nazi Party to German aristocracy. For example, Cecile was a Nazi Party member, Sophie named her son after Hitler and Margarita's husband was a German army commander. In fact, when Cecile was killed in an air crash in 1937, Prince Philip attended the funeral and was photographed alongside uniformed Nazi soldiers.

Undoubtedly, the most prominent British personage to have close links with Hitler was King Edward VIII (23 June 1894–28 May 1972), the great grandson of Queen Victoria and the German Prince Albert of Saxe-Coburg-Gotha. Born Edward Albert Christian George Andrew Patrick David Saxe-Coburg-Gotha, his family name was changed to Windsor in 1917 for political reasons to shroud the German ancestry of the royal family. He was invested as Prince of Wales on 13 July 1911 and succeeded to the British Crown on his father's death on 20 January 1936. He was very proud of his German origins, spoke German fluently, and felt an emotional, racial and intellectual solidarity with the Nazi leaders.

After the First World War, Edward had pursued a number of dangerous hobbies. He had learned to fly and rode in steeplechases until he suffered a bad fall. He also developed an enthusiasm for nightlife, nightclubs, and dancing, which the style of post-war London life encouraged, and he soon became a leader of fashionable London society. As a youth, Edward had two long-term relationships. The first during the First World War with Mrs Winifred (Freda) Dudley Ward, the wife, with two small daughters, of Lord Esher's grandson, William Dudley Ward, a Liberal MP and chamberlain of the royal household. She was described by Lady Cynthia Asquith as 'a pretty little fluff'. The second was with Thelma, Viscountess Furness, a married American woman. Later, in the early 1930s, Edward immersed himself in the 'Ritz Set', described by Robert Worth Bingham, the American ambassador, as a 'pro-German cabal',[1] especially Maud Alice (Emerald) Cunard, an American hostess and the widow of Sir Bache Cunard, the shipping tycoon. Together they extolled the virtues of the charismatic new dictators, Mussolini and Hitler. It was Lady Cunard who first introduced the Prince of Wales to Oswald Mosley and Joachim von Ribbentrop. By 1933, the young Edward and his brother, the glamorous Prince George, Duke of Kent, were genuinely intrigued by Nazi politics and both equally enthusiastic about Hitler's new regime.

This all took place while Germany's first concentration camp opened at Dachau on 20 March 1933 to hold 'wasters, idlers, social undesirables, Jewish profiteers and riffraff' by re-educating them under the slogan *Arbeit Macht Frei* (Freedom through Work). The British Member of Parliament, Victor Cazalet, described the camp in 1934 as 'not very interesting but quite well run'. Another parliamentarian, Sir Arnold Wilson, observed that the men [in Dachau] seemed well housed and fed.[2] Vice Admiral Sir Barry Domvile visited Dachau and agreed that the Nazis were giving the 'dregs of humanity' a new start. He praised the camp's efficiency and comfort and condemned the British press for printing 'lies about Germany'. Lloyd George would visit Hitler at his Bavarian retreat in September 1936 and, from his discussions, concluded that Germany did not want war with Britain but was mortally afraid of the Soviet Union. He virtually justified the German treatment of the Jews, saying that the Jews had always been persecuted for one reason or another and what was happening in Germany was really no worse than what had happened in Russia and other countries over the centuries.

Hitler actively pursued an effective and largely overlooked backdoor foreign policy by recruiting German aristocrats with close family ties across Europe. He used German aristocrats such as Otto von Bismarck, the grandson of the man who unified Germany in 1871, to call on their English cousins. He influenced right-wing aristocrats such as the Duke of Connaught, the Earl of Kincardine and his brother, Lord Ronald Graham, all of whom were eager to visit the German 'labour camps' in order to understand how the Nazis effectuated 'race purity and fitness'.[3] Bismarck also established a close relationship with the Prince of Wales and Wallis Simpson.

On 19 October 1933, 4,000 Nazi stormtroopers marched in a torchlight parade through the town of Coburg to celebrate the wedding between Princess Sibylla of Saxe-Coburg and Gotha, the daughter of Duke Charles Edward of Coburg, and Prince Gustaf Adolf, heir to the Swedish throne.

The whole town was bedecked in Nazi flags and Hitler sent a congratulatory telegram. Princess Alice, the Countess of Athlone, Prince Arthur of Connaught and his sister, Princess Patricia, all members of the British royal family attended the Coburg wedding. Princess Alice was the sister of Charles Edward, a grandson of Queen Victoria. Charles Edward had been born and raised in England and held the British titles of Duke of Albany, Earl of Clarence and Baron Arklow. At the age of fourteen, in July 1900, he was sent by his grandmother to become the sovereign Duke of Saxe-Coburg and Gotha. His support for Germany during the First World War led to him being stripped of his British titles and Germany's defeat also saw him lose his constitutional position in that country. He went on to support far-right movements in Germany and joined the Nazi Party in 1933.

In a 1935 speech, the Prince of Wales had called for a closer understanding of Germany in order to safeguard peace in Europe, and in response Sir Thomas Moore MP set up a study group of pro-German MPs that evolved into the Anglo-German Fellowship (AGF). It was established in September 1935 with its headquarters in a flat at 223 Cranmer Court in Chelsea and Lord Mount Temple was its chairman, with historian Philip Conwell-Evans and merchant banker Ernest Tennant its secretaries. Members of the establishment dominated the Fellowship; their wealth and influence were considerable, but MI5 quickly infiltrated agents Kim Philby and Guy Burgess into the organisation. A German sister society, the *Deutsch-Englische Gesellschaft* (DEG), was established at 30 Bendlerstrasse in Berlin. Hitler selected Duke Charles Edward to be his emissary to the British royal family and this pro-German lobby to foster political, professional, commercial and sporting links with Germany. Charles Edward had visited Sandringham in 1932 and 1933 to stay with George V and Queen Mary and had travelled to England several times a year, often to coincide with important political events.

Charles Edward met influential Nazi-sympathisers at Claremont House in Surrey, the home of his sister, Princess Alice. Many Conservatives were prepared to embrace almost any alternative to the status quo and turned to the AGF, created with the intent of targeting the rich and the powerful and which claimed to have 'fifty members of both Houses of Parliaments, three directors of the Bank of England, and many generals, admirals, bishops and bankers' as well as the Duke of Wellington, Lord Londonderry, Lord Galloway, Lord Nuffield and Unity Mitford's father, Lord Redesdale.[4] It was funded by powerful British business interests, patronised by Anglo-German royalty, influenced by the German high command, welcomed by elements of the British establishment and infiltrated by British, German, Russian and Jewish intelligence agents.[5] While there was no direct involvement of Ribbentrop in setting up the AGF, there is evidence that, subsequently, he made substantial cash donations to fund travel and accommodation for its members.

The AGF was dominated by businessmen and by 1937 had 347 members, who included the Bank of England Director Frank Cyril Tiarks, its Governor Montagu Norman, and Geoffrey Dawson, editor of *The Times*, but Diana and Unity Mitford were also members. A number of Conservative Members of Parliament also joined, including Sir Peter Agnew, Lawrence Dundas, Ernest Bennett, Sir Robert Bird, Robert Tatton Bower, Douglas Douglas-Hamilton, Robert Vaughan Gower, Thomas Guinness, Norman Hulbert, Archibald James, Alfred Knox, John Macnamara, Sir Thomas Moore, Assheton Pownall, Frank Sanderson, Duncan Sandys, Charles Taylor and Ronald Tree. Members of the House of Lords who joined up were Lord Brocket, Lord Galloway, the Earl of Glasgow, Lord Mount Temple, Lord Londonderry, Lord Nuffield, Lord Redesdale, Lord Rennell and the Duke of Wellington. Lord Mount Temple, who was the original chairman, would later resign on account of the treatment of the Jews in Germany and the attitude of the Germans towards the Catholic and Lutheran communities. The AGF and its German counterpart the DEG would often unite to host banquets, where the guests of honour included Rudolf Hess, Joachim von Ribbentrop and the Duke of Coburg. At one AGF dinner held in Mayfair on 14 July 1936, Bastille Day, guests sat at tables adorned with swastikas as a direct provocation to the French.

The Prince of Wales, meanwhile, was addressing the British Legion's annual conference on 11 June 1935, urging British veterans of the First World War to visit Germany and 'stretch forth the hand of friendship to the Germans'.[6] While *The Times* reported the speech as a pro-German stance that was helping to make the Nazi Party acceptable, even fashionable, in London society, it upset both the British Foreign Office and the French government as well as infuriating Edward's father, King George V, who summoned him to Buckingham Palace to be severely reprimanded. Also at the time, Edward, in discussion with the German ambassador in London, Leopold von Hoesch, was heard to criticise the British Government's hard-line stance in the Anglo-German naval talks. Von Hoesch immediately reported the indiscretion to Hitler.

Edward VIII and Mrs Simpson

'Every drop of blood in my veins is German,' Edward once bragged to Oswald Mosley's wife. He spoke fluent German and had travelled to Germany regularly in his student days. When the Nazis came to power, he welcomed them as a counterweight to the Soviet communists, whom he had never forgiven for killing his godfather, Czar Nicholas II. Hitler was greatly encouraged by Edward's remarks and came to believe that when he took over the throne, the pro-German Prince of Wales would be a vital ally in keeping Britain out of any future war. Joachim von Ribbentrop was appointed as representative at the Anglo-German naval talks in London and the Duke of Coburg accompanied him. 'I am convinced [Edward's] friendly disposition towards Germany will have some influence on the formation of British foreign policy,' Ribbentrop reported to Hitler in March 1936.

Hitler suggested that the Kaiser's granddaughter, Princess Frederica, who was attending an English school near Broadstairs in Kent, would make a suitable German bride for the Prince of Wales, despite the twenty-three year gap in their ages. In 1934, Frederica was invited to Buckingham Palace by George V and Queen Mary, who were close friends and cousins of her parents, the Duke and Duchess of Brunswick. Eventually, it was Frederica's parents who refused permission for the marriage to go ahead. By 1934 the prince, who had never been remotely interested in Frederica, had cast aside his two current dalliances, Thelma Furness and Freda Dudley Ward, and had fallen under the spell of a twice-divorced American called Wallis Simpson. She had been born Bessie Wallis Warfield into a rich and comfortably off middle-class family in Baltimore. She married a young air force officer and soon became an important personality in Washington society. Among her many friends were Prince Gelasio Caetani, the Ambassador in Washington of the new fascist regime in Italy, and Felipe Espil, First Secretary at the Argentinian Embassy in Washington, an ardent fascist and a representative of the savage Irigoyen dictatorship in Buenos Aires.

Charles Higham, in his book *Mrs Simpson: Secret Lives of the Duchess of Windsor*, says that American state files produce clear evidence that Wallis Spencer, as she then was, was hired as an agent for US Naval Intelligence. In this role she was sent to China, along with her husband, where she acted as a courier taking secret papers between the American Government and Chinese forces fighting against the communists. Moving to Shanghai, she made another conquest in a dashing young fascist, Count Galeazzo Ciano, later to be Mussolini's son-in-law and Foreign Secretary. While there has never been any evidence produced to support the rumours, it has often been claimed that they became lovers and it is further believed that, as a result of the affair with Ciano, Simpson became pregnant and underwent what proved to be a bungled termination that left her infertile. What is known is that she became ill on a trans-Pacific Ocean liner en route from Japan to Seattle and underwent a serious operation when the vessel docked. The friendship with Ciano persisted, however, and when he became Italian Foreign Minister it gave Simpson a direct contact with the Italian leadership.

Edward had first met Wallis at Borough Court in Leicestershire, the home of his then mistress, Thelma Furness, in January 1931. He was immediately besotted with Wallis and very soon came to see her as his natural companion in life, both sexually and intellectually. Wallis was perceived as having 'complete power' over him.[7] The government was also convinced that Wallis was in fact involved in other sexual relationships at this time, including one with a 'very charming adventurer, very good-looking, well-bred' married car dealer called Guy Marcus Trundle. Wallis was also reported to be in a sexual relationship with William C. Bullitt, the allegedly pro-Nazi American ambassador to France in the years immediately before the war, and a third man, Ireland's premier peer, Edward FitzGerald, 7th Duke of Leinster. 'What a dear man,' said Wallis years later to journalist Michael Thornton, 'Please send Fitz my love. I have such happy memories of him.'

Rumours that Wallis had an affair with Ribbentrop refuse to go away, despite there being no reliable evidence to indicate that it was true. The main proponent of the theory was Father Odo, a Benedictine monk in a Franciscan monastery in the United States. Father Odo had once been the Duke of Wurttemberg, a minor German royal with connections to Queen Mary, her brother the Duke of Athlone, then Governor General of Canada, and Odo's mother.

He told FBI agents that Ribbentrop had been Wallis' lover when he was ambassador to Britain in 1936. While it is not clear whether or not the two actually did have an affair, it is the case that Ribbentrop was in the habit of sending seventeen carnations (some say roses) to Wallis whenever he was in London from the florist shop of Mrs Simpson's great friend, Constance Spry, supposedly, Odo claimed, to represent the number of times they had slept together.

Accustomed to getting his own way, Edward assumed that matters would turn out as he desired and from an early stage he seems to have wanted Simpson to be his queen, making no effort to prepare the ground. In her second marriage after a divorce from US Navy officer Earl Winfield Spencer Jnr, Wallis already had a reputation for having affairs. How much of Simpson's history Edward was acquainted with is uncertain, but it is clear that however much he did know he was quite willing to overlook it all.

When those around him raised the matter with Edward, they were confronted by evidence of his passion for Wallis and his plans for a life with her that clouded all his judgements. The Royal household fell into what is best described as a political and constitutional limbo. In October 1934, Edward and Wallis had arrived in Paris on the Orient Express, having travelled in a luxury railway carriage supplied by Mussolini. A month later they attended the wedding celebration of Edward's youngest brother, Prince George, Duke of Kent, to Princess Marina of Greece, at Buckingham Palace and embarrassed Ernest, Wallis' husband, by flirting on the dancefloor. This was at a time when every effort was being made by everyone except Edward and Wallis to keep the affair secret from the public. To the embarrassment of all present, who had 'dressed down' so as not to outshine the bride, Wallis wore over £100,000 worth of diamonds given to her by Edward as a Christmas present.

British Intelligence had started to take an interest in the Simpsons at the instigation of King George. Officers followed Wallis and interviewed her acquaintances to ascertain the character of her relationship with the Prince of Wales. In the process, detectives also investigated the activities of the 'Ritz Set' that surrounded Edward and Wallis that included Lady Maud Alice (Emerald) Cunard, Sir Oswald Mosley, Diana Mitford, Edward Dudley (Fruity) Metcalfe, Lady Alexandra Curzon, Princess Stephanie von Hohenlohe, and Alice (Kiki) Preston. Wallis' social set was widely thought to be 'closely identified with a certain foreign government and the ambassador of that foreign government'. According to a Metropolitan Police Special Branch report, Edward had met Mosley for the first time at the home of Lady Cunard in January 1935. At one of her parties it was noted that Edward had delighted his guests by putting on a German army helmet and goose-stepping around the room making Nazi salutes.

Wallis was a frequent visitor to the home of the German diplomat Prince Otto von Bismarck, where she socialised with the German ambassador, Leopold von Hoesch. Her neighbour at Bryanston Court was Stephanie von Hohenlohe who, despite her Jewish background, held soirées for pro-Nazi British aristocrats in her apartment, whose drawing room had a large, signed portrait of Hitler. After a tip-off from French Intelligence, MI6 had begun intercepting Princess Stephanie's mail and tracking her movements in and out of the country as early as 1928. A frequent visitor to these events at Bryanston Court was Hitler's roaming envoy, Joachim von Ribbentrop. Another regular guest was the influential Lord Rothermere, an ardent Nazi sympathiser.

A British Intelligence report claimed that Stephanie had become a 'talent spotter' for Hitler and was given the job of suggesting which of the British establishment might be inclined to become friends of Nazi Germany.[8] Intelligence reports from 1938 (released in 2005) suggested that she was one of the very few women who had any influence over Hitler. It was she who came up with the idea, favoured by Hitler, of a morganatic marriage between Edward and Wallis when he succeeded to the throne as a means of keeping Edward in power in Buckingham Palace. This would have allowed Edward to marry Wallis on the understanding that she would merely be his consort and would not take the title Queen of England.

Stephanie had reputedly had a relationship with Edward's younger brother, Prince George, Duke of Kent, who, like Edward, also showed a deep interest in Nazi political philosophy. George had met Hess and Alfred Rosenberg, and dined frequently in London with Ribbentrop. There is no doubt that George and Stephanie saw a great deal of one another and shared political views. Indeed, both were at the lavish party given by Ribbentrop at the German Embassy in London to mark the coronation of King George VI in May 1937.

On 20 January 1936, King George V died, and Edward succeeded to the throne as King Edward VIII. When the news broke, he was at Princess Alice's apartment in Kensington with Charles Edward, Duke of Coburg, who, knowing that King George was dying, had arrived a few days earlier to be at Edward's side when he became King. While he had been there, Alice had invited Anthony Eden, Neville Chamberlain, Lord Astor and Duff Cooper to dinner. Charles Edward reported to Hitler that King Edward VIII now felt that a German–British alliance was a clear possibility and was willing to hold talks with Hitler in London or in Germany. Only days before King George had died, Edward had spoken to ambassador von Hoesch to express his support for Hitler and let it be known that he was planning to attend the Olympic Games in Berlin in the summer. At George's funeral at Windsor Castle on 28 January, Charles Edward raised eyebrows by wearing his SS uniform as he walked behind the coffin and sat with King Edward at the funeral dinner. In a move that only came to light years later, the security surveillance against Edward that was instigated by King George V was continued, under the orders of the Prime Minister Stanley Baldwin, even after Edward became King. The Permanent Under-Secretary at the Foreign Office, Robert Vansittart, also suspected Wallis Simpson of passing sensitive information to the Germans. Information that she may have become aware of through Edward's Foreign Office briefings.

On 7 March 1936, in the first of Hitler's moves to break free from the constraints of the Versailles Treaty, German troops reoccupied the Rhineland, a de-militarised zone that acted as a *cordon sanitaire* to increase the security of France, Belgium, and the Netherlands against future German aggression, which was also an important area of coal, steel, and iron production. Edward was quick to reassure von Hoesch that he would do all he could to prevent 'complications of a serious nature' arising as a result of the reoccupation.

When this news was conveyed to Hitler he was visibly relieved and became convinced that Britain would not oppose his plans in Europe militarily. Charles Edward, Duke of Coburg, rushed to London to speak to Edward to ascertain his state of mind but was greatly reassured when the King sent Hitler a birthday greeting wishing him 'happiness and welfare'.[9]

When von Hoesch died in April 1936 he was replaced as ambassador to Britain by von Ribbentrop, who set about reaching an understanding that would leave Germany free to pursue its ambitions in eastern Europe. Wallis Simpson was close to von Ribbentrop and a great admirer of his, which caused great concern over the risk of security breaches. Rumours abounded that she was passing information to Germany about secret codes used by British embassies. The Foreign Secretary, Anthony Eden, complained that Edward interfered in foreign policy while knowing little about it and as a result began to withhold sensitive information from him. This, of course, may well have been because of suspicions that Wallis was getting access to the information through Edward's indiscretion.

Edward, meanwhile, was planning to make Wallis his queen. He came to an agreement with Ernest Simpson to support Wallis financially if he would agree to an uncontested divorce settlement. Wallis, however, was livid that such an agreement had been arrived at behind her back and was only mollified by a large settlement of money and expensive gifts from Edward. The future Prime Minister, Neville Chamberlain, wrote in his diary that she was 'an entirely unscrupulous woman who is not in love with the King but is exploiting him for her own purposes. She has already ruined him in money and jewels.'

In the light of public perceptions about the 'idyllic romance', it is interesting to examine their relationship through the eyes of someone close to Wallis. Lady Diana Cooper would later claim that Wallis was irritated and 'bored stiff' by Edward, frequently criticised him and was cold towards him. In September 1936 Wallis had actually written to Edward telling him that for them to continue would 'create disaster' and that she planned to return to Ernest, with whom she still had 'the deepest affection' and it was clear from the way that Ernest hung around her all the time in public, even when she was with Edward, that he had never lost his dependence on her. Edward reacted in the most dramatic way by threatening to commit suicide if Wallis left him. Whatever has been said about Wallis, and for whatever reason, it cannot be doubted that she held an enduring fascination for men she met, but also that she seemed to develop an ambiguous relationship with any man who fell for her. She both craved their affection and, at the same time, was disdainful towards them. Months after she and Edward had married, Wallis was still writing to Ernest in the most loving terms, having treated him with utter contempt.

The King, who, up to the point of accession had enjoyed a glamorous playboy lifestyle, was becoming bored with royal duties and took off on a Mediterranean cruise with Wallis and Lady Diana Cooper, Duff Cooper, Lord and Lady Brownlow, Lord Sefton, Helen Fitzgerald, Lady Cunard and two American friends of Wallis, Katherine and Herman Rogers. When they returned to London, Wallis took up residence at 16 Cumberland Terrace. Divorce proceedings had been started in the Ipswich County Court but thanks to the severe censorship imposed on their newspapers by Lord Beaverbrook and Lord Rothermere, Wallis Simpson's name was never mentioned in the press and she remained largely unknown to the British public. A decree nisi was granted on 27 October 1936 but it would be 27 April 1937 before it would become effective. Edward had already chosen 12 May as his coronation day and he was determined to have Wallis by his side as his queen.

Much to the chagrin of the government, Wallis sat in the Strangers' Gallery when Edward opened Parliament on 3 November 1936. It was feared that the press would not remain silent much longer and a scandal was expected. Baldwin threatened that his government would resign in protest if the King married a twice-divorced woman, but Andrew Morton, in his book *17 Carnations: The Royals, The Nazis and the Biggest Cover-Up in*

History, claims that the whole marriage question was a false front that Baldwin utilised to get rid of the King because of the latter's pro-German views. The government had awakened to a danger that had nothing to do with any question of marriage. Throughout the centuries archbishops and prime ministers had easily overcome their moral objections to royal idiosyncrasies in the bedchamber. The real objection to the liaison between the King and Wallis was that both were Nazi sympathisers. As King, Edward would have access to all manner of secret documents and the close relationship between Wallis and Ribbentrop was a clear security issue. In fact, by midsummer 1936, all confidential documents were being withheld from the King. Baldwin suggested that there would be no objection to the King continuing his relationship with Wallis as long as it remained a private affair but Edward, certain that his popularity with the people would carry him through, insisted that he would marry her before his coronation and make her Queen of England and Empress of India.

In December, Edward's plans were thrown into disarray when Bishop Blunt of Bradford implied at a diocesan conference that Edward was not a committed member of the Christian religion. When the bishop went further and denounced the proposed royal marriage from his pulpit, the story was picked up by a local reporter and published on the Press Association's national newswire, resulting in a wave of articles and photographs of the couple. In Germany press censorship ensured that there was no such coverage of the crisis there. Wallis fled to Cannes but her house there was besieged by the press. Prime Minister Baldwin contacted Sir Vernon Kell, head of MI5, and ordered him to put the King and Wallis under close surveillance, effectively treating them as potential enemies of the state, despite the fact Kell did not consider it to be a security issue.

Edward now sought permission from the government to appeal to his people over the radio but, worried that he would try to provoke a constitutional crisis and force the government to resign, the idea was rejected by the Cabinet. The Minister for War, Duff Cooper, wrote that: 'So long as the king is king, every utterance that he makes must be on the advice of ministers who must take full responsibility for every word. If, therefore, we could not advise him to make a speech, we could not allow him to.'[10] When Thomas Robertson, a security operative, tapped the King's phone from a junction box in Green Park, he overheard Edward suggest to his younger brother that he was contemplating abdication if he was prevented from marrying Wallis. Robertson was the first commoner to become aware of that development.

The *Daily Mail* and *Express* rallied in support of Edward, and Mosley's BUF frantically put out pro-Edward propaganda lauding him as 'a symbol of the modern age'. The establishment feared revolution; some worried that Edward might dismiss the government and launch a right-wing takeover.[11] Edward briefly contemplated aligning with Mosley but in the end he baulked at the thought of civil war. After sending Mosley 'a polite thanks for his offer of support', of which he had 'felt unable to take advantage', the next day Edward decided to abdicate.[12] On 10 December he signed six copies of the Instrument of Abdication and on the following day made a radio broadcast, which he had composed with Churchill's help, telling the nation that he had abdicated because he found he could not 'discharge the duties of king as I would wish to do without the help and support of the woman I love'. That night, he stayed at Wootton with Diana Mosley and left the country the next day.

BUF youths led 800 protesters to Downing Street, and other marchers plastered posters all over the Parliament buildings calling for the people to 'Stand by the King!' Fearing a popular uprising, Scotland Yard flooded central London with extra police officers. A band of women marched from Marble Arch to Buckingham Palace to 'let the King know we are with him'.[13] In the East End, 3,000 people attended a meeting in Stepney, where Mosley demanded the question of the abdication be put to the British people in a referendum. His Blackshirts smashed windows, and there was a street battle with anti-fascists. In the end, the police made only five arrests that night, quashing Ribbentrop's alarming prediction that 'there would be shooting in the streets'. Joseph Goebbels, the Nazi propagandist, said that: '[Edward] has made a complete fool of himself ... lacking in dignity and taste.' In the Commons, Churchill, in an ill-judged outburst, tried to persuade the government to stay its judgement, but he was howled out of the House and suffered a serious blow to his prestige as a result.

Chapter Fifteen

Lord Londonderry

Charles Stewart Henry Vane-Tempest-Stewart, the 7th Marquess of Londonderry, and a descendant of one of Britain's grandest and wealthiest aristocratic families, had been appointed Minister for Air in 1931 and held the post at a time when Hitler and Göring were frantically rebuilding the German Air Force. Londonderry was about as well-connected in British society as it was possible to be. He could have lived quietly outside politics but felt obliged to go against the trend of aristocratic decline and use his position for what he believed to be the nation's best interests. He had somewhat idealistic ambitions to avoid another war by developing friendly relations with Germany, but also saw the necessity of building up Britain's air power as a deterrent to German aggression.

The policy he advocated, however, which was to oppose disarmament and build a formidable offensive bomber force, was at odds with the ideas of his Cabinet colleagues, whose preference was for a strong defensive capability alongside a pursuit of multilateral disarmament, which Londonderry was sure would not be reciprocated in Germany. He found himself increasingly isolated in Cabinet and even gently mocked by his colleagues. The government seemingly was focused on reducing the military budget, even at a time when other countries were increasing theirs.

By 1934, however, all hope of disarmament was gone and the British government announced a series of rearmament programmes but did little in practice. While Londonderry was vindicated, he was again at odds with many in government because of his desire to address German grievances in the hope of reducing tensions. War, he thought, was not inevitable if some sort of air parity could be achieved, but that would not happen if Britain continued to make promises without taking any action. When public opinion started to turn and vocal critics of government policy, such as Churchill, were drawing attention to Britain's laggardly approach to rearmament, it was Londonderry who came in for criticism even though it was he who had warned all along about Britain's weakness in air power.

He urged acceleration of Britain's rearmament programme but Chancellor of the Exchequer Neville Chamberlain objected to the level of expenditure that would entail. He argued that reports of German capabilities were overblown, and that Britain's defences were sound. With rearmament decidedly not popular with the electorate, the government, he said, was doing all that was required under the circumstances. It was soon clear, however, that Germany was outstripping Britain in air power and alarm bells were ringing all over Whitehall. Londonderry was thrown onto the defensive as Churchill attacked him in Parliament and Rothermere did the same in print. He failed to respond robustly and was left fighting for his political life. In the face of plots to remove him, Londonderry refused to resign but on 22 May, however, a debate in the House of Lords left him badly wounded and when Stanley Baldwin became Prime Minister on 7 June 1935, his Cabinet had only one change; a new Minister for Air. Londonderry, however, was retained as Lord Privy Seal for a few months before being eventually shown the door. As part of the justification for his removal, it was argued that he had been pro-German, but it was only afterwards that he began to express any genuine sympathy with the Nazi regime and within a year he would be seen as the most prominent pro-German lobbyist in Britain.

On 29 January 1936, he made his first private visit to Germany in a German Junkers Ju 52, when he met Hitler and other leading Nazis. After his humiliation at the hands of Baldwin, it was some relief to be treated as an honoured guest at Berlin's best hotel, the Adlon. On his first evening, Londonderry witnessed a torchlight parade of some tens of thousands of stormtroopers to mark the third anniversary of Hitler's rise to power. This was followed by a sumptuous banquet hosted by Göring and then a visit to Carinhall. The next day it was Ribbentrop's turn to entertain him in Dahlem. On the fourth day, Londonderry had a two-hour meeting with Hitler, whom he found ill at ease and awkward but agreeable.[1] Two days later he was Hitler's guest at the Winter Olympics at Garmisch-Partenkirchen.

Even though he was essentially shunned on his return by a government that took a dim view of his amateur diplomacy, Londonderry was now primed to laud the new Germany at every opportunity. He would not, however, make public declarations in favour of Germany but would make full use of his connections 'in quiet and suitable fashion in appropriate places'.[2] Despite this, he was quoted in the press, ever quick to pour fuel onto a spark of controversy, as saying that German rearmament was not directed towards Britain but was simply essential for the country's own security. This was gleefully interpreted in print as characterising him as a spokesman for Nazi propaganda in Britain. The *Guardian* said that Baldwin had done well to push him out of government. At the same time, his entreaties to his ex-colleagues in government were ignored as public opinion began to harden against Germany and Londonderry became synonymous with pro-Nazism.

He was undaunted, however, and believed that he had an important role to play in preventing war. Ribbentrop persuaded him to join the AGF and Londonderry, with his wife, were now also beginning to cultivate their recently made acquaintance with leading Nazis. They wrote to Göring in the most flattering terms. The Germans, apparently unaware that Londonderry was quite out of step and out of favour, responded in similar vein and expressed the hope that he might act as an informal channel to the British government to establish 'understanding' for the German position. To Ribbentrop, Londonderry admitted that he harboured racial prejudices and had 'no great affection for the Jews', blaming them for much of the trouble in the world. However, there is no evidence that either he or his wife held extreme anti-Semitic views, and neither was either ever associated with Mosley's BUF. The Nazi anti-Jewish policies were seen by Londonderry as an unfortunate and unnecessary obstacle to better relations between Britain and Germany.

When Hitler marched his troops into the 'demilitarised' Rhineland on 7 March 1936, there was little outcry. The act itself was seen as too trivial a matter to upset the fragile peace that prevailed in Europe but Londonderry, and others like Lothian who were of similar opinion, wrote to the newspapers to encourage public understanding of Germany's position. This, they said, was a perfectly understandable reaction to the recent Franco-Soviet Treaty.

Lady Londonderry, who had proved to be particularly susceptible to Göring's charms, hosted Ribbentrop, now tipped to be the next Ambassador to Britain, at the family home in Mount Stewart, Northern Ireland, on 29 May. Ribbentrop was accompanied by his formidable wife and among the other guests was the Chief of the Air Staff, Sir Edward Ellington, and the *Mail* journalist, George Ward Price. Stepping from his aircraft at Newtownards airport, Ribbentrop announced to the waiting newsmen that he was there in a private capacity as 'a great friend of Lord Londonderry', but privately Londonderry thought him rude and his wife apparently could not stand him. The press was quick to characterise the visit as a political event and speculated widely on its significance, which was a great embarrassment and irritation to Londonderry. Officials in the German Foreign Ministry apparently believed that Ribbentrop was bringing proposals from Hitler aimed at a pact that would guarantee Britain's security in return for a free hand for Germany in the east, which is indicative of the way in which the Germans still, mistakenly, thought that Londonderry had influence with the government. Londonderry extended an invitation to Ribbentrop for a second weekend visit, this time in Wynyard, north of Stockton-on-Tees in County Durham, in November 1936.

Londonderry now turned to the Lord Privy Seal, Lord Halifax, whom he perceived as one of the few ministers who had taken notice of his entreaties. He argued for an anti-communist strategy alongside Germany, however much other issues might separate them. For himself he expressed annoyance that his valuable contacts inside Germany were being wasted by the government that was woefully mishandling the whole German issue and pandering to French opinion. As was his wont, Halifax listened politely but little of what Londonderry said seemed to have any effect on his judgement or subsequent actions.

Chapter Sixteen

Sir Barry Domvile

The peppery, short-tempered Barry Edward Domvile had risen through the naval ranks with commendable speed having won the prestigious Gold Medal of the Royal United Service Institution and been appointed the Secretary to the Committee of Imperial Defence. During the First World War he had commanded both destroyers and cruisers, and was seen as a likely candidate for high office in Naval Intelligence when he attended the Versailles peace negotiations in 1919. He emerged with the distinct impression that the Treaty was doomed to failure because 'if the peace conditions are harsh, it is obviously necessary to arrange that they can be enforced and maintained without danger of retaliation, involving a further breach of the peace. To make a peace treaty which can neither be expected to endure, nor yet to be capable of enforcement, even after a further recourse to arms, is just silly.'[1]

In February 1916, Domvile married his cousin, Alexandrine von de Heydt, the daughter of a German Baron, Daniel von de Heydt, a banker and later a director of a German company. The Baron's bank was liquidated by the British government in 1917. After the war, Domvile became Director of the Plans Policy Division of the Admiralty Naval Staff, in which capacity he represented Britain at many conferences throughout the world. He later became Chief of Staff to Sir Osmond Brock with the Mediterranean Fleet, and went on to achieve the rank of rear admiral as Director of Naval Intelligence. Domvile was invited to go to Germany as Hitler rose to power and fully enjoyed his experiences, praising the positive changes that the Führer was making in an economically ravaged society.[2] He retired from the Navy with the rank of admiral in 1936 and the honour of Companion of the Order of the Bath (CB), as well as a knighthood.

During his retirement, he continued to retain a close interest in military matters and foreign affairs and had strong views on how Britain should avoid becoming embroiled in another war. His conclusion was that the only solution to the situation was amicable relations with Germany.

Before his retirement, Domvile had been introduced to Anton Walter de Sager, a Swiss businessman and German spy, which led to a lengthy relationship with leaders of the German Reich.[3] De Sager arranged for him and Sir Arnold Wilson to visit Germany for the first time in 1935, when he met Himmler and visited Dachau concentration camp, where he found that the inmates had 'very pleasant work to do' [and the camp was] very comfortable and the food was very good'.[4] He came away from his trip apparently favourably impressed with what he saw as 'freedom in everyday matters [in Germany]' but he was also very aware of the atrocities being inflicted on the Jewish community in German cities. Wilson was appalled at what he saw. Writing in *The English Review*, he described 'things were being done of which no reasonable person could approve'. Stanislav Zámečník, who was a prisoner at Dachau, later described how, in what he called a theatre of the absurd, the camp was prepared for foreigners to present a model prison environment. Clearly Domvile, unlike Wilson, chose to see only what he wanted to see. By no means did he hold extreme anti-Semitic views before going to Germany, but he still tended to trivialise Germany's anti-Jewish policies and find excuses for them by suggesting that the Jews were somehow architects of their own downfall. This changed from about 1936 onwards after he had met some of the Nazi leaders and fallen under their spell. He found Himmler to be 'very charming and capable', and described Hitler as having 'magnetic, honest eyes [and] great charm of manner'.[5]

He had become a member of the Anglo-German Fellowship, established at the end of 1935, but found it too narrowly focused on the interests of wealthy entrepreneurs and large business. As a result, and with Ribbentrop's help, he founded the Link in July 1937 as an independent non-party organisation to promote Anglo-German friendship through its journal, the lavishly illustrated *Anglo-German Review*, 'a sort of celebrity magazine for the Third Reich, with extensive photo spreads showing Hitler and other Nazi officials relaxing and spending time with children featured in nearly every issue'.[6] Although it held pro-Nazi views and attracted a number of anti-Semites and pro-Nazis, membership of the Link never exceeded about 4,500 spread over some thirty branches, the first ones opening in Chelsea, Southend and Birmingham. There were also partner branches in Cologne and Düsseldorf and Salzburg under the name *der Ring*. The Link encouraged its members to visit Germany and it arranged trips to various German destinations. While not having a huge membership, the organisation did include a large number of aristocrats, including the dukes of Westminster, Marlborough, Wellington, Buccleuch, Bedford, and Hamilton.

Among those founding the Link along with Domvile was Professor Arthur Pillans Laurie, a Scottish chemist and a member of many of the leading British colleges and academies. Laurie was described by Mosley as 'the mildest man alive [but a man of] violent opinions [yet] a perfectly honest Englishman'. In 1939, Laurie published a book entitled *The Case for Germany*, in which he praised Hitler as having 'a charming personality [who] stands apart and like all men of genius who have led great movements he is simple and direct'.[7] Domvile supplied the forward to the book, in which he wrote of Germany: 'I recommend this with confidence to all people who are genuinely impressed with the desire to understand one of the greatest and most bloodless revolutions in history.'[8]

Describing to an audience in Southend what the Link stood for, Domvile lauded Hitler as a man in whom the German people had found a saviour and stressed that the sole aim of his organisation was to encourage friendship with Germany. Domvile's ambition was to extend the appeal of friendship with Germany to a wider audience. Looking at the original supporters of the Link, however, we see a coterie of extreme Nazi sympathisers and anti-Semites, including Sir John Brown of the British Legion, Susan Fass of the Anglo-German Kameradshaft, and Professor Raymond Beazley, a regular contributor to the *Anglo-German Review*.

The *Anglo-German Review* was founded by Cola Ernest Carroll because he was unhappy about the way he saw the mainstream British press, which, he claimed, was controlled by Jews, as taking an anti-German tone. It was funded by the Trans-Ocean News Service, a German news agency, ostensibly by advertising through its London contact, the Nazi diplomat Otto Karlowa. Karlowa was *Landesgruppenleiter* of the Ausland organisation, tasked with coordinating the activities of the many German Nazis living in Britain. He wrote to his Ausland members encouraging them to attend events organised by the Link and, if possible, take along 'young ladies as dancing partners'.[9] MI5 files also record that Carroll received a total of £750 from Ribbentrop through the German Embassy. The *Anglo-German Review* regularly carried excerpts of speeches by Hitler and Goebbels. Others who wrote for the review were the extreme pro-Nazi Lord Redesdale; Sir Albert Lambert Ward MP; Captain Edward Unwin VC; Councillor W.J. Bassett-Lowke; the Scottish Peer Lord Sempill, who was later shown to have been a spy for both Germany and Japan; A.E.R. Dyer; Archibald Crawford KC; and Hubert Maddocks, who was considered by Domvile as 'one of Mosley's best men'.[10] Carroll was able to report to Goebbels that many of the thirty branches of the Link showed German news and 'instructional' films monthly and the Studio One cinema in Oxford Street had agreed to show German films not otherwise available in England, all of which played to capacity audiences.

John Parker, Labour MP for Romford, raised the matter of the Link in Parliament on 21 December 1937 when he called it 'a camouflaged fascist organisation'.[11] He later wrote to the Home Secretary, Sir Samuel Hoare, saying that the Link did all it could to glorify Hitlerism and derived financial support from Germany. From its inception, the organisation had come under MI5 scrutiny and several intelligence agents were infiltrated into its ranks. One such mentioned that during her stay in Germany as a member of the Link, she was asked to copy German propaganda newsletters for free at her home in Britain and distribute them as widely as possible. Despite a donation of £180 a month from Dr Erich Hetzler of the *Dienststelle Ribbentrop*, an unofficial German foreign affairs organisation, the Link was always short of money and was unable to establish a central office of administration.

The tone of the articles in the *Anglo-German Review* and interpretations of political events was completely pro-Nazi and often no more than thinly veiled anti-Semitism, but the Link would not hesitate to support the British government stance if it agreed with the publication's views. In particular, the *Anglo-German Review* was effulgent in its praise of Chamberlain's apparent success at Munich, when Domvile recorded in his diary that he was 'feeling so happy especially at Hitler and Chamberlain's peace pact'.[12] In a letter to *The Times*, Domvile, Carroll and others wrote:

> [We] believe that real friendship and co-operation between Britain and Germany are essential to the establishment of enduring peace not only in Western Europe but throughout the world [and] strongly deprecate the attempt which is being made to sabotage an Anglo-German rapprochement by distorting the facts of the Czecho-Slovak settlement. We believe that the Munich Agreement was nothing more than the rectification of one of the most flagrant injustices of the Peace Treaty. It took nothing from Czecho-Slovakia to which that country could rightly lay claim and gave nothing to Germany which could have been right-fully withheld.

MI5 had a keen interest in Domvile, whom they described as being enormously enamoured of all Germans, a great snob and an anti-Semite, but someone of no great intellectual ability and, furthermore, one who drank too much. In spring 1939, they gave Domvile a 'friendly warning' that, in its opinion, the Germans were using the Link as a state-controlled propaganda tool. However, Domvile refused to accept this. Although its membership was still growing at this time, there was an increasing anxiety over German intentions after its annexation of Bohemia, Moravia and Silesia and the Italian invasion of Albania. The extreme far right tried to use the Link to resurrect the conspiracy theories based on *The Protocols*, but it was now becoming increasingly difficult to drum up support for Germany.

When war broke out, Domvile urged his supporters to support the King and he voluntarily dissolved the Link in early September 1939. MI5 scrutiny intensified and a number of incriminating letters were intercepted. In one, Domvile wrote of his 'close' contact with Mosley and their mutual plans that were 'maturing well'. Although the Link had been notionally suspended, Domvile met with Beckett, Gordon-Canning and Benjamin Greene to plot the formation of a new organisation, the British Council for Christian Settlement in Europe (BCCSE), financed by Tavistock, to lobby for a negotiated settlement with Hitler. Its first action was to publicly appeal to the government to 'terminate the war [and] call an international conference for [a] peaceful settlement'. MI5 reported that the first meeting of the BCCSE was treated to 'naked German propaganda' and those attending had listened to Hitler being praised for his 'wise statesmanship'. The audience of some 150 supporters, apparently cheered wildly.[13] Altogether MI5 estimated that the BCCSE had about 1,500 members and had evidence to show that they were 'in the early stages of planning for an armed fascist uprising'.[14] At another meeting at the Kingsway Hall in Holborn, MI5 agent-runner Maxwell Knight's insider reported that it was 'one of the most seditious meetings they had ever attended' and they had heard a speech that was 'particularly treasonable'.[15]

Benjamin Greene was a long-time peace campaigner and cousin to the novelist Graham Greene. He had been active in the Labour Party and seemed to have become a Nazi sympathiser after acting as deputy Chief Returning Officer in the 1935 Saar Plebiscite. He came to the attention of MI5 in 1939 when he was suspected of receiving a large sum of money from Germany to set up a Peace and Progress Information Bureau, which was simply a front for Nazi propaganda. He was subsequently removed from the bench of local JPs in Herefordshire.

Maxwell Knight had infiltrated agents into the BCCSE, one of which, German-born Harald Kurtz, was introduced to Greene in March 1940 and thereafter dined with him often. Kurtz convinced Greene that he was a German agent in touch with Nazis, which led Greene to request that he convey to his contacts in Germany that there were 'men in [England] ready to take over the government after a German victory [but that] Mosley was not the right person to lead it'.[16]

The intelligence services were also aware of a secret meeting Mosley held with Domvile and other fascists on 7 February 1940, and understood that Lady Domvile was paying the salary of a BUF employee. Letters that Domvile were writing and articles he submitted to fascist periodicals were considered by MI5 to be influencing 'public opinion in a manner likely to be prejudicial to the defence of the Realm or the efficient prosecution of the war'.[17] He was described by Richard Carter of Naval Intelligence as a potential quisling (collaborator) and he was recommended for detention under Defence Regulation 18B. Domvile was interned in Brixton Prison on 7 July 1940, the justification for his detention being as follows:

- He is a founder and essential supporter of the Link, without whom it could not continue.
- He is closely associated with prominent Nazi leaders in Germany and in this country.
- He is sympathetic to Germany and the Nazi system of Government.
- He has been closely associated with Sir Oswald Mosley and other prominent leaders of the BUF.
- He has been active in the furtherance of the objects of the BUF.
- He has since the outbreak of war discussed with Sir Oswald Mosley and other prominent members of the BUF the coordination of fascist activities and the achievement of fascist revolution in this country.[18]

The extent of control with which Regulation 18B empowered state officials was draconian. Detainees were not shown any of the allegations or 'evidence' for their detention. They could appeal to an Advisory Committee to ask for a review but were not allowed any legal representation, nor could they ask any question as to the sources for the case against them. Domvile was brought to Berystede Hotel in Ascot for questioning on 22 October 1940, which according to his own testimony 'passed off very pleasantly',[19] but he was recalled two weeks later when the mood was quite different. Apparently the Advisory Committee had received intelligence from an MI5 agent, Sidney Noakes, whom they were not obliged to identify in court, and this time Domvile was questioned rather more aggressively. Why had he written in the preface to Laurie's book *The Case for Germany*: 'It is with admiration and gratitude for the great work that [Hitler] has done for the German people'? Did he not see that every word he wrote was seen in the eyes of Germans in the context of him being an admiral of the fleet and an ex-Director of Naval Intelligence? Apparently not. Why had the Central London branch of the Link entertained pro-German speakers and handed out pro-German and anti-Semitic literature? He had no knowledge of that, in fact he had specifically forbade it. Did he know that the *Anglo-German Review* was financed from Germany? Only through advertising. Had he signed a letter to Hitler with a 'heil Hitler'? Yes, but that was mere politeness.

There was some suggestion that Margaret Bothamley, an extreme fascist and a member of the International Fascist League as well as the Right Club, who had travelled with Domvile to Germany in 1939, was his lover. She travelled around the Link branches making speeches and promoting her fascist views but was kept under close surveillance by the security service. As a result, she fled to Germany and became active in broadcasting German propaganda back to England. When she returned to England she was tried and sentenced to a year in prison.

Among Domvile's associates were Henry Luttman-Johnson, a Scottish landowner and, along with Robert Forgan, a founder member of the January Club with Carroll and Gordon-Canning, and Olive Baker. The Club was essentially a front organisation for Mosley's BU and arranged dinners to bring British fascists into contact with the political establishment. Sir Charles Petrie said that it was a 'spontaneous effort of a number of disinterested people [who] are very anxious with regard to the present trend of events [and which has] received very substantial support both inside and outside parliament'. Members of the club professed an admiration for Italian fascism but were careful to distance themselves from Nazism and the club's relevance essentially rose and fell in step with Mosley's own popularity.

Olive Evelyn Baker was an unrepentant admirer of Hitler and member of both the BU and the Link. She would later receive a five-year sentence of penal servitude for spreading German propaganda in the form of 'a large quantity' of material published by the BU and other right-wing organisations, despite MI5 raising 'no objections on security grounds' to her release. She was a forty-year-old West Country nurse who had worked as a teacher in Germany in the 1930s and who corresponded with Domvile on matters pertaining to fascism. In one letter she spoke of 'the depths of degradation and depravity under our Jewish teachers'.[20] Domvile instructed her on how to tune in to the short-wave New British Broadcasting Station (NBBS), a 'black propaganda' organisation run by Büro Concordia, a division of Goebbels' propaganda ministry, based in the Charlottenburg district of Berlin. In addition to providing false 'news' about the progress of the war, there is some evidence that NBBS was also sending coded messages to German intelligence agents in Britain.

Ramsay had used parliamentary privilege, without rebuke, to publicise the frequency of the NBBS transmissions in a speech in the House of Commons, while William Bruce Tomkins had been arrested for giving the exact same information to his landlady. Tomkins, a BUF activist from Kingston, had been sentenced at the Old Bailey to six months' imprisonment for doing acts 'likely to prejudice' the efficient prosecution of the war. This had included him being found in possession of 'sticky-back slips' on which were printed the same NBBS radio wavelength. To his credit, the judge, Mr Justice Atkinson, refused to hand down a more severe punishment for Tomkins 'when the real criminals responsible have not been brought to justice'.[21]

Baker's punishment throws a bright light on the way that Nazi sympathisers were treated differently according to their social status. Something that has not been sufficiently recognised was the way that wealthy or politically well-connected fascists, such as members of the Right Club, were being treated with 'kid gloves', while lower-ranking activists received lengthy prison sentences, often with hard labour. Many files pertaining to the right-wing activity of prominent persons during the Second World War continue to be withheld from public scrutiny seventy-five years after the end of the war. One can only speculate on the reasons why.

Chapter Seventeen

Archibald Maule Ramsay and the Right Club

Captain Archibald Henry Maule Ramsay was a man of impeccable credentials: ex-Army, Eton, Sandhurst and Coldstream Guards, he had been Conservative MP for Peebles and South Midlothian since 1931. For the first few years of his political career he had focused his attention on local matters, but turned abruptly towards international affairs during the Spanish Civil War, when his attention was drawn to what he saw as left-wing bias in the press supporting the Republican cause. This quickly led him to perceive threats to Britain from the 'intellectual and spiritual poison' of international communism.[1] He would become second only to Mosley as a significant figure on the fascist fringe of British politics.

When a conference of the International Federation of Freethinkers was planned in London for 1938, Ramsay and others, including Sir Thomas Moore, saw it as a 'Godless Conference' held by the 'League of the Militant Godless', or in simple terms a subversive communist plot to undermine democracy. In June Ramsay introduced a Private Members' Bill entitled the 'Aliens Restriction (Blasphemy) Bill', the object of which was 'to prevent the participation by aliens in assemblies for the purpose of propagating blasphemous or atheistic doctrines or in other activities calculated to interfere with the established religious institutions of Great Britain'. That same year, anti-Semitism became part of Ramsay's message when he declared that 'that the power behind World Revolution was not just a vague body of internationalists, but organised World Jewry'.[2]

Ramsay was quickly establishing himself as the unofficial leader of the extreme right in Britain. He objected to having Jews in government and started a campaign to have Leslie Hore-Belisha removed from his post as Secretary for War. Chamberlain did eventually move Hore-Belisha to the Ministry of Information, a move that Lord Halifax objected to, claiming that it was 'inappropriate to have a Jew in charge of publicity'. Ramsay was invited by the Link to co-sign a letter to *The Times* calling for friendship and cooperation between Britain and Germany and then, in November 1938, a few weeks after Kristallnacht, attended a dinner at the German embassy in London along with Moore and Domvile. At this time, Ramsay was convenor of the fourteen-strong Council of the Nordic League, the driving force behind the Militant Christian Patriots, whose perceived enemy was conspiratorial Jewry and whose main purpose was to keep Britain out of any European war. Both organisations had been infiltrated by intelligence agents, whose reports of meetings convinced MI5 that Ramsay was 'unbalanced and suffering from a persecution mania'.[3]

In May 1939, Ramsay founded a secret society called the Right Club, whose stated objective was to 'oppose and expose the activities of Organised Jewry ... [and] to clear the Conservative Party of Jewish influence'. Its secondary aim was to 'avert war which we considered to be mainly the work of Jewish intrigue centred in New York'. The club operated out of a number of quiet and inconspicuous locations in South Kensington, including a flat belonging to Margaret Bothamley at 67 Cromwell Road.[4] Members of the Right Club included William Joyce, A.K. Chesterton, Lord Redesdale, the Duke of Wellington and a dozen Members of Parliament. All members' names, a total of 235, were handwritten by Ramsay in a Red Book and kept strictly secret for fear of 'Jewish retaliation of a serious nature'.[5] Membership fees were high, as much as £25 joining fee and £10 per annum for the most senior members. This restricted membership to the well-off and allowed Ransey to award himself an annual salary of £600.

The MI5 agent-runner Maxwell Knight was given the task of infiltrating the Right Club. He had a long history of espionage work, having first joined Lintorn-Orman's British Fascisti in 1924 as an undercover agent of MI5, although his early work for the intelligence agencies had been primarily in surveillance of communist organisations. He claimed that his motivation had been purely professional but one who worked with him at the time said that he 'had no time for democracy and believed the whole country should be ruled by the social elite'. When he was elevated to lead section B5(b), he ran agents through a 'shadow' operation run from his flat in Sloane Street. His qualifications for the job apparently included 'a willingness to break the law in the service of his employers'.[6] Knight objected strongly to the prevailing view within MI5 that women were not considered suitable as agents and proceeded to employ several. He valued their intuition and emotional complexity. In 1933 he turned his attention to fascist movements in Britain, when it was Ramsay's pro-Nazism rather than his anti-Semitism that came under his scrutiny. He was one of the few in MI5 who had insider knowledge of fascist movements and was considered to be their expert on the subject. At this point he was still downplaying the importance of the BU, which, he said was motivated by a genuine, if wrong-headed, patriotism.

In the absence of any directive from above, Knight had created an intelligence strategy all of his own and brought with him a collection of informants, some of whom had infiltrated the CPGB and various small fascist groups. At this time he was still sympathetic to fascist organisations and reported to his superiors that he had never found them to act in any unconstitutional manner. He did not believe in 'golden rules' when it came to recruitment of agents, and when they were deployed in the field, all agents in one particular field of activity, which he limited to six, would come under a single handler. His comments on the running of his agents is instructive. The handler must be 'a man of wide understanding' and be, at all times, 'at the beck and call of his agent'. He must make friends with them, get to know their strengths and limitations thoroughly, and establish mutual trust.[7] In the field, an agent, he believed, should infiltrate an organisation by a gradual process of assimilation and if possible be invited into a relationship rather than instigating it themselves. This meant initially attending public meetings, getting recognised, and then making known their views, which they would have researched from an organisation's literature.

Knight infiltrated three agents into the Right Club, all of them women. The first was Marjorie Amor (aka Marjorie Mackie, agent M/Y) described as a 'cosy middle-aged woman' in the mould of Agatha Christie's Miss Marple.[8] Amor had previously done work for MI5 and was therefore experienced in tradecraft. She had met the Ramsays through another organisation, the Christian Protest Movement, a few years earlier and Knight suggested that she find a pretext for re-establishing contact with Ismay, Ramsay's wife. She did so and was invited to have tea at the Ramsay house at 24 Onslow Square. After a number of such meetings, during which the two discussed politics, Amor gave the impression of supporting right-wing movements and was invited to join the Right Club. Ismay then suggested that Amor become active in support of her husband by applying for a position with the Postal Censorship section of the Foreign Office and acting as an undercover agent of the Right Club. Knight made sure that her application was successful, which left Amor now working undercover twice over.

Quite unaware that Amor was a 'plant', Ramsay invited her into the 'inner circle' and hoped to use her to find out just how much attention was being paid to the Right Club within government circles. On the other hand, Amor was finding out the extent of Ramsay's penetration of Scotland Yard, MI5 and other government departments. Already she had warned Knight that Anthony Ludovici, who worked in the Military Censorship Department, was passing information to Ramsay. She would later report on Right Club informants in the Ministry of Economic Warfare, the Air Ministry censorship branch and, crucially, exposed Francis Hemming, who was a member of Churchill's War Cabinet secretariat. Amor would later play an important role in the arrest and prosecution of Tyler Kent, who was charged with passing classified information to Anna Wolkoff.

The Russian Tea Rooms off Queen's Gate Mews, run by Admiral Nicolai Wolkoff, had become a meeting place for the Right Club, which is where the admiral's daughter, Anna, met Ramsay. She had previously met both Hans Frank and Rudolf Hess in Germany, which had first brought her to the attention of MI5. Later she would also form a close relationship with Wallis Simpson. During May and June 1940, Anna Wolkoff met Hélène Louise de Munck, a twenty-five-year-old Belgian national, on an almost daily basis and had taken her into her confidence, unaware that, like Amor, de Munck (agent M/I) was also working for Knight. She was denied membership of the Right Club because of her Belgian nationality but she was able to gain favour by insinuating that she had a contact, Jean Nieuwenhuys, in the Belgian embassy through whom communications with Nazi Germany might be established, even with William Joyce in Berlin. Knight now employed his dark, and highly illegal, arts by having one of his agents, a fascist sympathiser, James McGuirk Hughes, write an encoded letter to Joyce containing 'facts' about Jewish activity in Britain, which was given to Anna Wolkoff. Wolkoff then gave the letter to Munck, who now promised to use a contact in the Romanian embassy to have it sent to Joyce, c/o Radfunkhaus, Berlin. This act of Wolkoff would be an important piece of evidence at her subsequent trial.

When Britain declared war on Germany on 3 September 1939, the Right Club officially disbanded itself, but members continued to meet in secret. For his part, Ramsay had continued his anti-Jewish propaganda both in and out of Parliament. Many who had been active members of the Right Club, and were still members of the NL, would continue their subversive activities under Ramsay's guidance. Two of these, Oliver Gilbert and T.W. Victor Rowe, were the first members of the Right Club to be arrested and interned on 22 September under Defence Regulation 18B. Gilbert was accused of having 'hostile associations' with German and Japanese agents in London, while Victor Rowe had boasted that he could travel from Croydon to Germany without passing through airport control. He was found to have festooned his flat with Nazi regalia and was considered to be 'mentally unstable'.[9]

On the previous day, Knight's agent, Marjorie Amor, had met Ramsay, who told her that the Right Club was continuing its activities clandestinely and Special Branch had filed a report stating that it expected the club would only attempt 'a bloody revolution' once the Germans had made a successful landing on the British mainland.[10] All the names of Right Club members had been recorded in what became known as the Red Book. In late 1940 questions were raised in Parliament and the Home Secretary was requested to publish the contents of the book, a copy of which had been seized by Special Branch, in light of the fact that it contained the names of 'distinguished persons' but he declined, saying that he did not think 'it would be in the public interest'. The contents of the Red Book remained under wraps for the next sixty years.

No charges were brought against Ramsay but he was interned under Defence Regulation 18B and joined Mosley and Nikolai Wolkoff in Brixton Prison. Claims were made that he had made some sort of deal in order to avoid being charged with treason. While in custody, his wife, Ismay, a Nazi-sympathising toff, was allowed to bring him fine food and wine to ensure he served his time in the comfort of his rank.

About one third of all documents relating to internments of 1940 are considered to be so sensitive that they have been retained under Section 3(4) of the Public Records Act and never released by the Home Office. Richard Thurlow believes that there was and still is a sophisticated cover-up to prevent the release of information pertaining to secret meetings all across the fascist political fringe in 1939 and 1940.[11] However, there is no evidence that the vast majority of interned native fascists were engaged in subversive or terrorist activities, which raises questions over the government action.

If election results are anything to go by, support for fascist groups was extremely low after the outbreak of war and even though rallies were supported enthusiastically, the number of people attending them was in the hundreds rather than the thousands. At first, in 1939, the government had made no concerted move to rein in fascist groups but they became increasingly nervous after the German occupation of Denmark and Norway, and especially after the invasion of France in May 1940. Public opinion moved decisively against the fascists like Mosley, but the security services lacked the resources to come up with evidence to justify taking further action. A frantic recruitment drive had been started by MI5 after 1939, which led to its administration reaching a crisis point close to collapse. Some recruits proved to be quite unsuitable for the role, while experienced people were tied up with training programmes. All this at a time when the workload was increasing at a furious rate.[12]

However, the arrest of Tyler Kent on 20 May 1940 forced the government to act. There was a fear that fascist groups were unifying in a concerted effort to undermine the government position. This in itself shows how badly the security services misread the situation. Evidence of the schismatic and doctrinal rifts within the right-wing organisations shows just how improbable close cooperation between them would be. Try as they might, however, the government was unable to uncover definite proof of subversive activity. There was never any evidence that Ramsay had intended to break the law by publishing the information he had been given by Kent. A case against him could not be made under Section 1 of the Official Secrets Act, and indeed was not desirable given that he could choose to be tried by his peers. It was felt that greater benefit could be derived from interning him and interrogating him in confinement to discover exactly what he had been planning. Neither could a case be brought against Mosley, who had broken no laws.

Defence Regulation 18B was amended to 18B(1a), which permitted the Secretary of State to make a detention order against any person who had been a member of or active in any organisation subject to foreign influence or control or had associations with any government with which Britain was at war. While the Right Club had been regarded as a semi-secret society primarily concerned with promulgating anti-Semitism and not overtly pro-Nazi, it now found itself in the government's firing line as the authorities desperately tried to boost public confidence and morale just days after the German attack against France and the Low Countries. A meeting chaired by Chamberlain and addressed by the Home Secretary chose to see Ramsay's group as subversive, disruptive of the Home Front and hindering the prosecution of the war. It was decided that Ramsay should be interned. Two others whose names were in the Red Book and who were also known to be members, or had been members, of other far-right organisations were taken in with him.

The BU was proscribed on 10 July. It has been argued that on this day the government, facing the prospect of either a German invasion or an intensification of the Luftwaffe air assault, lost its sense of proportion and went far beyond what was necessary or legally permissible to protect British security. Unfortunately almost all documents relating to the Link and Right Club are withheld so it is not possible to even open a debate on the rights and wrongs of government policy towards them over internment and what reasons they might have for keeping so much information about prominent people under wraps.

Up until 1937, Hitler had made it clear that Britain was to be seen not as a potential enemy but a country with which he would negotiate a non-aggression treaty, leaving the British Empire intact and with him as lord and master of mainland Europe. For this reason the Abwehr had made no attempt to establish an intelligence network in the country and when Britain started a programme of intensive rearmament and Hitler began to change his approach to Britain, it was too late to change tack. By then, MI5 was alert to the danger and stepped up its surveillance of potential or suspect German agents, while Knight's B5(b) section had infiltrated agents into all the major fascist organisations active in the country. The Nazis were never able to establish anything like an efficient intelligence presence in the country, which actually made internment an irrelevance in security terms and was simply used as a propaganda tool to boost morale and impress the public that all necessary steps were being taken to protect them. An Advisory Committee was set up to hear appeals from all internees who petitioned to be released. Richard Thurlow believes that this committee did a particularly good job in resisting pressure from the security services and that the Rothermere press 'kept the erosion of civil liberties [of those detained and of the population generally] to a necessary minimum'.[13]

In an attempt to get them to give up information about the BU, some of its members were taken to Latchmere House on Ham Common, where they were initially held in solitary confinement with minimal rations. They were then interrogated aggressively, usually in the middle of the night, under fierce arc lights. When Mosley became aware of this he threatened legal action and the practice was stopped.

In 1941 the *New York Times* claimed that Ramsay had been guilty of spying for the Nazis and had sent treasonable information, which had been given to him by Kent, to the German Legation in Dublin. Ramsay sued the owners of the *New York Times* for libel and won his case but, was awarded only a farthing in damages and ordered to pay his own costs. Ramsay was released from Brixton Prison on 26 September 1944 and later lost his seat in the 1945 General Election.

Chapter Eighteen

The Windsors after the Abdication

Edward had moved to Austria and stayed with friends until Wallis obtained her divorce from Ernest, at which point she changed her name back to Wallis Warfield. On 3 June 1937, the couple were married just south of Tours in France at the sixteenth-century Château de Candé. The house was owned by the French-born, naturalised American businessman Charles Eugene Bedaux, who was suspected of being a Nazi agent, and who also had a villa near Hitler's Alpine retreat at Berchtesgaden. The ceremony was presided over by the Mayor of Monts, Dr Charles Mercier, but the actual ceremony was conducted by the Reverend R. Anderson Jardine with Fruity Metcalfe acting as best man. The small number of guests included Randolph Churchill and Baron Eugène Rothschild. At the ceremony, Herman Rogers, a friend from Wallis' days before she arrived in England and who was said by Morton to be her 'one true love', walked her to the altar and acted as all-round host at the ceremony. Wallis had been staying at the home of the Rogers on the Côte d'Azur before moving to the Château de Candé in March. Afterwards the couple departed on the Simplon-Orient Express overnight to Venice, where the train stopped for several hours and thus allowed them to take a motorboat ride and stroll in the gardens of the Hotel Excelsior. They then continued to southern Austria, where they spent their three-month honeymoon in the Schloss Wasserleonburg. This castle in southern Austria, all Florentine fountains and cosy wooden cottages, was owned by Count Paul Münster, a German with close ties to Mosley and the BUF. Bedaux and his wife Fern joined the newly-weds for part of their honeymoon.

Afterwards, George VI bestowed upon Edward the title of Duke of Windsor but refused to extend to the new Duchess of Windsor the rank of 'royal highness', and Edward was forbidden from ever returning to Britain. While living in France, the Duchess of Windsor employed the Parisian Nazi Armand Grégoire as her lawyer. French Intelligence described him as 'one the most dangerous of Nazi spies' and showed that he was also working as a lawyer for Ribbentrop and Hess.

In October 1937 the couple decided to visit Germany. The trip was organised by Fritz Wiedemann and Stephanie von Hohenlohe, with all the costs of their stay in Germany met by the German government. The couple, who were then staying in their luxurious nine-room hotel suite overlooking the Tuileries Gardens at the Hotel Meurice in Paris, would be the official guests of Robert Ley, the head of the German Labour Front (*Deutsche Arbeitsfront*). This organisation had replaced trade unions in Germany and had as its stated aim the registering of all Germans abroad to provide information for the Nazi Party organisation. Ley was a notorious drunk and embezzler who would eventually commit suicide while awaiting trial at Nuremberg in October 1945. Rothermere flew to Paris to try to persuade the couple to decline the invitation, but all to no avail. This was all deeply embarrassing for the British government and the royal family, but there was little they could do to prevent it. On 11 October 1937, the Duke and Duchess arrived on the Nord Express at the Friedrichstraße station, where they were greeted with as much pomp as if it had been a state visit. Strings of Union flags decorated the platform, interspersed with Nazi swastikas. Their first stop was the Death's Head Division of the Elite Squad of the SS training school in Pomerania, where they were greeted by an SS band playing the British national anthem. At one point, Ley, heavily intoxicated, had crashed their car into a gate post.

They also visited Göring's estate at Carinhall and later had dinner with Ribbentrop, Albert Speer and Joseph Goebbels, who wrote of the meeting in his diary; 'The Duke is wonderful – a nice sympathetic fellow who is open and clear and with a healthy understanding of people ... It is a shame he is no longer King. With him, we would have entered into an alliance.' On 19 October the Duke and Duchess had dinner in Nuremberg with the Duke of Saxe-Coburg and Gotha, who was a male-line grandson of Queen Victoria and Prince Albert.

The Duke and Duchess then met Hitler himself at the Berghof in the Obersalzberg on 22 October. To spite the British royal family, Hitler addressed the Duchess as 'Royal Highness'. Afterwards, Hitler gave them an affectionate farewell, taking both of their hands warmly, after which he stiffened and gave a rigid Nazi salute, which the Duke returned.

The Duke later wrote a thank you letter to Hitler in which he said:

Beim Verlassen Deutschlands danken die Herzogin von Windsor und ich Ihnenaufrichtig fur die grosse Gastfreundschaft, die Sie uns gawaehrt und

The Windsors after the Abdication

fur die wielen Moeglichkeiten das du zehen, was fuer das Wohl der Schaffend Deutschen Getan wird.

Wir nehmen einen tiefen Eindruck von unserer Reis durch Deutschland mit und werden nie vergessen, mit welcher Aufmerk amkeit wir von ihren Beauftragten ungeben worden sind, und eine wie heraliche Aufnahps wie uberall gefunden haben.

[On leaving Germany, the Duchess of Windsor and I sincerely thank you for the great hospitality you have shown us and for the many opportunities you have to show what is being done for the good of the working Germans.

We take with us a deep impression of our trip through Germany and will never forget the attention with which we were given by their representatives and found such a wonderful reception everywhere.]

The Windsors celebrated their first wedding anniversary on the yacht *Gulzar* with Hermann Rogers and his wife somewhere off the Amalfi coast. They had two expensive homes, one at 24 Boulevard Suchet in Paris and the other at the Château de la Croë in Cap d'Antibes. In Antibes, where Churchill was a frequent guest, they were attended by sixteen servants, including liveried footmen wearing scarlet coats with gold collars, cuffs and buttons.[1] When Churchill visited in August 1939, French Intelligence warned of a possible assassination plot against him. True or not, Churchill quickly packed his bags and went back to London.

Chamberlain declared that 'a state of war' now existed with Germany on 3 September 1939. The Duke and Duchess of Windsor quickly made their way back to Britain and arrived in Portsmouth ten days later to be met by a red carpet, but no royal welcome. Neither his mother, Queen Mary, nor his sister-in-law, Queen Elizabeth, would, on any account, receive the Duchess. The couple were even denied accommodation at the Palace and were forced to stay with the Metcalfes in Sussex, but they were met with loud cheers whenever they were recognised by the public. King George VI, eager to have Edward removed from public attention, contacted the Secretary of State for War, Leslie Hore-Belisha, and requested that Edward be found some employment abroad. He was assigned to the British Military Mission in Vincennes but had to waive his rank of field marshal and become a mere major general. The King, however, would not allow Edward to visit his former military commands accompanied by his wife. Throughout the whole of his stay in England, Edward had a single meeting with the King and none at all with any other member of the royal family.

The couple returned to France on 29 September, when Wallis went to Paris while Edward went to Nogent-sur-Marne to report to his new commander, Major General Sir Richard Howard-Vyse. Wallis became honorary president of the French relief organisation Colis de Trianon. Their respective work kept the couple apart for much of the Phoney War. On 28 May 1940, by his own request, Edward was transferred to an attachment with the Armée des Alpes on the Italian frontier so that Wallis could join him there. They rented a villa in Cap d'Antibes but when Mussolini brought Italy into the war on the side of Germany and the French were signing away their freedom at Vichy, it was thought prudent for the Duke and Duchess to move quickly.

They set out for the Spanish border on 19 June without visas and with no guarantee that the Spanish would not have them interned, with Spain hovering on the point of joining the Axis powers. At Perpignan they were halted by Spanish officials and refused entry. Edward hurriedly contacted the British ambassador at Madrid and the Spanish consul at Bordeaux, and eventually was allowed to pass at 1800 on 20 June, then set up in a luxury hotel in Barcelona. When he became aware of this, the German ambassador, Eberhard von Stohrer, telegraphed Ribbentrop for advice, saying: 'We might perhaps be interested in detaining the Duke of Windsor here and eventually establishing contact with him.' Ribbentrop replied immediately: 'Is it possible to detain the Duke and Duchess in Spain for a couple of weeks to begin with before they are granted an exit visa? It would be necessary to ensure, at all events, that it did not appear in any way that the suggestion came from Germany.'[2] At the same time Ribbentrop sent a telegram to General Franco's foreign minister, Colonel Juan Beigbeder y Atienza, requesting that the Windsors be detained in Spain as long as possible. Beigbeder offered Edward a chance to stay in Spain indefinitely as a guest of the Spanish government at a romantic Moorish palace in Andalusia.

In conversation with Alexander Weddell, the US Ambassador to Spain, Edward said: 'The most important thing to be done now was to end the war before thousands more were killed or maimed to save the faces of a few politicians.' Understandably, the British government was getting very nervous about Edward's public statements and worried about possible intrigues involving Edward and Wallis. They requested that they return to England, but Edward was adamant that he would not do so unless both he and Wallis were received back into the royal fold, which seemed very unlikely to happen. The Palace had received intelligence that: 'Germans expect assistance from Duke and Duchess of Windsor. Latter desiring at any price to become Queen. Germans have been negotiating with her since June 27th.' Edward, meanwhile, had moved to Madrid and had been in touch with both the German and Italian Embassies there, anxious to ensure that their two properties in France were protected from looting.

There was an intense three-way conversation between the Palace, Churchill and Edward over a possible return to England for the royal couple. Edward was adamant that Wallis had to be accepted at the Palace but the Queen was equally adamant that she would never agree to that. Jealous of his brother's popularity with the public, King George was equally opposed to Edward returning to England, fearing that it might diminish his own status and authority. Churchill pleaded for reconciliation without success and Edward became even more embittered towards the country that he had once served as King. For his part, the Prime Minister became seriously concerned that the people Edward and Wallis were socialising with in Spain were, if not pro-German, certainly anti-English. It was becoming a conundrum to know what to do about them.

On 1 July, Edward's younger brother, the Duke of Kent, completed an official visit to Lisbon and returned home, leaving the way clear for Edward to move to Portugal. Ribbentrop was informed at midnight on 2 July that Edward and Wallis had moved to Lisbon and flew into a rage. The British embassy in Lisbon arranged for the Windsors to stay at the Boca do Inferno, or Mouth of Hell. It was an isolated but beautiful seaside villa owned by a Portuguese banker named Ricardo Espirito Santo Silva. This man was a close friend of the German Minister in Lisbon, and though he had strong English as well as German connections and had entertained the Duke of Kent on his recent visit, British Intelligence was increasingly coming to regard him as pro-German. Throughout his stay in Portugal, the Duke was constantly under the surveillance of MI6 and the British Embassy did everything to see to it that the couple had no contact with the local British community. It was vital that as little as possible was written about them in the local press and that there was never any suggestion that their visit had political significance.

Then Edward received a telegram from Churchill that appeared to threaten him with court martial if he did not return to England immediately: 'Your Royal Highness has taken active military rank and refusal to obey direct orders of competent military authority would create a serious situation. I hope it will not be necessary for such orders to be sent. I must strongly urge immediate compliance with wishes of the Government.' Two flying boats of RAF Coastal Command were waiting in the Tagus to take the couple back to England. Edward replied furiously: 'You threatened me with what amounted to arrest, thus descending to dictator methods in your treatment of your old friend and former King,'[3] but agreed without conditions. On the following day, however, the situation changed dramatically. Edward received a telegram from the Foreign Office telling him that he was being offered the position of Governor and Commander-in-Chief of the Bahamas. After some consideration, Edward replied that he would accept the posting. German and Italian observers took this as a sure sign that the Duke was in disgrace and Ribbentrop planned to take advantage by hatching up a plot to kidnap the royals.

On 11 July he sent a top-secret telegram to Stohrer: 'We are especially interested in having the Duke of Windsor return to Spain at all events,' it said. It went on:

> We are ... convinced that [British agents] will try to get him out of Lisbon as soon as possible [but] we may be able to get him back into Spanish territory without further trouble ... After their return to Spain the Duke and Duchess must be persuaded or compelled to remain on Spanish soil. For the latter eventuality we would have to secure the agreement of the Spanish Government to the internment of the Duke under the neutrality regulations for as a British officer and a member of the British Expeditionary Force the Duke could be arrested as a deserting military refugee ... When the time comes you will receive more detailed instructions in this matter.'[4]

Ribbentrop's plan involved, first of all, persuading the Duke that it was safer for him to return to Spain and once there to have him held against his will if necessary. Then, when he was there, he would be approached by a German emissary, who would advise Edward to hold himself in readiness to play a role if Germany and Britain got down to discussing peace terms. Whatever Ribbentrop's intentions, it seems that he discussed his plan with Hitler, who personally sanctioned it and was consulted at every stage. Edward was to be approached by a reliable Spanish confidential emissary who had been a friend of the Duke for a long time. This person would request the Duke and Duchess to return to Spain for a short time so that the Interior Minister could discuss with him certain questions regarding Spanish–English relations.

Wallis, meantime, was preoccupied with retrieving from her Paris and Antibes homes possessions that had been left behind during their hurried departure. Edward was conscripted to help and made an appeal to Beigbeder to instead send a Spanish agent to Lisbon for discussions. This turned out to be Tiger Bermejillo, who stayed with the Windsors for five days, during which time they all discussed ways and means of retrieving their possessions. It was decided to send one of their maids, Mademoiselle Moulichon, to Paris, where she might arrange to have a number of items packaged and sent on to them in Portugal. Edward had been travelling with quite a large sum in cash but his French bank account was frozen and his liquid assets in London were unavailable to him. Bermejillo also warned the Duke against taking up the Bahamas post, which he said was beneath the Duke's dignity and dangerous to boot. He advised Edward that he would be much safer in Spain. Stohrer then sent a telegram to Ribbentrop saying: 'The Duke of Windsor through the confidential emissary of the Foreign Minister has again expressed thanks for co-operation in the matter of his house in Paris ... I recommend that the wish of the Duke and Duchess be fulfilled since, if necessary, the maid's journey to Paris and above all the return journey to Lisbon could be held up by us as required in order to postpone further their departure [to the Bahamas].'[5]

Now enters the Machiavellian German Intelligence officer Walter Schellenberg, who was called in to see Ribbentrop regarding the situation of the Duke and Duchess. Ribbentrop had discussed the matter with Hitler, who was confident that Edward was sympathetic to Germany and would welcome the opportunity to 'escape from his present environment'. Much of what is known about Schellenberg's involvement in the plot is derived from his own testimony made after the war and must be treated with circumspection given the way he tended to rewrite history. According to Schellenberg, Ribbentrop told him to be prepared to 'circumvent British plans [to have Edward returned to England], if need be, by the use of force' and have him relocated to Switzerland, where a large sum of money would be made available to him. Schellenberg went back and told his intelligence chief, Reinhard Heydrich, about the meeting with Ribbentrop. Heydrich had no time for Ribbentrop and was contemptuous of the whole plan. Furthermore, he expected that any plan concocted by Ribbentrop would be prone to disaster, so he advised Schellenberg not to take it too seriously and, just to be on the safe side, to take a couple of 'reliable and experienced men' with him.[6]

Edward was in limbo, dithering between angling for an arrangement that would allow him to return to England and delaying any move to have him sent to the Bahamas. He confided to an old friend, Don Miguel Primo de Rivera, that he felt like a prisoner surrounded by spies, apparently unaware that he was now quite literally surrounded by spies. Don Miguel tried to persuade Edward to return to Spain as soon as possible, hinting that he had heard the British were planning to kidnap him. In Spain, he would be much safer, he said and suggested a plan whereby he might go there without the knowledge of either the British or Portuguese authorities. Edward and Wallis would go on a hunting trip to Guarda close to the Spanish border, but once there they would quietly slip over the border into Spain to Ciudad Rodrigo. Schellenberg flew to Madrid on 25 July, where he met Stohrer and he brought him up to date on the situation. He then flew to Lisbon on the following day, where the German ambassador Dr Oswald Baron von Hoyningen-Huene told him that Edward was rumoured to have shown 'dissatisfaction about his situation' but there was no certainty about the extent to which he was willing to do anything about it. Von Hoyningen-Huene confided to Schellenberg that he had no confidence in any plan to coerce the Duke into moving to Spain but when he was told that Hitler had authorised it he agreed to render all assistance he could. Agents were infiltrated on to the Duke's staff at Boca do Inferno and kept Schellenberg informed of movements and conversations within the household. He made certain that Edward was made aware of rumours British Intelligence was planning unspecified operations against the royal couple that endangered them.

Schellenberg made secret arrangements with the Portuguese–Spanish border police to effect the handover at Vilar Formoso and Fuentes de Oñoro on the Spanish–Portuguese border since the Duke and Duchess would have no entry visas. With stories of kidnappings, frustration of continued rejection from his family and entreaties from the British government, the atmosphere at Boca do Inferno became stifling. On top of that, Edward was constrained from making any decision while Wallis was still preoccupied with getting her personal effects brought from their French residences. Mademoiselle Moulichon had not been heard from since she left. While not really addressing any of the issues, Edward decided to move into Hotel Aviz in Lisbon, which, quite unbeknown to him, was an establishment much utilised by British Intelligence. When Schellenberg heard about this he intensified his whispering campaign, getting various people around the couple to suggest that that once in the Aviz, the

The Windsors after the Abdication

Windsors would be at the mercy of Churchill, whom, they would be told, had hostile intentions towards them. They were left to imagine for themselves what that might mean.

Don Miguel had written to Edward on 24 July with a warning about 'something of extreme gravity which directly affects the personal safety of Your Highness and that of the Duchess, should you manifest an opinion or act in some way contrary to a decision of the British Government. It is a danger which can become a reality not only in the Bahamas but also in Portugal.' He went on to outline the arrangements, careful to avoid any mention of German involvement, whereby the Duke would travel to Guarda via Estoril and Coimbra with all the accoutrements of hunting such as guns and fishing apparel and once there he would meet them, apparently by chance, in the middle of the village before crossing the border into Spain. The Duke, however, prevaricated and met Sir Walter Monckton, who had flown in on 28 July with a message from Churchill urging him to take up his appointment in the Bahamas without delay, but warning him to avoid expressing 'views about the war and the general situation which are not out of harmony with those of His Majesty's Government'. Churchill signed off 'Your faithful and devoted servant'.[7] It is probable that Monckton, at the same time, informally told the Duke of suspected German plots to kidnap him.

Schellenberg became convinced that the Duke had no intention of accepting the preposterous hunting invitation but was seriously concerned by the attentions of British Intelligence and was still against taking up his new role in the Bahamas. Neither was he happy about living either in a neutral or an enemy country. His forlorn hope was for King George to relent and allow him and Wallis to return to England but there was no sign of that happening and his mistrust of British intentions was deepening. He wrote to Churchill despondently, 'the King and Queen do not wish to bring our family differences to an end, without which I could not accept a post in Great Britain'. Of all the options, the Bahamas one was starting to look like the best of a bad bunch. Edward, however, had been left to arrange his own transport to Nassau and so made enquiries of the American Export Line for passage to New York on the American packet steamer *Excalibur*, which was due to leave Lisbon on 1 August.

Both the British and US governments were concerned at the prospect of Edward setting foot on American soil and attracting a great deal of unwanted media attention, unwanted by the governments at least. The prospect of an indiscrete remark by the Duke or the opportunity for the

American press to splash his and Wallis' picture all over the front pages was not appealing to them. A compromise was reached whereby the vessel would call at Bermuda en route to New York and the royal couple would disembark and go on to Nassau from there. The Duke was livid at being 'messed about with' and threatened to 'reconsider [his] position'.[8] He was adamant that Wallis had to go to New York 'for medical reasons' and they would expect to stay there for some time before carrying on to the Bahamas. However, in the end, he had no choice but agree to the government's plan, but confided to a friend that he '[viewed] the prospect of an indefinite period of exile on those islands with profound gloom and despondency'.

After a couple of weeks during which the Duke showed no signs of preparing for his hunting trip, Ribbentrop contacted Schellenberg to say that Hitler was getting bored with the idea and had ordered an immediate abduction of the couple. Schellenberg said that he suspected it was Ribbentrop's idea alone and privately considered it madness to try. He now decided to arrange things to convince his superiors that the plan was completely impractical. The next day, Schellenberg arranged with Portuguese police that they increase the guard around the Duke's residence. When he reported to Berlin that security had been tightened, the reply to him was that he was 'responsible for measures suitable to the occasion'.[9]

He felt that in order to come out of the episode with some credibility, Schellenberg was ready to make one last effort to prevent Edward and Wallis sailing on 1 August. The Duke had reconciled himself to the Bahamas posting. He made arrangements on 31 July for his departure on *Excalibur* and gave an eve-of-departure dinner for his Portuguese friends at the Hotel Aviz. A new maid and Detective Sergeant Harold Holder of Special Branch, who would accompany them to the Bahamas, arrived by flying boat. Unfortunately, that same morning Mademoiselle Moulichon was detained by SS officers in Paris and sent to stay with her widowed mother in the Nièvre. She would eventually arrive in the Bahamas at the end of November. When the Sud Express train arrived in Lisbon at noon on 1 August, the much-awaited Parisian possessions were not on it.

The royal couple sailed into Nassau on 18 August and stepped onto British soil for the first time since 1936. The tone of their stay would be set when, at a luncheon laid on by the Royal Bermuda Yacht Club, in what Edward considered to be a deliberate snub, none of the wives curtsied to the Duchess.

Appendix

Edward's Abdication Statement

At long last I am able to say a few words of my own. I have never wanted to withhold anything, but until now it has not been constitutionally possible for me to speak.

A few hours ago I discharged my last duty as King and Emperor, and now that I have been succeeded by my brother, the Duke of York, my first words must be to declare my allegiance to him. This I do with all my heart.

You all know the reasons which have impelled me to renounce the throne. But I want you to understand that in making up my mind I did not forget the country or the empire, which, as Prince of Wales and lately as King, I have for twenty-five years tried to serve.

But you must believe me when I tell you that I have found it impossible to carry the heavy burden of responsibility and to discharge my duties as King as I would wish to do without the help and support of the woman I love.

And I want you to know that the decision I have made has been mine and mine alone. This was a thing I had to judge entirely for myself. The other person most nearly concerned has tried up to the last to persuade me to take a different course.

I have made this, the most serious decision of my life, only upon the single thought of what would, in the end, be best for all.

This decision has been made less difficult to me by the sure knowledge that my brother, with his long training in the public affairs of this country and with his fine qualities, will be able to take my place forthwith without interruption or injury to the life and progress of the empire. And he has one matchless blessing, enjoyed by so many of you, and not bestowed on me – a happy home with his wife and children.

During these hard days I have been comforted by Her Majesty my mother and by my family. The ministers of the crown, and in particular, Mr Baldwin, the Prime Minister, have always treated me with full consideration. There has never been any constitutional difference between me and them, and between me and Parliament. Bred in the constitutional tradition by my father, I should never have allowed any such issue to arise.

Ever since I was Prince of Wales, and later on when I occupied the throne, I have been treated with the greatest kindness by all classes of the people wherever I have lived or journeyed throughout the empire. For that I am very grateful.

I now quit altogether public affairs and I lay down my burden. It may be some time before I return to my native land, but I shall always follow the fortunes of the British race and empire with profound interest, and if at any time in the future I can be found of service to His Majesty in a private station, I shall not fail.

And now, we all have a new King. I wish him and you, his people, happiness and prosperity with all my heart. God bless you all! God save the King.

Notes

Introduction
1. Paxton, Robert O., *The Anatomy of Fascism* (Harmondsworth, 2005), p. 6.

Chapter 1: The Radical Right in Britain Before 1914
1. Thurlow, Richard, *Fascism in Britain: A history 1918–1985* (Basil Blackwell, 1987), p. 8.
2. Linehan, Thomas, Norman, *British Fascism, 1918–1939* (Manchester University Press, 2000), p. 91.
3. Bloom, Cecil, 'The Politics of Immigration, 1881–1905' (*Jewish Historical Studies*, Vol. 33, pp. 187–214, 1992), p. 189.

Chapter 2: The Emergence of Fascism in Italy and Germany
1. Gentile, Emilio, *Storia del partito fascista 1919–1922* (Cultura Storica, 2021), p. 496.
2. Paxton, Robert O., *The Anatomy of Fascism* (Harmondsworth, 2005), p. 28.
3. Corni, Gustavo, 'Fascism and the Radical Right' (*International Encyclopedia of the First World War*, 2015), p. 6.
4. Griffiths, Richard, *Fellow Travellers of the Right: British Enthusiasts for Nazi Germany* (Kindle edition).

Chapter 3: British Fascist Movements in the 1920s
1. Darwin J.G., 'The Fear of Falling: British Politics and Imperial Decline Since 1900' (*Royal Historical Society* Vol. 36, 1986), p. 34.
2. Ibid., p. 41.
3. Griffiths Richard, *Fellow Travellers of the Right: British Enthusiasts for Nazi Germany* (Kindle edition).
4. Gottlieb Julie V., 'Body Fascism in Britain: Building the Blackshirt in the Interwar Period' (*Contemporary European History*, Vol. 20, No. 2, 2011), p. 16.
5. Linehan, p. 61.
6. Gottlieb, Julie V., *Feminine Fascism*, (Bloomsbury Publishing, Kindle Edition), p. 14.
7. Linehan, p. 65.
8. Gottlieb, Julie V., *Feminine Fascism*, p. 19.
9. Linehan, p. 69.
10. Griffiths, Richard, *Patriotism Perverted Captain Ramsay: the Right Club and British anti-Semitism 1939–1940* (Kindle edition).
11. Brustein, William A. and King, Ryan D., 'Anti-Semitism in Europe Before the Holocaust' (*International Political Science Review*, Vol. 25, No. 1, 2004), p. 39.
12. Griffiths, Richard, *Patriotism Perverted* (Kindle edition).

13. Griffiths, Richard, *Fellow Travellers of the Right* (Kindle edition).
14. Linehan, p. 71.
15. Thurlow, p. 71.
16. Linehan, p. 77.
17. Ibid.
18. Thurlow, p. 58.
19. Darwin, p. 37.

Chapter 4: The Suffragette Movement and Fascism
1. Riddell, Fern, *Death in Ten Minutes: The forgotten life of radical suffragette Kitty Marion* (Hodder & Stoughton, 2018), p. 137.
2. Webb, Simon, *Suffragette Fascists* (Pen & Sword, 2020), p. 131.
3. Ibid., p. 66.
4. Crawford, Elizabeth, *The Women's Suffrage Movement: A Reference Guide 1866–1928* (Routledge, 1999), p. 597.
5. Richardson, Mary S., *Laugh a Defiance* (Weidenfeld & Nicolson, 1953), p. 168.
6. *The Blackshirt* (29 June 1934).
7. *The Times* (14 August 1918).
8. Pugh, Martin, *Why Former Suffragettes Flocked to British Fascism* (slate.com).
9. Newsinger, p. 836.

Chapter 5: British Press Coverage of Nazi Germany in the 1930s
1. Dack, Janet Elizabeth, *In from the Cold? British Fascism and the Mainstream Press 1925–1939* (Teesside University, 2010), p. 284.
2. Kershaw, Ian, *Making Friends with Hitler: Lord Londonderry and Britain's Road to War* (Kindle edition).
3. McDonough, Frank, 'The Times, Norman Ebbut and the Nazis, 1927–37' (*Journal of Contemporary History*, Vol. 27, No. 3, 1992), p. 409.
4. Griffiths, Richard, *Fellow Travellers of the Right* (Kindle edition).
5. McDonough, p. 411.
6. Galbraith, Kylie, *From Our Own Correspondent: The British Press and Nazi Germany, 1933–1939* (University of Adelaide, 2017), p. 25.
7. McDonough, p. 415.
8. Shirer, William, *Berlin Diary* (Alfred A. Knopf, 1941), p. 42.
9. Galbraith, p. 197.
10. Dack, p. 279.

Chapter 6: Lord Rothermere
1. Gannon, F.R., *The British Press and Germany 1936–1939* (Oxford, 1971), p. 25.
2. Griffiths, Richard, *Fellow Travellers of the Right* (Kindle edition).
3. Wilson, Jim, *Nazi Princess: Hitler, Lord Rothermere and Princess Stefanie Von Hohenlohe* (Kindle edition).
4. Palmer, p. 128.
5. Wilson.
6. Ibid.
7. Kershaw.

Notes

8. Pugh, Martin, 'The British Union of Fascists and the Olympia Debate' (*The Historical Journal*, Vol. 41, No. 2, 1998), p. 48.
9. Wilson.

Chapter 7: Nazi Camp Followers

1. Griffiths, Richard, *Fellow Travellers of the Right* (Kindle edition).
2. Ibid.
3. Spicer, Charles, *Ambulant Amateurs: the rise and fade of the Anglo-German Fellowship* (University of London, 2018), p. 17.
4. Griffiths, Richard, *Fellow Travellers of the Right* (Kindle edition).
5. Ibid.
6. Spicer, p. 73.
7. Ibid., p. 72.
8. Griffiths, Richard, *Fellow Travellers of the Right* (Kindle edition).
9. Ibid.
10. Dorril, p. 263.
11. Griffiths, Richard, *Fellow Travellers of the Right* (Kindle edition).
12. Ibid.
13. Chesterton, p. 202.
14. Dorril, p. 418.
15. Belloc, Hillaire, *The Cruise of the Nona* (Constable and Co., 1947), p. 164.
16. Shirer, p. 256.
17. Lewis, David Stephen, *Illusions of Grandeur: Mosley, Fascism, and British Society, 1931–1981* (Manchester University Press, 1987), p. 5.
18. Mosse, George L., *The Fascist Revolutionaries: Towards a General Theory of Fascism* (Howard Fertig, 1999), p. 42.
19. Griffiths, Richard, *Fellow Travellers of the Right* (Kindle edition).
20. Chandler, Andrew, *British Christians and the Third Reich* (Cambridge University Press, 2022), p. 97.
21. Ibid., p. 193.
22. Tate, Tim, *Hitler's British Traitors* (Icon Books, 2019), p. 53.
23. Ibid., p. 115.
24. Ibid., p. 120.
25. *London Review of Books*, 19 January 2023, p. 13.
26. Ibid.
27. Griffiths, Richard, *Fellow Travellers of the Right* (Kindle edition).
28. *London Review of Books*, 19 January 2023, p. 14.
29. Griffiths, Richard, *Fellow Travellers of the Right* (Kindle edition).
30. Thurlow, p. 142.
31. Tate, p. 188.
32. Griffiths, Richard, *Fellow Travellers of the Right* (Kindle edition).

Chapter 8: The Mitford Sisters

1. Lovell, Mary S., *The Mitford Girls: The Biography of an Extraordinary Family* (Abacus, 2002), p. 147.
2. Mosley, Diana, *A Life of Contrasts* (Gibson Square Books, 2017), p. 121.

3. Lovell, p. 147.
4. Ibid., p. 176.
5. Mosley, p. 108.
6. Lovell, p. 216.
7. Ibid., p. 274.
8. Dorrill, p. 386.
9. Pryce-Jones, David, *Unity Mitford: An Enquiry into Her Life and the Frivolity of Evil* (Dial Press, 1997), p. 76.
10. Lovell, p. 121.
11. Ibid., p. 133.
12. Mosley, p. 106.
13. Lovell, p. 190.
14. Young, p. 23.
15. Lovell, p. 205.
16. Palmer, p. 128.
17. Guinness, Jonathan, *The House of Mitford* (Weidenfeld & Nicolson, 2015), p. 424.
18. Lovell, p. 307.
19. Ibid., p. 328.
20. Ibid., p. 334.

Chapter 9: The Cliveden Set
1. Rose, Norman, *The Cliveden Set* (Kindle edition).
2. Ibid.
3. Ibid.
4. Young, p. 45.
5. Rose.
6. Ibid.
7. Young, p. 48.
8. Rose.
9. Ibid.
10. Ibid.

Chapter 10: Oswald Mosley and the British Union of Fascists
1. Gottlieb, Julie V., *Feminine Fascism*, p. 186.
2. Mosley, p. 122.
3. Dorrill, Stephen M., *Blackshirt: Sir Oswald Mosley and British Fascism* (Viking, 2006), p. 187.
4. Gottlieb, Julie V., *Feminine Fascism*, p. 144.
5. Ibid., p. 115.
6. Ibid., p. 43.
7. Ibid., p. 52.
8. Thurlow, p. 93.
9. Gottlieb, Julie V., *Feminine Fascism*, p. 123.
10. Newsinger, p. 829.
11. Cullen, p. 247.
12. Thurlow, p. 96.

Notes

13. Gottlieb, Julie V., 'Body Fascism in Britain', p. 189.
14. Public Records Office, HO 144/20142.
15. Barnes, p. 129.
16. Ibid., p. 132.
17. Ibid., p. 131.

Chapter 11: Olympia

1. Public Records Office *PRO HO 144/20140, 674, 216/66*.
2. Pugh, Martin, 'The British Union of Fascists and the Olympia Debate', p. 53.
3. Piratin, Paul, *Our Flag Stays Red* (Lawrence & Wishart Ltd, 2007), p. 8.
4. Newsinger, p. 829.
5. Thurlow, p. 103.

Chapter 12: Mosley after Olympia

1. Benewick, Robert, *Political Violence and Public Order* (Allen Lane, 1969) p. 152.
2. Newsinger, John, 'Blackshirts, Blueshirts, and the Spanish Civil War' (*The Historical Journal*, Vol. 44, No. 32, 2001), p. 832.
3. Chesterton, Arthur Kenneth, *Portrait of a Leader* (Action Press, 1937), p. 126.
4. Dorrill, p. 368.
5. Copsey, Nigel, *Anti-Fascism in Britain* (Routledge, 2016), p. 171.
6. Steel, Peta, *The Battle of Cable Street* (Sertuc, 2017), p. 8.
7. Dorrill, p. 384.
8. Steel, p. 11.
9. Cullen, Stephen M., 'Political Violence: The Case of the British Union of Fascists' (*Journal of Contemporary History*, Vol. 28, No. 2, 1993), p. 263.
10. Linehan, p. 99.
11. Tate, p. 220.
12. Gottlieb, Julie V., 'Body Fascism in Britain', p. 69.
13. Dorrill, p. 250.
14. Love, Gary, '"What's the Big Idea?": Oswald Mosley, the British Union of Fascists and Generic Fascism' (*Journal of Contemporary History*, Vol. 42, No. 3, 2007), p. 453.
15. Dorrill, p. 406.
16. Love, p. 455.
17. Keeley, Thomas Norman, *Blackshirts Torn: Inside the British Union of Fascists, 1932–1940* (Simon Fraser University, 1995), p. 78.
18. Ibid., p. 81.
19. Public Records Office, HO 144/21060, 692, 242/20.
20. Public Records Office, HO 144/20142, 674, 216.
21. Gottlieb, Julie V., *Feminine Fascism*, p. 59.
22. Newsinger, p. 837.
23. Dorrill, p. 442.
24. Ibid., p. 448.
25. Gottlieb, Julie V., *Feminine Fascism*, p. 59.
26. Dorrill, p. 450.
27. Quinlan, p. 124.
28. Dorrill, p. 492.

29. Ibid., p. 490.
30. Hansard, Vol. 117 cc. 247–68.
31. Dorrill, p. 497.

Chapter 13: The British Legion

1. Barnes James J. and Patience P. Barnes, *Nazis in Pre-War London 1930–1939* (Sussex Academic Press, 2010), p. 153.
2. Ibid., p. 150.
3. Ibid., p. 149.
4. Ibid., p. 151.
5. Ibid., p. 157.
6. Ibid., p. 160.

Chapter 14: Edward VIII and Mrs Simpson

1. Palmer, Dean, *Tea with Hitler* (The History Press, 2022), p. 104.
2. Ibid., p. 109.
3. Young, Lauren, *Hitler's Girl* (Kindle edition), p. 25.
4. Griffiths, Richard, *Fellow Travellers of the Right* (Kindle edition), p. 51.
5. Spicer, p. 8.
6. Palmer, p. 115.
7. Rhodes, J., *Chips: The Diaries of Sir Henry Channon* (Weidenfeld & Nicolson, 1967), p. 41.
8. Palmer, p. 128.
9. Morton, Andrew, *17 Carnations: The Windsors, the Nazis and the Cover-up* (Michael O'Mara Books, 2015), p. 79.
10. Phillips, Adrian, *The King Who Had To Go: Edward VIII, Mrs Simpson and the Hidden Politics of the Abdication Crisis* (Biteback Publishing, 2018), p. 186.
11. Dorrill, p. 404.
12. Palmer, p. 152.
13. Higham, Charles, *Mrs Simpson: Secret Lives of the Duchess of Windsor* (Sidgwick and Jackson, 2005), p. 185.

Chapter 15: Lord Londonderry

1. Londonderry Marques of, *Wings of Destiny* (Macmillan & Co., 1943), p. 156.
2. Kershaw.

Chapter 16: Sir Barry Domvile

1. Connolly, Martin, *Hitler's Munich Man: The Fall of Admiral Sir Barry Domvile* (Pen & Sword, 2017), p. 20.
2. Domvile, Barry, *By and Large* (Hutchinson and Co., 1936), p. 233.
3. Tate, p. 53.
4. Connolly, p. 97.
5. Soukupová, Martina, *The British Pro-German Organisation The Link on the Eve of The World War II* (Charles University, 2017), p. 11.
6. Spicer, p. 33.
7. Connolly, p. 60.

8. Tate, p. 57.
9. Ibid., p. 55.
10. Connolly, p. 57.
11. Ibid., p. 59.
12. Soukupová, p. 15.
13. Tate, p. 191.
14. Ibid., p. 196.
15. Ibid., p. 202.
16. Ibid.
17. Connolly, p. 84.
18. Ibid., p. 64.
19. Thurlow, p. 206.
20. Tate, p. 257.
21. Ibid., p. 42.

Chapter 17: Archibald Maule Ramsay and the Right Club

1. Griffiths, Richard, *Patriotism Perverted* (Kindle edition).
2. Ibid.
3. Thurlow, p. 79.
4. Young, p. 38.
5. Ramsay, A.H.M., *The Nameless War* (Britons Publishing Society, 1952), p. 83.
6. Tate, p. 37
7. Quinlan, Kevin, *The Secret War Between the Wars* (Boydell & Brewer, 2014), p. 90.
8. Ibid., p. 115.
9. Thurlow, p. 193.
10. Tate, p. 172.
11. Thurlow, p. 189.
12. Brinson, Charmian and Dove, Richard, *A Matter of Intelligence* (Manchester University Press, 2014), p. 100.
13. Thurlow, p. 207.

Chapter 18: The Windsors after the Abdication

1. Palmer, p. 192.
2. Bloch, Michael, *Operation Willi: The Plot to Kidnap the Duke of Windsor, July 1940* (Kindle edition).
3. Ibid.
4. Ibid.
5. Ibid.
6. Schellenberg, Walter, *The Schellenberg Memoirs: A Record of the Nazi Secret Service* (Kindle edition).
7. Bloch.
8. Ibid.
9. Schellenberg.

Bibliography

Barnes, James J. and Patience P. Barnes, *Nazis in Pre-War London 1930–1939* (Sussex Academic Press, 2010).
Belloc, Hillaire, *The Cruise of the Nona* (Constable and Co., 1947).
Benewick, Robert, *Political Violence and Public Order* (Allen Lane, 1969).
Bloch, Michael, *Operation Willi: The Plot to Kidnap the Duke of Windsor, July 1940* (Little Brown Book Group, Kindle edition, 1984).
Bloom, Cecil, 'The Politics of Immigration, 1881–1905' (*Jewish Historical Studies*, 33, pp. 187–214, 1992).
Brinson, Charmian and Dove, Richard, *A Matter of Intelligence* (Manchester University Press, 2014).
Brustein, William A. and King, Ryan D., 'Anti-Semitism in Europe Before the Holocaust' (*International Political Science Review*, Vol. 25, No. 1, 2004).
Chandler, Andrew, *British Christians and the Third Reich* (Cambridge University Press, 2022).
Chesterton, Arthur Kenneth, *Portrait of a Leader* (Action Press, 1937).
Clough, Bryan, *State Secrets: The Kent-Wolkoff Affair* (Hideaway Publications, 2005).
Connolly, Martin, *Hitler's Munich Man: The Fall of Admiral Sir Barry Domvile* (Pen and Sword, 2017).
Copsey, Nigel, *Anti-Fascism in Britain* (Routledge, 2016).
Copsey, Nigel and Tilles, Daniel, *Uniting a Divided Community? Re-appraising Jewish Responses to British Fascist Antisemitism, 1932–1939* (Holocaust Studies).
Corni, Gustavo, 'Fascism and the Radical Right' (*International Encyclopedia of the First World War*, 2015).
Crawford, Elizabeth, *The Women's Suffrage Movement: A Reference Guide 1866–1928* (Routledge, 1999).
Cullen, Stephen M., 'Political Violence: The Case of the British Union of Fascists' (*Journal of Contemporary History*, Vol. 28, No. 2, 1993).
Dack, Janet Elizabeth, *In from the Cold? British Fascism and the Mainstream Press 1925–1939* (Teesside University, 2010).
Darwin, J.G., 'The Fear of Falling: British Politics and Imperial Decline Since 1900' (*Royal Historical Society*, Vol. 36, 1986).
Domvile, Barry, *By and Large* (Hutchinson and Co., 1936).
Dorril, Stephen, *Blackshirt: Sir Oswald Mosley and British Fascism* (Viking, 2006).
Fleming, N.C., 'Diehard Conservatives and the Appeasement of Nazi Germany, 1935–1940' (*Journal of the Historical Association*, 2015).
Galbraith, Kylie, *From Our Own Correspondent: The British Press and Nazi Germany, 1933–1939* (University of Adelaide, 2017).

Gannon, F.R., *The British Press and Germany 1936–1939* (Oxford, 1971).
Gentile, Emilio, *Storia del partito fascista 1919–1922* (Cultura Storica, 2021).
Godfrey, Rupert, *Letters from a Prince: Edward, Prince of Wales to Mrs Freda Dudley Ward* (Little Brown & Co., 1998).
Gottlieb, Julie V., 'Body Fascism in Britain: Building the Blackshirt in the Interwar Period' (*Contemporary European History*, Vol. 20, No. 2, 2011).
Gottlieb, Julie V., *Feminine Fascism* (Bloomsbury Publishing, Kindle edition).
Griffiths, Richard, *Fellow Travellers of the Right: British Enthusiasts for Nazi Germany* (Kindle edition).
Griffiths, Richard, *Patriotism Perverted: Captain Ramsay, the Right Club and British anti-Semitism 1939–1940* (Kindle edition).
Guinness, Jonathan, *The House of Mitford* (Weidenfeld & Nicolson, 2015).
Heyen-Dubé, Thomas, 'Fascism, War and the British Officer Class: The Case of Robert Gordon-Canning' (*War & Society*, Vol. 40, 2021).
Higham, Charles, *Mrs Simpson: Secret Lives of the Duchess of Windsor* (Sidgwick and Jackson, 2005).
Kean, Hilda, 'Some problems of constructing and reconstructing a suffragette's life: Mary Richardson, suffragette, socialist and fascist' (*Women's History Review*, Vol. 7, No. 4, 1998).
Keeley, Thomas Norman, *Blackshirts Torn: Inside the British Union of Fascists, 1932–1940* (Simon Fraser University, 1995).
Kershaw, Ian, *Making Friends with Hitler: Lord Londonderry and Britain's Road to War* (Kindle edition).
Lebzelter, Gisela C., *Political Anti-Semitism in Britain 1918–1939* (Oxford University Press, 1978).
Lewis, David Stephen, *Illusions of Grandeur: Mosley, Fascism, and British Society, 1931–1981* (Manchester University Press, 1987).
Linehan, Thomas, *British Fascism, 1918–1939* (Manchester University Press. Kindle Edition, 2000).
Londonderry, Marquess of, *Wings of Destiny* (Macmillan & Co., 1943).
Love, Gary, '"What's the Big Idea?": Oswald Mosley, the British Union of Fascists and Generic Fascism' (*Journal of Contemporary History*, Vol. 42(3), 2007).
Lovell, Mary S., *The Mitford Girls: The Biography of an Extraordinary Family* (Abacus, 2002).
McDonough, Frank, 'The Times, Norman Ebbut and the Nazis, 1927–37' (*Journal of Contemporary History*, Vol. 27, No. 3, 1992).
Miller, Joan, *One Girl's War* (Mount Eagle Publications, 1986).
Morton, Andrew, *17 Carnations: The Windsors, the Nazis and the Cover-up* (Michael O'Mara Books, 2015).
Morton, Andrew, *Wallis in Love: The untold true passion of the Duchess of Windsor* (Michael O'Mara Books, 2018).
Mosley, Diana, *A Life of Contrasts* (Gibson Square Books, 2017).
Mosse, G.L., *The Fascist Revolutionaries: Towards a General Theory of Fascism* (Howard Fertig, 1999).
Mosse, G.L., *Fallen Soldiers: Reshaping the Memory of the World Wars* (New York, 1990).
Newsinger, John, 'Blackshirts, Blueshirts, and the Spanish Civil War' (*The Historical Journal*, Vol. 44, No. 32, 2001).

Bibliography

Palmer, Dean, *Tea with Hitler* (The History Press, 2022).
Paxton, Robert O., *The Anatomy of Fascism* (Harmondsworth, 2005).
Phillips, Adrian, *The King Who Had To Go: Edward VIII, Mrs Simpson and the Hidden Politics of the Abdication Crisis* (Biteback Publishing, 2018).
Piratin, Phil, *Our Flag Stays Red* (Lawrence & Wishart Ltd, 2007).
Pryce-Jones, David, *Unity Mitford: An Enquiry into Her Life and the Frivolity of Evil* (Dial Press, 1977).
Pugh, Martin, *Why Former Suffragettes Flocked to British Fascism* (slate.com, 2017).
Pugh, Martin, 'The British Union of Fascists and the Olympia Debate' (*The Historical Journal*, Vol. 41, No. 2, 1998).
Pugh, Martin, *Hurrah for the Blackshirts!: Fascists and Fascism in Britain Between the Wars* (Pimlico, 2006).
Quinlan, Kevin, *The Secret War Between the Wars* (Boydell & Brewer, 2014).
Ramsay, A.H.M., *The Nameless War* (Britons Publishing Society, 1952).
Rhodes, J., *Chips: The Diaries of Sir Henry Channon* (Weidenfeld & Nicolson, 1967).
Richardson, Mary, *Laugh a Defiance* (Weidenfeld & Nicolson, 1953).
Riddell, Fern, *Death in Ten Minutes: The forgotten life of radical suffragette Kitty Marion* (Hodder & Stoughton, 2018).
Rose, Norman, *The Cliveden Set* (Jonathan Cape, 2000).
Sachs, Adam J., *The Fascist Sympathies of Britain's Aristocracy* (Tribune Magazine, 2020).
Scellenberg, Walter, *The Schellenberg Memoirs: A Record of the Nazi Secret Service* (Carlton Books, 2006).
Shirer, William, *Berlin Diary* (Alfred A. Knopf, 1941).
Soukupová, Martina, *The British Pro-German Organisation The Link on the Eve of The World War II* (Charles University, 2017).
Spicer, Charles, *Ambulant amateurs: the rise and fade of the Anglo-German Fellowship* (University of London, 2018).
Steel, Peta, *The Battle of Cable Street* (Sertuc, 2017).
Tate, Tim, *Hitler's British Traitors* (Icon Books, 2019).
Tate, Tim, *Treason, Treachery and Pro-Nazi Activities by the British Ruling Classes During World War Two* (Berkeley Centre for Right-Wing Studies, 2019).
Thurlow, Richard, *Fascism in Britain: A History 1918–1985* (Basil Blackwell, 1987).
Urbach, Karina, *European Aristocracies and the Radical Right 1918–1939* (Oxford University Press, 2007).
Valli, Roberta Suzzi, 'The Myth of Squadrismo in the Fascist Regime' (*Journal of Contemporary History*, Vol. 35, No. 2, 2000).
Webb, Simon, *Suffragette Fascists* (Pen and Sword, 2020).
Wheatcroft, Geoffrey, 'Not even a Might-Have Been' (*London Review of Books*, Vol. 25, No. 2, 2023).
Wilson, Jim, *Nazi Princess: Hitler, Lord Rothermere and Princess Stefanie Von Hohenlohe* (Kindle edition).
Worley, Matthew, 'Why Fascism? Sir Oswald Mosley and the Conception of the British Union of Fascists' (*History*, Vol. 96, No. 1, 2011).
Yadlin, Michal Rebecca, *Radical Politics of Rich People: British Upper Class Support of Interwar Communism and fascism* (Boise State University, 2014).
Young, Lauren, *Hitler's Girl* (Kindle edition).

Index

Agnew, Peter 134
Air Time Limited 120
Allen, Mary Sophia 29, 31, 32
Allen, William E. 73, 91, 120
Amery, Leo 3
Amor, Marjorie (Marjorie Mackie, agent M/Y) 124, 157, 158, 159
Anglo-German Fellowship (AGF) 50, 148
Astor, Nancy 30, 36, 81, 82
Astor, William Waldorf 81, 82
Athlone, Countess of 133
Athlone, Duke of 136
Aussenpolitische Amt (APA) 36
Auswärtiges Amt 36, 47

Baldwin, Stanley 50, 104, 115, 139, 141, 144, 145, 173
Barker, A.L. 39
Barrington, Mercedes 31
Barrington-Ward, Robert 39
Beamish, Henry Hamilton 21, 22, 24
Beaumont, Colin 120
Beigbeder y Atienza, Juan 166, 169
Bell, Doreen 113
Belloc, Hilaire 54
Bene, Otto 99
Bennett, Ernest 134
Bermejillo, Tiger 169
Bingham, Adrian 33
Bingham, Robert Worth 131
Bird, Robert 134
Bishop Blunt of Bradford 141
Black, James 21
Boothby, Robert 69
Bothamley, Margaret 49, 65, 66, 123, 153, 156

Bowerman, Elsie 31
Box, F.M. 117, 118
Braun, Eva 72, 76
British Commonwealth Union (BCU) 16
British Council for Christian Settlement in Europe (BCCSE) 63, 151
British Democratic Association 108
British Empire Union 18
British Fascisti (BF) 17, 18, 19, 20, 23, 25, 95, 96
British People's Party (BPP) 63
British Union (BU) 118, 119, 120–3 passim, 125, 126, 153, 154, 157, 161, 162
British Union of Democrats (BUD) 108
British Union of Fascists (BUF) 13, 19, 21, 24, 28, 29, 30–2, 33, 23, 40, 44, 51, 54, 57–60 passim, 65, 71, 75, 87–99 passim, 101–5 passim, 107–19 passim, 122, 124, 126, 142, 145, 152, 154, 163
Brocket, Lord 24, 62, 134
Broekhuizen, Herman Dirk van 49
Brown, John 127, 128, 149
Bryans, James Lonsdale 62
Bullitt, William C. 136
Burgess, Guy 133

Cadogan, Alexander 83
Caetani, Gelasio 135
Capello, Luigi 10
Cazalet, Victor 132
Chamberlain, Austen 12, 15
Chamberlain, Houston Stewart 6
Chamberlain, Joseph 3, 4, 34
Chamberlain, Neville 43, 64, 84, 88, 90, 115, 121, 124, 138, 139, 144, 150, 155, 160, 165

Chamberlain, J. 34
Channon, Henry 63, 64
Chesterton, Arthur Kenneth 24, 53, 54, 65, 107, 116, 118, 119, 123, 156
Childers, Erskine 4
Christie, Malcolm 52
Churchill, Randolph 70, 163
Churchill, Winston 12, 25, 46, 62, 65, 69, 73, 90, 122, 124, 126, 142–4 passim, 158, 165, 167, 170, 171
Clarke, Mick 112, 118
Clausen, Fritz 48
Cockburn, Claud 83
Cohen, J.B. Brunel 130
Cole, E.H. 54
Colfax, Lady 82
Communist Party of Great Britain (CPGB) 92, 95, 101, 112, 119, 157
Connaught, Duke of 132
Conwell-Evans, Thomas Pugh (Philip) 39, 51–2, 133
Crawford, Archibald 49, 149
Cripps, Sir Stafford 77
Crozier, W.P. 39
Cunard, Maud Alice (Emerald) 69, 70, 77, 82, 132, 137, 140
Cunard, Sir Bache 132
Curzon, Cynthia Blanche 'Cimmie' 71, 88, 90, 96, 97

D'Annunzio, Gabriele 11
Davison, Emily 31
Dawson, Geoffrey (*aka* Geoffrey Robinson) 34, 35, 36, 39, 83, 85, 134
Defence Regulation 18B 122, 124, 152, 159, 160
Dell, Robert 37
Deutsch-Englische Gesellschaft (DEG) 133
Die-Hards 2, 15, 25
Domvile, Barry 132, 147–54 passim, 156
Donavan, H.J. 17
Douglas-Hamilton, Douglas 134
Downe, Viscountess 125
Drummond, Flora 31
Dudley Ward, Winifred (Freda) 131, 135

Dundas, Lawrence 134
Dunn, Lady 125

Ebbutt, Norman 34–40 passim
Eckersley, Frances 65, 66
Eckersley, Peter 120
Eddy, Mary Baker 81
Eden, Anthony 48, 65, 83, 84, 85, 138, 139
Edward VIII, Edward Albert Christian George Andrew Patrick David Saxe-Coburg-Gotha 64, 73, 128, 131–42 passim, 163–72 passim, 173
Ellington, Sir Edward 145
Emergency Powers (Defence) Act 1939 60

Federation of Democrats 108
Fetherston-Godley, Francis 127, 129, 130
FitzGerald, Edward (7th Duke of Leinster) 136
Fitzgerald, Helen 140
Fitzroy, Rt. Hon. Edward Algernon 83
Ford, Henry 22
Foster-Anderson, Herbert 48, 49
Fox, Norah Dacre (*aka* Norah Elam) 31, 32
Frankfurter, Solomon 84
Fraser, Sir John Foster 34
Fuller, John Frederick Charles 57, 62
Furness, Thelma 131, 135, 136

Galbraith, Kylie 35, 39
Galloway, Lord 133, 134
Game, Sir Philip 109, 111, 112
Gardiner, Henry Rolf 50, 51
Gärtner, Margarete 51, 52
Garvagh, Lord 17
Gedye, G.E.R. 37
German Secret Society of the Illuminati 25
Gilbert, Oliver 159
Glasgow, Earl of 134
Goebbels, Joseph 48, 72, 73, 103, 111, 115, 120, 142, 149, 150, 154

Index

Goebbels, Magda 73
Goelet, Mary (May) 83
Gordon-Canning, Robert (Bobbie) 57, 63, 76, 151, 153
Göring, Hermann 76, 129
Gower, Robert Vaughan 134
Graham, Lord Ronald 132
Grandi, Dino 71
Greene, Benjamin 63, 151
Grègoire, Armand 163
Griggs, Anne Brock 113
Grimm, Friedrich 48
Guinness, Bryan 69, 70, 72
Guinness, Desmond 69
Guinness, Jonathan 69
Guinness, Lady Honor 64
Guinness, Thomas 134
Gustaf Adolf, Prince 132

Hall, Howard 125
Hamilton, Duke of 24, 149
Hanfstaengl, Putzi 71, 72
Harmsworth, Harold Sidney (1st Viscount Rothermere) 41–6 passim
Harris, Henry Wilson 34
Hawkins, Neil Francis 17, 93
Hawks, Olive 113
Headlam, Arthur Cayley 34, 0
Henderson, Nevile 83
Hess, Rudolf 39, 48, 128, 134, 138, 158, 163
Hill, Derek 75
Himmler, Heinrich 48, 77, 129, 148
Hitler, Adolf 4, 11, 24, 30, 32, 33, 34, 35, 37, 41, 43, 44, 45, 47, 48, 49, 52, 53, 56, 59, 62, 64, 72–9 passim, 84, 85, 99, 115, 120, 121, 125, 128, 130, 132, 133, 135, 138, 139, 144, 148, 149, 151, 161, 163, 164, 168, 169, 170
Hoesch, Leopold von 134, 137, 138, 139
Hohenlohe-Waldenburg-Schillingsfürst, Julianne Stephanie Maria Veronika Richter von (Stephanie Richter) 41, 42, 43, 44, 45, 53, 77, 83, 137, 138, 164
Hohenlohe-Waldenburg-Schillingsfürst, Prince Friedrich Franz von 42

Holder, Harold 172
Hore-Belisha, Lesley 88, 155, 165
Houston, Richard Alister (Jock) 112, 118
Howard-Vyse, Richard 166
Hoyningen-Huene, Oswald baron von 170
Hughes, James McGuirk 158
Hulbert, Norman 134
Hutchison, Graham Seton 127, 128

Imperial Fascist League (IFL) 22–4, 95, 96, 117
Inskip, Thomas 85

James, Archibald 134
Jewish Ex-Servicemen's Legion (JEXL) 129
Jewish Labour Council (JLC) 108
Joyce, William Brooke 17, 24, 32, 60, 65–7, 87, 109, 112, 114–18, 156, 158, 159

Kell, Vernon 141
Keller, Dr. Hans 48, 49
Kennedy, A.L. 39
Kennedy, Joseph 83
Kent, Tyler 123, 124, 132, 135, 137, 138, 158, 160, 162
Kerr, Philip Henry (11th Marquis of Lothian) 38, 83, 85, 145
Kincardine, Earl of 132
King George V 31, 44, 62, 134, 137, 138, 139
King George VI 138
Kitson, Arthur 49
Knight, Maxwell 66, 123, 124, 151, 156, 157–61
Knox, Alfred 134
Ku Klux Klan ix

Leese, Arnold 17, 22, 23, 24, 95, 96, 117
Legion of Blue and White Shirts 108
Lewis, Ted (Kid) 95
Ley, Robert 164
Liddell, Guy 32
Liddell Hart, Basil 57

Lindbergh, Charles 83
Lintorn-Orman, Rotha 17, 18, 19, 146
Lloyd George, David 22, 28, 31, 83, 88, 90, 132
Lubbe, Marius van der 35, 36
Luxemburg, Rosa 10
Lymington, Viscount 49

MacDonald, Ramsay 50
Macnamara, John Foster 48, 134
Makgill, Esther Lady 93
Manchester, Duchess of 83
Mandeville Roe, E.G. 17
Marlborough, Duchess of 83
Marlborough, Duke of 149
Matthias, Ludwig 123
Maule Ramsay, Archibald Henry 24, 65, 122, 123, 124, 155–62 passim
Maxse, Leopold 3
Maxwell, John 92
Mercier, Dr. Charles 163
Metcalfe, Edward Dudley (Fruity) 71, 137, 163, 165
Middle Class Union 18
Militant Christian Patriots 24
Miller, Joan (Joanna Phipps) 123, 124
Milner, Lord 3
Mitford, Diana 69–79 passim, 121, 134, 137
Mitford, Unity Valkyrie 69–79 passim, 133, 134
Monckton, Sir Walter 171
Moore, Thomas Cecil Russel 52, 104, 133, 134, 155, 156
Morning Post 24
Morris, Sir William 90
Morrison, Herbert 21
Mosley, Cynthia 71, 88
Mosley, Oswald ix, 4, 12, 19, 22, 24, 30–3, 40, 44, 51, 56, 57, 59, 60, 65, 69, 70–5 passim, 87–99 passim, 107–26 passim, 132, 135, 137, 142, 149, 150–2, 159, 160
Mount Temple, Lord 133, 134
Munck, Hélène Louise de (agent M/I) 158

Murphy, James 48
Mussolini, Benito 11, 12, 17, 18, 23, 30, 54, 69, 91, 113, 114, 118, 137, 166

National Citzens Union 18
National Fascists 18
National Party (NP) 16
National Review 24
National Socialist German Workers' Party (NSDAP) 43, 48, 99
National Socialist League (NSL) 24, 65
Neurath, Konstantin von 36, 128
New World Fellowship (NWF) 108
Nicholson, Harold 12
Niemöller, Martin 34, 61, 62
Nieuwenhuys, Jean 158
Nordic League (NL) 22, 24, 158
Nordischer Gesellschaft 24
Northumberland, Duke of 24
Nuffield, Lord 133, 134

Pankhurst, Christabel 28
Pankhurst, Emmeline 27–32 passim
Panter, Noel 38
Pearson, Lady 125
Pfister, George A. 98, 99
Philby, Kim 133
Pitt-Rivers, George Lane-Fox 65
Plugge, Leonard Frank 120
Pownall, Assheton 134
Preston, Alice (Kiki) 137
Primo de Rivera, Don Miguel 169
Prince Arthur of Connaught 133
Prince George, Duke of Kent 137
Prince of Wales Fund 18

Rathenau, Walther 10
Red Cross Society 18
Redesdale, Lord 133, 134, 149, 156
Redwitz, Hans von 127
Rennell, Lord 134
Ribbentrop, Joachim von 39, 47, 48, 49, 50, 59, 62, 64, 73, 83, 84, 115, 127–30 passim, 132, 134, 135, 136, 138, 139, 141, 144, 145, 148, 163, 164, 166–9, 172
Richardson, Mary Raleigh 30–2, 93

Index

Right Club 24, 65, 123, 124, 125, 153, 154, 155–62 passim
Roberts, Mrs H. (Mayor of Stepney) 110
Robertson, Thomas 141
Rogers, Hermann 140, 163, 165
Rogers, Katherine 140
Röhm, Ernst 37, 75
Ropp, William de 36, 51
Rosenberg, Alfred 36, 47, 108, 138
Rothschild, Eugène 163
Rowe, T.W. Victor 159
Roxburghe, Duchess of 83
Russell, Hastings William Sackville (Lord Tavistock) 63, 151

Sanderson, Frank 134
Sandys, Duncan 134
Saxe-Coburg-Gotha, Edward Albert Christian George Andrew Patrick David (Prince Albert) 131
Schellenberg, Walter 169–72 passim
Schmidt, Paul 128
Scott, Elizabeth Montagu Douglas 71
Scott, Walter John Montagu Douglas (Duke of Buccleuch) 12, 62, 71, 149
Scrimgeour, A.C. 118
Sears, James Edmonds 47
Shirer, William 39
Shore, Olga 113
Silva, Ricardo Espirito Santo 166
Simpson, Wallis (Bessie Wallis Warfield) 73, 131–42 passim, 163–72 passim
Soldier's Parcel Fund 18
Somerville, Daniel Gerald 48
Speer, Albert 164
Spencer Jnr., Earl Winfield 137
Spry, Constance 136
Squire, John Collings 97
Stephens, Pembroke 37

Tatton Bower, Robert 134
Taylor, Charles 134

Tennant, Ernest William Dalrymple 48, 49, 50, 133
The Britons 21–2
The Fascist 22
The Hooded Men 54
The Patriot 24
The White Knights of Britain 54
Thwaites, Norman 48
Tiarks, Frank Cyril 134
Tiplady, Thomas 33
Tree, Ronald 134
Trundle, Guy Marcus 136

Valle, Consuelo Yznaga de 83
Vanderbilt, Consuelo 83
Vane-Tempest-Stewart, Charles Stewart Henry (Lord Londonderry) 143–6 passim
Vansittart, Robert 52, 127, 139
Voigt, Frederick Augustus 35

Ward Price, George 47, 52–3, 145
Waters, Florence 19
Webb, Simon 28
Weber, Nesta 17
Weddell, Alexander 166
Wellington, Duke of 24, 133, 134, 149, 156
Westminster, Duke of 12, 149
White Knights of Britain 24
Whitney, Jock 71
Wiedemann, Fritz 43, 45, 164
Wiesmes, Martin 33
Williamson, Henry 54–7 passim
Wilson, Sir Arnold 21, 38, 132, 148
Winn, Godfrey 39
Wolkoff, Anna 123
Wolkoff, Nicolai 123
Women's Social and Political Union, (WSPU) (Suffragette Movement) 27–32 passim
Women's Guild of Empire 31